The **PROBLEM** of the **FUTURE** World

The **PROBLEM** of the **FUTURE** World

W. E. B. DU BOIS AND THE RACE CONCEPT AT MIDCENTURY

Eric Porter

Duke University Press
Durham and London   2010

© 2010 Duke University Press

Printed in the United States of America on
acid-free paper ∞

Designed by Heather Hensley

Typeset in Carter and Cone Galliard by
Keystone Typesetting, Inc.

Library of Congress Cataloging-in-Publication
Data and republication acknowledgments
appear on the last printed page of this book.

For

CARMEN YAMILA RAMÍREZ Y PORTER

and

OMAR RAFAEL RAMÍREZ Y PORTER

My life had its significance and its only deep significance because it was part of a Problem; but that problem was, as I continue to think, the central problem of the greatest of the world's democracies and so the Problem of the future world. The problem of the future world is the charting, by means of intelligent reason, of a path not simply through the resistances of physical force, but through the vaster and far more intricate jungle of ideas conditioned on unconscious and subconscious reflexes of living things; on blind unreason and often irresistible urges of sensitive matter; of which the concept of race is today one of the most unyielding and threatening.

W. E. B. DU BOIS, *DUSK OF DAWN* (1940)

I remember once offering to an editor an article which began with a reference to the experience of last century. "Oh," he said, "leave out the history and come to the present." I felt like going to him over a thousand miles and taking him by the lapels and saying, "Dear, dear jackass! Don't you . understand that the past *is* the present; that without what *was*, nothing is? That, of the infinite dead, the living are but unimportant bits?"

W. E. B. DU BOIS, *THE WORLD AND AFRICA* (1947)

CONTENTS

ACKNOWLEDGMENTS

This book began life, albeit in a much different form, while I was teaching at the University of New Mexico. I thank all of my colleagues in the American Studies Department and friends across campus for their warmth and support during my brief sojourn there. I am especially indebted to Beth Bailey and Ruth Salvaggio for their generous mentoring and friendship. I also benefited from teaching two graduate seminars on race at UNM, and I thank participants in them for a series of enlightening discussions that helped me better understand the stakes of this research.

This book is very much a project of UC Santa Cruz. Colleagues in American studies were supportive through this process. I am grateful to chairs (Judy Yung, Michael Cowan, Tricia Rose, George Lipsitz, and Charles Hedrick) and deans (Wlad Godzich, Gary Lease, and Georges Van Den Abbeele) for helping me secure funding and time away from teaching and service to work on this project. I owe a huge debt to the broader community of friends and scholars at UCSC. They have sustained me with their keen intellects, wonderful senses of humor, wisdom about the bureaucracy, and excellent cooking. There are far too many people to name individually, and I fear leaving someone off the list. So let me just say thank you to the community and give special acknowledgment to Angela Davis, Rosa Linda Fregoso, Herman Gray, Susan Gillman, and George Lipsitz for their wise mentorship and the doors they helped to open, and to David Anthony and Bettina Aptheker for two very important conversations about Du Bois. And, of course, I am grateful to my students for their inspiration, especially the participants in my fall 2007 graduate seminar on Du Bois.

Preliminary research was supported by a UCSC Committee on Research grant, which funded excellent research assistance by Torie Quiño-nez and Barbara Texidor. Later, librarian Martha Ramírez helped immensely by bringing to our university a copy of Du Bois's papers on microfilm. Much of the initial drafting of chapter 2 was supported by a UCSC Institute for Humanities Research Fellowship. I benefited tremendously from a Stanford Humanities Center residential fellowship, which enabled me to write a significant portion of the manuscript. I am indebted to the entire SHC administration and staff and to the other fellows for creating a warm, collegial atmosphere and for many interesting discussions. A presentation to the SHC's American Cultures workshop and subsequent conversation was also very helpful, and I thank Shelley Fisher Fishkin and Nigel Hatton for that invitation.

I am grateful for the sustenance I received from many friends and mentors in American studies, ethnic studies, and history circles. Although there are, again, too many people to name, I want to give special recognition to Jonathan Holloway, Robin Kelley, George Lewis, Waldo Martin, and Sherrie Tucker for very concrete acts of support in recent years, and to Dennis Dworkin, Amy Tang, Alexandria White, and Matt Wray for reading and commenting on portions of the manuscript.

I am very happy to be working with Duke University Press. Ken Wissoker has been enthusiastic about and supportive of this project from the beginning, and his incisive feedback at various stages of its production made it better. Courtney Berger and Leigh Barnwell also provided important assistance through the process. Duke's anonymous readers helped to sharpen my focus and directed me to critical sources at the proposal stage. Their comments on the full manuscript helped me fine-tune it as it neared completion. I also benefited from the work of editors Pam Morrison and Rebecca Fowler, and from Trevor Sangrey's indexing.

Friends outside of the academy are often puzzled by the world I inhabit, but it always encourages me that they trust I am doing something useful. I give thanks to my immediate and extended families for continuing to believe in me, especially my parents, Scipio and Barbara Porter, and my brother, Scott Porter. My wife, Catherine Ramírez, has been a loving companion, a fantastic mother to our children, and a dedicated scholar who inspires me through her example and gives necessary scrutiny to my work. I couldn't have done this without her.

I started outlining this book several months after the birth of our daughter, Carmen. Around that time I had a dream in which I tried to escape a crumbling modernist office building with her in my arms. I suppose this was, on some level, a fairly typical dream for a new, anxious parent, and it no doubt had something to do with my unconscious processing of the collapse of the twin towers and my own experience, in full panic mode, trying to escape my workplace in downtown Oakland during the 1989 Loma Prieta earthquake. But it occurred to me upon awakening, with Du Bois's critique in mind, that the dream was an allegory for our crumbling state infrastructure, civic institutions, and social services at this neoliberal moment, with frightening prospects for future generations, particularly for colored folk and working people. I dedicate this book to my black-white-Mexican children, Carmen Yamila Ramírez y Porter and Omar Rafael Ramírez y Porter, hoping that they live to see a more just world than we have now, where their achievements and comfort will not be contingent on someone else's suffering.

W. E. B. Du Bois was an extraordinary thinker and an iconic and controversial activist. He also lived a long time. He turned seventy-two in 1940 but was politically and intellectually productive for two more decades. In 1940 he published an autobiography, *Dusk of Dawn*, and launched a new journal, *Phylon*, based at Atlanta University, where he taught from 1897 to 1910 and again beginning in 1934. This academic work bracketed two and a half decades of service to the National Association for the Advancement of Colored People (NAACP), which he helped found, as board member and editor of its journal, the *Crisis*. Du Bois edited *Phylon* until Atlanta University forced him into retirement in 1944, at which point he returned to the NAACP as director of special research. Although this position came to an abrupt end in 1948 as he diverged politically from the organization and clashed with its leadership, during his brief return he helped the NAACP develop an internationalist, antiracist, and anticolonialist platform. Among other activities, he assisted in reviving the Pan-African movement, was consultant to the U.S. delegation at the United Nations founding conference, and drafted petitions to the world body on behalf of people of African descent.

After leaving the NAACP Du Bois moved further to the left, devoting more time to the Communist Party–influenced, anticolonial organization Council of African Affairs (CAA). He also participated in the communist-led and Soviet-affiliated international peace movement. In 1951 Du Bois was indicted by a federal grand jury for failing to register as a foreign agent because of his peace movement activities and was subsequently arrested, tried, and acquitted. During this ordeal, and following the death of his wife of over fifty years, Nina Gomer Du Bois, he married the political activist, composer, performer, and writer Shirley Graham. He subsequently lost his passport, as did his wife, but he remained active as a peace advocate, proponent of U.S.–Soviet reconciliation, ally of anticolonial movements, and defender of civil liberties in the face of Cold War hysteria. Once his passport was returned in 1958, he traveled extensively in Europe, the USSR, and the People's Republic of China. He finally joined his wife in the Communist Party in 1961, and they subsequently moved to Ghana. The Du Boises eventually gave up their U.S. citizenship and became Ghanaian citizens after experiencing renewed passport problems. W. E. B. Du Bois died in Ghana in 1963. Between 1940 and his death, he published six more books, composed his posthumously published autobiography and manuscripts that remained unpublished, wrote for African American newspapers, academic journals, left publications and other venues, and maintained an active career as a public speaker.

Despite such activities — and in many respects, because of them — and despite the ways that the study of Du Bois has for decades inspired black political activity and been a staple of Africana scholarship, scholars have not sufficiently analyzed the late period of his career, when he moved from a socialist to communist political orientation and voiced an often uncompromising leftist and antiracist critique of the United States and its government's and corporate elite's actions. This book responds to this scholarly deficit by examining Du Bois's intellectual production during the 1940s and early 1950s, with an eye toward using it to help us address race and racism as multilayered, protean, global phenomena in the present. The book showcases four themes in Du Bois's writings as it proceeds in roughly chronological fashion: his understanding of race and racism's complex, shifting ontologies and paradoxical nature (their simultaneous reality and unreality) as intertwined with political-economic transformation and knowledge production; his assessment of the exclusions produced at the interface of race, war, militarism, peace, and human rights; his evaluation of the place of Africa in the world as both product of and determinant of racialization; and his insights into the linkages among race, citizenship, and expectations and acts of loyalty.

Although Du Bois addressed most of these issues earlier in his life, the specific ways he rearticulated them at midcentury makes his thinking valuable to the present. His work helps us understand a twenty-first-century world defined in part by social and ideological processes that emerged or developed during the 1940s and early 1950s, a period I call the *first post-racial moment*. Du Bois understood that the persistence and revision of slavery's and colonialism's racist legacies, and the faith that they were being overcome, produced emergent forms of racism in his present. He recognized how science, state reform, and liberal and left academic and activist projects made possible both racial transcendence and racial inequalities cloaked within this transcendence. The legacies of such projects today can be found in their institutionalization (in the academy, in public policy, and so on) and through their incorporation into the exceptionalist frameworks justifying U.S.–engineered capitalist restructuring, the concomitant project of empire, the terror and violence that has accompanied both, and our continued unwillingness to address legacies of those foundational racial pasts and those that were emergent at midcentury.

Du Bois's midcentury work insists that we remain attentive to the international and transnational dimensions of race and racism but also demands that we address the particular role that the United States — in its contradictory role as imperial power and engine for democratic reform — has played in reproducing them. Du Bois encourages us, at a moment when many dwell in complicated and often transhistorical ways on blackness as subjection and abjection, to not lose sight of historically specific political economic transformations and the changing contours of citizenship and possibilities of civic engagement. He emphasizes how U.S. subjects — even those on the margins — are implicated in the project of empire and bear responsibility for its reformation. We can thus locate in Du Bois's work a moral and epistemological orientation from which future analysis and activism against racism may be launched.

This book emphasizes texts and events situated temporally from Du Bois's autobiography *Dusk of Dawn* (1940) to his memoir *In Battle for Peace* (1952). I focus on what we can term the "early late period" in part because Du Bois's thinking was clearer and more rigorous during this period than at the very end of his life. Although I believe that scholars have often erred in overemphasizing the extent to which his post-1948 (or post-1944, or even post-1940) work was defined by the limitations brought by advancing age and political dogmatism, my view is that there does seem to be a point after 1952 where his criticism becomes significantly less nuanced. His take on communist states and leaders, for example, seems increasingly driven more by hagiography, wishful thinking, and a refusal to acknowledge disturbing facts than by analysis.[1] And while additional analysis of how subsequent texts (the semi-autobiographical *Black Flame Trilogy* and his posthumously published autobiography) reconfigure the race concept through imaginative self-reflection would be welcome, I believe there is greater value for present-day social analysis in examining the relatively earlier writings that respond more directly to a specific set of social and historical phenomena — war, peace, the politics of academic research, political loyalties, colonial and anticolonial politics, and so on — in their moment. Reading Du Bois's work in the 1940s and early 1950s remains important because he was at this point still invested in what he dismissively referred to later as a "middle-way" between capitalism and communism.[2] I find provocative, appealing, and analytically useful in the neoliberal and post-Soviet present a political and intellectual vision motivated by a hope for a reconstruction of democracy in the United States and elsewhere through this middle way.

My goal is not simply to recuperate the post-1940 Du Bois; nor do I dare to claim he provides all the necessary tools for addressing the contradictory persistence of race and racism in the present. But this book is based on the premise that additional work on Du Bois's midcentury writings helps open up the usable past of his intellectual history and the radical possibilities in mid-twentieth-century black intellectual life more generally. We accomplish this by examining Du Bois's insights and by exploring the limitations and contradictions that also defined his work. While I am not the first to address the post-1940 period, I seek to move the conversation about Du Bois and race forward by building on existing work on the period but also by looking more systematically at a range of texts and contextualizing them differently, in part by drawing on new scholarship on race, neoliberalism, empire, and some of the challenges of antiracist activism in the twenty-first century.

WRITING DU BOIS

Even a brief review of the extensive, multifaceted scholarship on Du Bois reveals lacunae that call out for more attention to his later life, as well as suggestive possibilities for how this period might be more productively engaged. Scholars writing about Du Bois shortly before or after his death tended, especially in their assessments of the late period, to reproduce the animus directed to him by the U.S. government, members of the civil rights establishment, Cold War liberals, and former communists because of his commitment to Marxist principles, estrangement from the NAACP, pro-Soviet statements, and decision to join the Communist Party in 1961. At best, scholars were ambivalent about the late period, describing his work then as inconsistent and paradoxical and finding it difficult to place it within normative models of black political and intellectual activity.[3]

Du Bois eventually received more favorable treatment, as scholars energized by the political moment of the late 1960s and 1970s turned to him for intellectual guidance. Some accounts still elided the late period or viewed his Marxist turn as a failure of theory, vision, or ethical fortitude, but others, even when recasting his project to fit contemporary political agendas, acknowledged the importance of his post-1940 insights.[4] Scholars on the left played particularly important roles. His friend and colleague the Marxist historian Herbert Aptheker engaged in heroic efforts, beginning in the sixties, to collect and organize his papers, publish edited collections of short writings, and reissue out-of-print books.[5] Later, Cedric Robinson's *Black Marxism* (1983), while focusing on *Black Reconstruction in America* (1935) and making only passing reference to later writings, validated Du Bois's turn to the left by recognizing him as one of the "deans of radical historiography."[6]

The major biographies of Du Bois written by Arnold Rampersad, Manning Marable, and David Levering Lewis sympathetically examined Du Bois's final two decades. And Gerald Horne's *Black and Red* focused specifically on this period. These surveys were critically important for documenting the events of Du Bois's late career, identifying key points in his writings, and situating them in their historical context. Rather than ignoring or dismissing this period, these authors made the case that scholarly and political imperatives demanded that it be engaged productively in our present, despite its limitations and contradictions. Horne and Marable more explicitly made this point, coming as they did from a left perspective, but one can also find validation of it in Lewis's more circumspect approach. Even if the history of the past few decades makes Du Bois's faith in communism and African liberation "ring so oddly as to cause doubt as to his standing as one of the twentieth century's intellectual heavyweights," Lewis writes, " . . . it may be suggested that Du Bois was right to insist that to leave the solution of systemic social problems exclusively to the market is an agenda guaranteeing obscene economic inequality in the short run and irresoluble political calamity in the long run."[7]

Yet these studies also suggest the need for further work on Du Bois's late period through their limitations. As intellectual and political biographies, all are constrained by their genre; they chart the general contours of thought alongside biographical detail rather than providing detailed readings of specific texts. The ideological orientations of these writers and their concomitant assumptions about Du Bois's ideological motivations also appear to constrain the analyses. With Rampersad and Lewis, the assessment of and limited attention to Du Bois's later ideas, relative to their treatments of other periods of his career, seems in part a product of their discomfort with his radical agenda and a sense that it was overly determinative.[8] With Horne and Marable, biography's generic limitation is augmented by a vindicationist project—a goal of legitimating late ideas and activities, of showing the consistency between them and early intellectual and political moves—that similarly narrows the analytical frame.[9]

Given that these biographical works opened the door to further engagements with the post-1940 Du Bois, it is striking that the period has not been more often and more rigorously addressed in the veritable explosion of theoretically and conceptually oriented work on Du Bois published over the past few decades. Produced within and across disciplines, much of this scholarship analyzes Du Bois's understanding of race and racism, while seeking to draw lessons from his work for contemporary analysis and activism.

This multidisciplinary conversation about Du Bois is overdetermined, but we can point to some fundamental factors directing scholars to this subject. There is, simply, the frame of historical imagination, which impels us to return to the past for solutions to current dilemmas. And Du Bois stands out as an icon of the twentieth-century black freedom struggle, which resonates so deeply across geographical and cultural boundaries. Du Bois's iconicity is, among other things, a result of his centering of "the race concept," of the prophetic aspects of his statement, made in 1900, borrowed from Frederick Douglass, and subsequently reproduced in *The Souls of Black Folk*, that the "problem of the Twentieth Century is the problem of the color-line," and of his unflagging commitment to social justice. Some of us may be drawn to Du Bois because of the masculinism of African American and critical race studies he helped to shape.

Du Bois revisited the "race concept" and the "color line" over the course of his career, and as the twentieth century drew to a close, other thinkers did as well, amid much anxiety and debate about the relevance of race as a social and analytical category and in light of an almost endless set of "racial" problems and issues apparent to those who were still willing to deploy the categories. Critically important to shaping the contours of the discursive field surrounding Du Bois was K. Anthony Appiah's essay "The Uncompleted Argument: Du Bois and the Illusion of Race" (1985). Among other things, Appiah's essay helped foreground in many assessments of Du Bois's work a fundamental, ethical-ontological question that has animated countless scholarly and activist interventions: Given that we know race is a scientifically flawed category, is it still a valid concept upon which to base antiracist theory and praxis? Appiah ultimately answered no, arguing that Du Bois failed in his stated attempt to leave behind the biological conception of race that had long served racism and craft instead a sociohistorical conception that could be the basis of healthy human identities and progressive political projects.[10] Appiah's essay, in turn, provoked a number of rejoinders and continues to be a reference point for scholars contemplating the value of Du Bois's work. Whether taking on Appiah's argument directly or obliquely, scholars argue that Du Bois demonstrated the undeniable existence of race as a social and political category and its legitimacy as a platform for accruing a collective sense of self-worth among and mobilizing people who have been racially subordinated.[11] Others emphasize that Du Bois's work provides insight into race as a multilayered "social construction" that has real social effects no matter its scientific status.[12]

There is no small irony in the fact that Appiah's piece about the limitations of Du Bois's thinking about race has inspired so many recuperations of his "race concept." Some scholars find Du Bois's work invaluable for understanding and interrogating whiteness as a social category that ascribes power and privilege to those who inhabit it. Others locate in Du Bois's writing a valuable conceptualization of nonessentialist, African American political identities.[13] Still others draw from Du Bois's valuable interrogation of the connections among race, national identity, and citizenship—for example, via his model of double-consciousness. Another key area of inquiry concerns Du Bois's insights into race, racisms, and racial identities as global phenomena, with determinative origins in the projects of slavery, European colonialism, and U.S. empire. A related project is to use Du Bois to explore possibilities and limitations of interracial, transnational affiliation and activism, organized around or in spite of racial identities.[14] Others bring his insights to the present in order to interrogate or justify assertions about specific social or political issues, like African American reparations.[15] Another approach is to show how Du Bois's scholarship, epistemological standpoints, or narrative strategies continue to provide a useful methodology for studying race.[16]

Feminist and sexuality studies scholars have emphasized both the possibilities and limitations of Du Boisean thought. Some feminist accounts during the early 1980s praised his early commitment to women's rights (particularly suffrage) and his attention, specifically in his *Darkwater* chapter "The Damnation of Women," to the restrictions posed to women, and black women in particular, by confining gender roles and their exploitation as workers.[17] Yet subsequent work noted that an attention to gender or sexuality is lacking in much of Du Bois's writings and that he did not treat female contemporaries like Anna Julia Cooper or Ida B. Wells-Barnett (not to mention his first wife, Nina Gomer Du Bois) as equals or encourage their ideas or careers.[18]

Others have moved the conversation in a somewhat different direction, arguing that Du Bois was engaged in a deeply gendered intellectual practice and style that was self-serving in his lifetime and which continues to shape academic field imaginaries and discourse. Du Bois thus becomes a negatively productive figure, with the limitations of his attitudes toward women and lacunae surrounding gender and sexuality in his work illustrating the need for more gender critical work in African American studies and other fields.[19] A more generous approach focuses on the theoretical and methodological possibilities that emerge when one teases out ideas that are only incipient in Du Bois's work. Ange-Marie Hancock argues that Du Bois, despite his limitations, provides a valuable precursor to contemporary intersectionality theory, which addresses how social categories like race, gender, sexuality, and class are mutually constitutive and are produced through the dynamic relationship of individual subjects and social structures.[20] Susan Gillman and Alys Weinbaum suggest we can identify in Du Bois's work a *"politics of juxtaposition* that positions multiple political issues and related world historical movements for social justice as associated, as necessarily juxtaposed, if not fully interlinked, or self-consciously interwoven" and then "push beyond the bounds of Du Bois's strictly associative or additive logic to animate the missing interrelations among available keywords, arguments, and textual parts."[21] Indeed several pieces in their recent collection show how an engagement with Du Bois's insights and limitations alike enables perspective on the linkages among race, gender, sexuality, nationalism, and imperialism.

Yet much of this recent work on Du Bois remains focused on texts ranging temporally from "The Conservation of Races" (1897) to *Dusk of Dawn*. Rarely does it address later writings in a rigorously contextual way. Some continue either to ignore or dismiss his late career. But even those who take post-1940 texts seriously often address them only as they reflect on and serve analyses of earlier events and writings. Or they read post-1940 texts as part of decades-long trajectories of thought, without much consideration for the particular contexts of commentary from different periods. We see one or more of these tendencies in many of the essays or book chapters discussed above, in some of the recent single-authored books on Du Bois, as well as in some of the most important edited collections or special journal issues surveying Du Boisean thought.[22]

This is not necessarily a problem in individual texts and analyses. I, for one, am indebted to the excellent work referenced above and to other studies focused on Du Bois's earlier years that facilitate a deeper understanding of his thought and its implications for studying race. This research offers necessary frameworks for analyzing Du Bois's late period. Yet while there is an array of practical and justifiable reasons why individual scholars have focused on earlier works, we must remain attentive to more problematic factors conditioning the temporal orientation as a whole.[23] Manning Marable and Adolph Reed have argued that the emphasis on earlier works stems at least in part from scholars' elitism, careerism, and political centrism.[24] And it is concomitantly clear that the generally scant attention to Du Bois's later work is a product of an unwillingness or inability to take on the political challenges of looking at it and of long-standing assumptions about its limited value.

But even the direct engagements with the period are often limited by what Kate Baldwin describes as "the deflection from politics and the overdetermination by politics."[25] Vindicationist scholarship on the late period, as well as that which points to a consistency of belief between the pre- and post-1940 periods, potentially challenges earlier interpretations of Du Bois's late thinking as contradictory, naive, or moribund. However, it can also elide the political and ideological context of the post-1940 period and the fundamental importance to his midcentury thought of his long-standing but growing interest in Marxism and his increasingly close relationships, especially after he split with the NAACP in 1948, with people in or aligned with the Communist Party, including his soon-to-be wife, Shirley Graham. We cannot comprehend the power of Du Bois's midcentury intellectual project without considering what he gained by being part of a radical intellectual milieu.[26] Yet we must avoid the problem of making leftist ideas and affinities overly determinative of his thought during these years in either positive or negative ways. Du Bois might have praised Stalin, for example, but he was not a Stalinist in any systematic way. Reading him as such relegates to the background his engagement with an array of issues that exceeded his procommunist or pro-Soviet positions. It also channels the focus to the mid- and late 1950s and away from his important writings from the 1940s or examines that earlier work primarily for clues to his eventual intellectual fall from grace.[27]

By not systematically addressing his post-1940 writings in a presentist yet historically grounded manner, we have not yet fully appreciated the value of Du Bois's perspective on race. There have, of course, been some important moves in this direction. Marable has called for a "reconstruction" of the "radical Du Bois" whose intellectual and political projects were transformed in important ways during his final decades. We must come to terms, he argues, with his "radical stance, an inherently critical posture located outside of the mainstream" and build upon his theoretical work, by "linking it to the pressing struggles for human dignity and liberation that increasingly transcend the geopolitical boundaries of what has now for us become twenty-first century global apartheid."[28] Notable short works that engage the late work with a presentist frame include Kenneth Mostern's analysis of Du Bois's autobiographies; Joel Olson's consideration of the "race concept" in texts ranging from *Black Reconstruction* to *The World and Africa*; Kate Baldwin's chapter on Du Bois's affinity with the Soviet Union in the 1940s and 1950s; and Abdul-Karim Mustapha's analysis of *The World and Africa*. Also encouraging is Oxford University Press's recent reissue of all twenty-two of Du Bois's single-authored books. In the introduction to the series, Henry Louis Gates Jr. suggests that the inclusion of Du Bois's later works in the series may inspire future generations to understand "the arc" of his thinking about race and racism, blackness, and modernity.[29] But, clearly, there is more work to be done right now.

The stakes of reexamining the 1940s and 1950s remain high today. These years witnessed what Howard Winant calls "a worldwide *crisis of racial formation*" and were a critical point of transition in the development of racial politics, practices, and ideologies that anticipated in significant ways our present-day social world.[30] Antiracist and anticolonial movements challenged white supremacy's edifices across the globe. And with a liberalizing social climate in some Western democracies, increasing knowledge of genocidal potential (eventually realized) of Nazi racial theory, and an egalitarian and cosmopolitan wartime rhetoric, African American researchers and nonblack researchers (most notably, Jews) in Britain, Europe, and the United States sought to undermine the biologistic bases of race and racism. When liberal opinion makers and antiracist activists alike embraced the findings of such studies — enabled in part by popular scientific titles such as Ruth Benedict's *Patterns of Culture* (1934) and *Race* (1940), Benedict and Gene Weltfish's *The Races of Mankind* (1943), M. F. Ashley Montagu's *Man's Most Dangerous Myth* (1942), and, of course, Gunnar Myrdal's *An American Dilemma* (1944) — they entered the public discourse.[31]

Scientific awareness of the fictiveness of race presented possibilities for reconstituting the human and the political subject while calling into question the racially exclusive definitions of these categories. Yet following this path toward racelessness called into question political and social formations situated in racial experience and potentially abandoned a powerful analytic for understanding the way the world operated. Moreover, it was precisely at the moment when the falsity of race was made public that its persistence and complexity became more apparent. For in the 1940s state reforms, the booming war economy, and the scientific and activist challenges to racial inequalities coalesced in ways that paradoxically challenged and perpetuated white supremacy.[32]

Therefore, we are compelled to return to this point of beginnings to contemplate the ways race structures the world today. This analytical project demands simultaneous attention to unyielding racisms and their stealth manifestations at midcentury that shaped political, intellectual, and social life in the past and continue to do so in the present; to the liberal and left reform projects that sought to ameliorate — but sometimes served—racism; to the development of the United States as a global hegemonic force that was in Winant's words "*both* the leading imperial power and the avatar of anti-colonialism," embodying, as it long had, contradictory commitments to egalitarianism and white supremacy;[33] and to contemporaneous and present-day claims that the middle of the twentieth century was the moment when, as Paul Gilroy puts it, the "conflict between 'race' and more inclusive models of humanity was concluded."[34]

So where precisely do we look at midcentury for, in Foucauldian terms, a history of the present? This book argues that one answer to the question is W. E. B. Du Bois. Another answer is the broader terrain of black political cultures at midcentury. Du Bois and other black intellectuals and activists addressed a range of issues—the antidemocratic practices of the liberal state, the problem of empire, enduring global wars, exclusionary definitions of citizenship status and applications of rights, civilizationist paradigms, and others—that continue to be sources of intractable political problems. They analyzed earlier permutations and antecedents of these phenomena as well as the ideological mechanisms that justified their existence. In other words, as they looked to the future world, they saw its arrival in exceedingly complicated terms.

One of the most exciting developments in African American and United States historiography in recent years is the publication of studies that examine the midcentury relationships among civil and human rights movements, anticolonialist struggles, World War II and the Cold War, emergent and residual racial ideologies, and the development and decline of black internationalism. I include in this group, while recognizing significant differences in orientation and ideology, works by Carol Anderson, Thomas Borstelmann, Mary Dudziak, Brenda Gayle Plummer, Vijay Prashad, Nikhil Singh, and Penny Von Eschen.[35] Du Bois is not the primary focus of these studies, although in some, like Von Eschen's, he is a major figure throughout. In others he is relegated analytically to the prehistory of the moment. In Plummer's study, for example, he is a symbol, first, for a kind of elitist internationalism held over from his early Pan-Africanist activism, and then for an anachronistic radicalism and racialism. Singh more sympathetically addresses Du Bois's radical commitment and proclaims his fundamental importance to midcentury black political cultures, but his analysis of Du Bois's work essentially ends in 1940. Yet all of these studies enable an understanding of the deep historical context in which Du Bois's midcentury work can be analyzed. They bring to light shifts in mass consciousness and ideological orientation, document in fine detail the activities of organizations in which Du Bois was involved or in dialogue with, link such details to political and economic developments across the globe, and in some cases provide ample details of Du Bois's activities missing from major biographical works. As will become clear, I draw substantially from these studies.

But to analyze Du Bois's ideas with contemporary concerns in mind and then bring those ideas to the present requires self-conscious reflection on method. Thomas Holt argues that "the concepts and tools we have developed for understanding the racism of the nineteenth and twentieth centuries" are not "adequate for the twenty first." In large part this is because "there are *new* anomalies, *new* ambiguities, and a *new* ambivalence in contemporary life that our standard definitions of race and racism simply cannot account for, and which render them somewhat anachronistic."[36] And Du Bois, as "the dean of modern race studies," demonstrates in some of this work that those who make anachronistic errors today are "in good company." Yet Holt also suggests there is still something potentially to "emulate" in Du Bois's basic move of situating his prognostication in a "close study of the past."[37] I, in turn, see the value of recuperating Du Bois's historicist orientation as well as his insights into phenomena he experienced in his present, in no small part because he was, at midcentury, making sense of an array of anomalies, ambiguities, and ambivalences.

So, as we map the present and future of race and connect it to the past, we benefit from keeping in mind Michael Omi's and Howard Winant's discussion of race as an often "nebulous" yet fundamental part of social structures and systems of "human representation." We should pay attention as well to race's protean and historically contingent aspects, and here their definition of "racial formation as the sociohistorical process by which racial categories are created, inhabited, transformed and destroyed" remains useful. They also remind us, as do others too numerous to cite, that the race concept is articulated with and through a wide array of social identities, institutions, patterns of common sense, political ideologies, and so forth.[38] Indeed, globalization, neoliberalism, and new migration and immigration patterns have complicated things immensely, drawing out new forms of racial anxieties and hostilities, and in some cases changing race's embodiment.[39] Yet familiar hatreds persist and even expand in the twenty-first century, as evident in the animus directed to poor black residents of the United States Gulf Coast and Haiti and to

African immigrants in southern and Eastern Europe in recent years. So we must remain attentive both to emergent phenomena and to how the exclusions wrought by European, American, and Asian slaveries and imperialisms and their racial justificatory frameworks of race and racism seep into the present in both full regalia and chameleonic guise.

I take to heart Stuart Hall's instructions to late-twentieth-century scholars wanting to employ Antonio Gramsci's "conjunctural" ideas for contemporary social analysis. "To make more general use of them," Hall argues, "they have to be delicately dis-interred from their concrete and specific historical embeddedness and transplanted to new soil with considerable care and patience."[40] We can locate the imperative for such moves in Du Bois's own intellectual project, which often sought to transform theory (empiricism, pragmatism, Marxism) to fit his contemporary social world. Yet we must remain aware of the ways historical investigation is shaped by the needs of the present, as well as of the ways that information from the past causes us to rethink what those present-day needs are.

I draw upon Adolph Reed Jr.'s "generative approach" to Du Boisean thought, which he offers as an alternative to hagiographic accounts. The latter have been useful, he admits, given Du Bois's fall from grace in his waning years and because of the general marginalization of black intellectual life in Americanist scholarship. However, this approach to intellectual history often falls into a vindicationist trap of anachronistically, uncritically, and even apolitically using a black historical subject's present-day relevance to make claims for his or her legitimacy.[41] Reed advocates instead "a vantage point that approaches examination of antecedent individuals and debates and the discourses within which they were embedded from an orienting concern to locate within them clues to sources of salient political problems and discursive tendencies in our present." The challenge is to understand the limitations of presentism and historicism alike, refusing the illusion that the past can be represented "purely on its own terms" while avoiding as well the tendency toward decontextualized historical readings that opportunistically serve the present. The generative approach, Reed argues, "establishes . . . connections between ["heroic" figures such as Du Bois] and ourselves—both by considering them and us as distinct yet related moments in a process and by bringing them down to earth as people just like us, the best of whom struggled in concert and debate with their peers to craft progressive visions and programs under adverse and uncertain conditions, with imperfect knowledge and constrained by the histories and *mentalités* through which they could construct meanings."[42]

David Scott's engagement with C. L. R. James's *The Black Jacobins* is also helpful for determining how to productively read midcentury radical and even revolutionary texts in a new context. Scott is concerned "with the conceptual problem of political presents and with how reconstructed pasts and anticipated futures are thought out in relation to them." He is interested in thinking about the "dead-end present" through both "the old utopian futures that inspired and for a long time sustained it" and "an imagined idiom of future futures that might reanimate this present and even engender in it new and unexpected horizons of transformative possibility."[43] Comparing the 1938 and 1963 versions of James's history of the Haitian Revolution, Scott finds embedded in James's use of the historiographical trope of "romance" (pace Hayden White) the teleological assumptions of anticolonialism, which do little good as inspiration for future movements given the histories of political failures that shape the postcolonial present. He finds greater value for apprehending the present and future in the complex narrative mode of tragedy evident in the materials that James added to the 1963 version of the book. Not only does an engagement with tragedy enable us to think beyond the teleological assumptions of anticolonialism; we also learn in more reflective terms how to connect the past, imagined futures situated in the past, and the ways those futures became our present in often unexpected ways.[44]

As I situate Du Bois's thought at midcentury, I explore his insight into longue durée processes that he saw shaping his past, present, and future. Just as he was aware of the ways that elements of racial regimes largely consigned to the past could make their way into new social formations, we can pay close attention to how he interrogated social and ideological projects that were emergent at this moment but which continue to shape our present. Yet I also recognize the ways that Du Bois and his analysis were bound by history. He did after all encounter a world that was materially, socially, and ideologically different from ours. Such differences affected fundamentally not just how he perceived it but the questions he asked as well. His quest for a fuller realization of democracy and his analysis of the present and future of the 1940s and 1950s were made possible by the political and analytical modes of Popular Front and statist Marxism, Keynesian economics, insurgent anticolonial nationalisms, social mobilizations against Jim Crow, and the state of civil rights and human rights discourse. Du Bois's critique would not have been possible without his immersion in these political modes, and it was precisely this immersion that enabled insights into the broad contours of race and other forms of power that continue to have resonance today. As Robin D. G. Kelley reminds us, there is great analytical possibility in engaging the utopian aspirations of radical imaginations in the past.[45] We can also locate deep moral commitment to changing the world in such aspirations that remains useful and, indeed, necessary.

But we must also contend with the ways Du Bois's political affiliations limited the possibilities of his critique. The social analysis that inspired and drew from these movements was rooted in a social configuration that has changed. And while such movements clearly achieved great victories and transformed the world in important ways, we live at a moment when the limitations and failures of such projects have been spectacularly apparent for decades. African independence was central to Du Bois's vision for a more just world, but now most postcolonial African nations suffer from severe neocolonial deprivations and a host of internal problems, not the least of which are the rising, at times genocidal formations of state and extrastate violence. China and Russia, the countries in which Du Bois put so much faith as socialist utopias and anodynes against white supremacy, now flex their imperial muscle across the global South, while Eastern Europe stands as ground zero for a resurgent and explicit antiblack racism.

So I consider how Du Bois's ideas might be revised as they are brought to bear on a very different present than he imagined. I find such a directive in both his practice of revising his understanding of terms like "the race concept" and "the color line" *and* in his own willingness to imagine alternative futures. I also explore what some have viewed as the "tragic elements" of his story: his often tentative and misguided steps toward solving social problems, his affinity for political projects with obvious flaws, his alienation from different communities in which he was immersed, and the pessimism that sometimes informed his project. This, as Kate Baldwin suggests, requires "resist[ing] assignments of 'positive' or 'negative' assessments of Du Bois's political alignment."[46] Instead, we should examine the ways such alignment, as well as political divergence, dovetailed with and were structured by his larger goal of a fully realized democracy — a still unrealized yet always relevant goal in our increasingly polarized world.

My project is also energized by feminist work on Du Bois and black intellectual life more generally. I consider the significance of his coming to an insightful understanding of the mutually constitutive relationship of race and class while, like most antiracist activists then and in the decades that followed, saying little about how other social categories, like sex and gender, might be factored into a race conscious social analysis. I keep in mind how, even when he was not talking explicitly about sex or gender, Du Bois was engaged in modes of analysis, intellectual performance, and conceptual mapping that reproduced certain gendered exclusions and sexualized means of interpreting the world. Yet, in keeping with the idea that we can think through the contradictions and limitations of Du Bois's work in order to come to a deeper understanding of race in the past and present, I extract relevant insights from his omissions, his problematic gendered assumptions and performances, and from those aspects of his project that dovetail with the concerns of contemporary feminist scholars.

ORGANIZATION

Chapter 1 begins with an examination of Du Bois's presentation of himself as a scientist and propagandist in *Dusk of Dawn*. I read this text, first, as a generalized critique of modernity and the racial knowledge supporting it. But I also examine it as an engagement with the contemporaneous scientific, political, and moral imperatives to move beyond race and with the putatively colorblind nature of the liberal state and academy. Even as I use this autobiography as a means of familiarizing the reader with aspects of Du Bois's pre-1940 biography and thought, I argue that we should consider *Dusk of Dawn* not as a culmination of his thinking about race, as many have done, but as a jumping-off point. I then examine Du Bois's journal *Phylon*. Both venues illustrate an antiracism that was morally against racism *and* colorblindness yet ethically committed to investigating fully the logic of each at a crucial, transformative moment. Among his primary concerns was the persistence of race and racism not just in spite of but as a consequence of collective beliefs that their exclusions were being overcome. This became all the more worrisome to him as the United States proclaimed itself an agent of racial reform while assuming a more hegemonic role in the world. I conclude by discussing how Du Bois offers a trenchant analysis of forces that continue to reconstitute race and racism in the present as well as grounds for intellectual and ethical commitments to investigate and respond to them.

Chapter 2 focuses on what Du Bois identified as the problem of "color and democracy" during World War II. Updating his long-standing understanding of the links among war, imperialism, and race, Du Bois contemplated future social costs if war remained or became even more fundamental to modernity. He saw the various ways that the United States was taking on the mantle of imperialism, ameliorating its project but reproducing to some degree its racial exclusions. He viewed the inability of global leaders to take race into account adequately and transcend their own racial myopia when planning for the postwar global reconstruction as an act of exception that laid the groundwork for future exclusions. Moreover, Du Bois understood how the pursuit of "peace" without a commitment to addressing legacies of colonialism and their articulation with new imperialisms would mean perpetual war and destruction for those already deemed racial subjects and potentially create new categories of "homines sacri."[47] Finally, Du Bois's analysis helps us understand how the justificatory frameworks for Allied power during World War II and U.S. power during the Cold War may continue to serve our "colonial present."

Chapter 3 explores the ways Du Bois imagined the relationship between Africa and the rest of the world during the 1940s and 1950s. Du Bois had, of course, identified with, lobbied on behalf of, and written about Africa and Africans for decades. Yet he was drawn somewhat differently to the continent during the 1940s and 1950s. I explore his participation in the revival of the Pan-African movement in the mid-1940s, and his work on Africa with the NAACP and Council of African Affairs. Throughout this period one major concern, symbolized by his book *The World and Africa* (1947), was to identify and then reimagine the "worldliness" of Africa — historically, politically, culturally, and economically — as a necessary step in the creation of a more democratic world. Africa presented perhaps *the* ethical challenge facing humankind at a moment when questions about the scope of human rights were paramount. Despite significant problems with Du Bois's vision, his project suggests an alternative global imaginary that holds value in the present for developing a more focused or at least differently focused moral concern for Africa and therefore a more substantial challenge to the global racial order.

Chapter 4 concludes the study by examining Du Bois's participation in the midcentury peace movement, his subsequent trial and acquittal, and his own representations of these events. The discussion is informed by readings of twenty-first-century African American responses to the "war on terrorism" and analyses that have sought to make sense of the changing contours of racialized citizenship more generally during the post-9/11 period. Exploring Du Bois's complex loyalties at midcentury allows me to move beyond some of the moralizing that is often directed to his career in the 1950s and to focus more deeply on the antiracist potential of his analysis. I examine Du Bois's account of loyalty as a racial project articulated with various forms of power and consider the ways he charted the pethical responsibilities for both the individual intellectual and racialized body politic that were simultaneously made marginal by and complicit in U.S. hegemony. This, of course, is a challenge that continues to resonate in our contemporary world: for African Americans at the neo-imperial, twenty-first-century moment, given our historical, contradictory imbrication in empire; and for those otherwise implicated in the economy of black inclusion and exclusion that helped define modernity and continues to shape the world.

W. E. B. Du Bois's *Dusk of Dawn* (1940) begins with an "Apology." In this brief prefatory section Du Bois justifies his book's unexpected turn, for the imperatives of reflection upon the occasion of his seventieth birthday shifted its generic moorings closer to autobiography than originally anticipated.[1] And autobiographies, he suggests, are often limited by hubris and selective memory. But Du Bois more subtly defends his use of the "concept of race," a term intimately connected to his life story by the book's subtitle, "An Essay toward an Autobiography of a Race Concept." At a moment when liberal and radical scholars and activists contended that race was an atavistic category that should be transcended, Du Bois, as he put it later in the book, "rationalize[s] the racial concept and its place in the modern world," retaining it as a social scientific analytic, mode of personal identification, and vehicle for political mobilization.[2] Autobiography, in the end, provides "a way of elucidating the inner meaning and significance of that race problem by explaining it in terms of the one human life that I know best."[3]

Du Bois has since, in a sense, been asked to apologize for his use of race in *Dusk of Dawn*. K. Anthony Appiah concludes his well-known critique of Du Bois's use of the "race concept" by arguing that despite his claim that *Dusk of Dawn* represents a move forward, he "lead[s] us back into the now familiar move of substituting a sociohistorical conception of race for the biological one; but that is simply to bury the biological conception below the surface, not to transcend it."[4] Others have set themselves up as Du Bois's apologists, arguing that *Dusk of Dawn* is an erudite account of the complicated social and political life of race as a "social construction" and convincing argument for the need to continue to mobilize around it in a white supremacist world.[5]

Despite their competing viewpoints, such accounts generally reproduce Du Bois's own assessment that the book represented the maturation of his thinking about race.[6] This chapter instead considers *Dusk of Dawn* as a window onto his and the world's future in 1940. During the 1930s, as he witnessed both the successes and limitations of New Deal reforms, left activism, and scholarly inquiry, Du Bois had developed a powerful critique of liberalism's and Marxism's inattention to race. Common to the failures of left and liberal projects alike was a belief that new scientific research debunking the category would tear away the veil separating black and nonblack bodies and minds. But racial inequities clearly persisted into the first postracial moment, and Du Bois feared they might even be enhanced in the future if the promise of colorblindness supported by these findings turned into a refusal to see race (and racism) in its various manifestations or enabled its morphology to change. So Du Bois insisted on remaining attuned to the persistence and complexity of race, which remained a central "problem of the future world." As he asked a few years later, "Today as we stand near halfway through a century which has proven the biological theories of unchangeable race differences manifestly false, what difference of action does this call for on our part?"[7]

I explore here Du Bois's account in *Dusk of Dawn* of how science, as an intellectual endeavor and institutional practice central to modernity, invented and upheld racial categories (and, more to the point, white supremacy) but in certain circumstances could still be used to promote racial justice at both the practical and rhetorical levels. Through his ambivalent portrayal of science and his role as scientist, Du Bois addresses the ways race, as it became destabilized as a concept and lost some of its scientific credibility, also became in some ways more powerful and more insidious through its articulations with and through the market, state policies, and academic discourses. Du Bois was attuned to domestic manifestations of race and to the ways its shifting ontological status was connected with U.S. imperialism.

To gain additional purchase on Du Bois's thinking about race during the early 1940s, I examine his contributions to the journal *Phylon*, which he edited from 1940 until 1944. I consider the "Apology" he wrote for the journal's first issue and discuss one of *Phylon*'s regular features, "A Chronicle of Race Relations," which consisted of clippings from journalistic and academic writing, compiled and interspersed with commentary by Du Bois. His contributions to *Phylon* illustrate how he extended his mapping of the multifaceted, simultaneous unreality and reality of race at a crucial historical juncture. The Chronicle's perspective was international and transnational, addressing various spheres of racial activity (juridical, political, cultural, economic, and the like) and cataloging concepts and theories emanating from academia, civil rights and anticolonial struggles, and popular discourse.

Much of my analysis here focuses on Du Bois's negotiation of the scientific, political, and moral imperatives to move beyond race, which provides a particularly useful way to enter into a consideration of his midcentury thought. Not only do these imperatives continue to resonate within the critical and antiracist genealogies he helped establish; they also serve, ironically, to perpetuate racial hierarchies in the present. By attuning ourselves to the difficult questions Du Bois raised and the answers he posed about white supremacy's survival in the first postracial moment, we gain insights through his eyes into some of the social phenomena shaping our lives today. We also see the makings of an antiracism that was simultaneously against racism and colorblindness yet committed to investigating fully the logic of each at a crucial, transformative moment.

RACE, SCIENCE, AND MODERNITY

Du Bois had long theorized the centrality of race and racial terror to the development of modernity, its institutions, and its political languages. Paul Gilroy identifies in Du Bois's early work, especially *The Souls of Black Folk*, a "theory of modernity [that] pursues the sustained and uncompromising interrogation of the concept of progress from the standpoint of the slave," and which points out a "democratic potential disfigured by white supremacy." Through his multidisciplinary method, Gilroy argues, Du Bois posed a challenge to Marxian teleology. Not only did his deployment of "the history of slavery" challenge "the assumptions of occidental progress that Marxism shared" but his foregrounding of race and his attention to the complex, mutual articulations of racial hierarchies and identities "produced a theory of political agency in which the priority of class relations was refused and the autonomy of cultural and ideological factors from crudely conceived economic determination was demonstrated."[8] In *Dusk of Dawn*, however, it is Du Bois as scientist, rather than the figure of the slave, that propels the critique of modernity as well as the retooling of Marxism, in which he was at this point more invested. Although Du Bois's account of his investments in scientific method and discipline displays an elitist and masculinist intellectual authority, he also represents himself here, as Arnold Rampersad notes, as a "troubled hero," one whose perspective is energized by self-criticism and ambivalence about the scientific enterprise.[9]

In his opening chapter, Du Bois situates his birth in 1868 as coinciding with the flowering of human sciences: a moment that witnessed great progress save for the ways that

> the mind clung desperately to the idea that basic racial differences between human beings had suffered no change; and it clung to this idea not simply from inertia and unconscious action but from the fact that because of the modern African slave trade a tremendous economic structure and eventually an industrial revolution had been based upon racial differences between men; and this racial difference had now been rationalized into a difference mainly of skin color. Thus in the latter part of the nineteenth century when I was born and grew to manhood, color had become an abiding unchangeable fact chiefly because a mass of self-conscious instincts and unconscious prejudices had arranged themselves rank on rank in its defense. Government, work, religion and education became based upon and determined by the color line. The future of mankind was implicit in the race and color of men.[10]

He then tells of an initial faith in science to challenge the racial order, a subsequent belief in the power of agitation to secure immediate results, and then a more "mature," post–World War I understanding that what was needed for racial justice was a kind of fusion of science and propaganda dedicated to struggle over the long term.

These passages set the stage in the narrative for the dialectical unfolding of his life's work as scientist and propagandist. They propel him toward a revised, Marxian understanding of race that builds from previously held ideas. Yet complicating the narrative and adding another layer of meaning is the way he often implicates himself as subject of and agent in science as a racial project. Du Bois describes himself as both an interested investigator and a racialized mind and body whose social experiences as such are determined by the interface of race and science. He notes his nineteenth-century faith in Euro-American civilization and political culture, the systems of scientific knowledge it produced, and its imperialist logic. "I was blithely European and imperialist in outlook; democratic as democracy was conceived in America."[11]

We learn subsequently of his colorblind orientation, developed in the largely white New England community of his youth, and of the racial insults that this perspective did not quite enable him to process. Describing his academic course of study through and following the Ph.D., he notes how his idealist commitments to the disciplines of philosophy and history eventually give way to a more empirical sociology: an intellectual shift motivated in part by the hope that careful social scientific research would disprove assumptions about black inferiority and provide a path toward equality through scientifically planned uplift strategies and reasoned discussion of black contributions to and marginalization from the fabric of society. This perspective informed several programmatic essays on the social sciences during the 1890s and 1900s, his path-breaking sociological study *The Philadelphia Negro* (1899), and his influential collection of essays *The Souls of Black Folk* (1903). He describes his leadership of the Atlanta Conferences, annual gatherings of black researchers and a concomitant series of social scientific studies of black life that Du Bois administered primarily from his faculty post at Atlanta University. He was hired by the school in 1897 and took over the conferences shortly thereafter. He notes as well during this period a shift in his thinking about the scientific basis of race, moving him away from a biological conception and toward a Boasian culturalism.[12]

Du Bois worked at Atlanta until 1910 and had a hand in administering the conferences and editing the publications until 1913. However, the later years of his tenure at the school were marked by growing doubt about his chosen role of scientist. At odds with Booker T. Washington's accommodationist, self-help philosophy, he helped found the middle-class male African American civil rights organization, the Niagara Movement, in 1905. After participating in its founding conference in 1909, Du Bois agreed to join the NAACP as director of publicity and research. Moving to New York in 1910, he soon began editing the organization's journal, the *Crisis*; this after a number of events eroded his faith in measured scientific inquiry for solving entrenched racial problems. He was disappointed that he did not receive better financial support for his scientific work from the U.S. government and from black and white academic institutions, including Washington's powerful Tuskegee machine. Discouraging as well were his encounters with institutional racism and pseudoscientific racial discourse. Also calling into question the value of science was the consolidation of de jure segregation and discrimination and concomitant instances of barbaric racial violence. In *Dusk of Dawn* he describes in haunting detail the aftermaths of the Sam Hose lynching outside Atlanta in 1899 and the city's race riot of 1906, including coming across Hose's knuckles on display in a grocery store window. Such events constituted a "red ray" that "cut across the plan which I had as a scientist. . . . one could not be a calm, cool, and detached scientist while Negroes were lynched, murdered and starved."[13]

Eventually, he would come to an understanding of "Empire; the domination of white Europe over black Africa and yellow Asia, through political power built on the economic control of labor, income and ideas. The echo of this industrial imperialism in America was the expulsion of black men from American democracy, their subjection to caste control and wage slavery." Such understanding compelled a further shift in orientation. Thereafter, "my career as a scientist was to be swallowed up in my role as master of propaganda."[14] In *Dusk of Dawn*'s final two chapters, Du Bois covers his participation in the NAACP, Pan-African Congresses, post–World War I peace planning efforts, and other political activities. During this time he developed a linked and growing antiracist and anti-imperialist critique, evident in writings like *John Brown* (1909) and the essays that eventually made it into *Darkwater* (1920), and influenced by the scientism of socialism and progressivism. As many have noted, Du Bois's analysis was pushed to greater urgency in the 1920s by Garveyism, New Negro protest, the political agitation of the growing black urban population in the United States, anticolonial agitation abroad, and revolutionary Marxism in the Soviet Union, which Du Bois visited in 1926.

Yet Marxist analysis was valuable only to the extent it could be made more attentive to race. Du Bois was contemplating via Marxian dialectics the place of African Americans and colonial subjects in the world at the same time that the Communist International—in dialogue with activists like Jamaican American Claude McKay, Dutch Guianan Otto Huiswood, and M. N. Roy from India—sought to work out "the Negro Question" and the "Eastern Question," that is, to link global anticapitalism to nationalist antiracist and anticolonial struggle.[15] In his essay "The Negro Mind Reaches Out" (1925), for example, Du Bois noted the growing critique of global capitalism and the place of labor in the wake of the

Bolshevik revolution. However, he insisted that one must remain attuned to the global dimensions of and different situations facing labor, which by definition were related to race. "Modern imperialism and modern industrialism are one and the same system; root and branch of the same tree. The race problem is the other side of the labor problem; and the black man's burden is the white man's burden."[16]

Into the 1930s Du Bois remained dissatisfied with Marxism's and liberalism's theoretical blind spots regarding race, although Marxism held growing potential given the ways liberalism did not seem up to the task of addressing the current economic crisis of overproduction, the negative influence of capitalism on cultural production, and the crisis of democracy that accompanied these trends. In early 1933 Du Bois used the *Crisis* to promote a Marxian analysis while revising the economist's theories to address its racial limitations. Yet his faith in Marxist doctrine was tempered by the Communist Party's manipulation of the Scottsboro case, and he believed that a Soviet-style revolution or economic centralization would be harmful to African Americans.[17] Moreover, Freudian insights into unconscious desires helped him understand how race complicated historical materialism. The fact that white workers had largely forsaken the possibilities of intraclass, cross-racial solidarity helped shape Du Bois's understanding that race could not be reduced to an epiphenomenon of class relations but was, rather, a semi-autonomous social category, mutually constitutive with class, and which clearly persisted in spite of, as he put it in *Dusk of Dawn*, "the new scientific argument that there was no such thing as 'race.'"[18]

Multiracial democracy remained his ultimate goal, but given the limitations of liberalism and interracial labor activism, the short-term response by African Americans, Du Bois argued for much of the 1930s, should be an economic plan based on a kind of voluntary segregation and organization of African Americans in their current roles as consumers, led by intellectuals like himself.[19] This program for African American self-activity drew upon yet revised Marx's dialectical unfolding of history, the story of the Soviet revolution, a Leninist vanguardism, and the Comintern's Black Belt thesis holding that southern blacks in the United States composed a distinct nation whose political activity could be a stepping stone toward a socialist revolution.

As he discussed in an extant fragment from an unpublished manuscript, an African American consumers movement might be but one component of a coordinated effort by "minority groups the world over" to find an effective political strategy located somewhere between the undesirable option of "becom[ing] segregated, narrowly racial, nationalistic and sectarian, iconoclastic" and the equally objectionable path of "seek[ing] quiet unobtrusive self-suppression with eventual absorption into the larger groups or even self annihilation or group suicide." Du Bois believed group self-activity could help redistribute wealth while enabling a radical mass politicization that would ultimately serve a future, multiracial socialist project. Minority social movements should also be internationalist in orientation, working in coordinated fashion with other movements toward the "equalization of wealth and income." This would be no easy feat given that minority group struggles had often relied upon, ignored, or even promoted the exclusion of other groups. Still, he believed there was possibility in "the cooperation and free voice of the peoples of the earth and the assuming of responsibility by all groups. A new conception of democracy must come—a democracy of minorities which becomes a reservoir of openly expressed opinion and desire, out of which those who rule the state may know the truth."[20]

Du Bois discussed his plan for an African American consumers movement in some detail in the *Dusk of Dawn* chapter "The Colored World Within." He noted that the plan put him at varying odds with young radical black social scientists at the second Amenia Conference in August 1933. This gathering of prominent and up-and-coming black leaders and intellectuals was designed to reassess the African American civil rights agenda in light of liberalism's failure to address black poverty and unemployment and in the wake of the growing influence of the Communist Party. Rejecting Du Bois's plan, Ralph Bunche, E. Franklin Frazier, and Abram Harris were among those who argued instead that the path toward black liberation would come through more rigorous economic and class analysis and alliances with white workers in the labor movement. And while Frazier was more sympathetic to Du Bois and helped disseminate his ideas at the conference, others publicly criticized him for what they viewed as outdated racial and elitist thinking.[21]

Not that his plan received a better hearing at the NAACP. In *Dusk of Dawn* Du Bois describes his growing alienation from the organization under the leadership of Walter White and Roy Wilkins. When facing the Great Depression, members of the NAACP and other supporters of African Americans, he argues, erred in their thinking that gaining political rights within the present system was sufficient as an "end in itself rather than as a method of reorganizing the state."[22] The conflict between Du Bois and other NAACP officials over his self-segregation plan in the spring and summer of 1934, in the pages of the *Crisis* and in behind-the-scenes machinations, provided the final impetus for Du Bois's resignation from the organization and from his position as editor of the *Crisis* that July. He resumed his professorial career in the sociology department at Atlanta University, where he hoped to revive his Atlanta Conferences with money from the Rockefeller family's General Education Board.[23]

Du Bois, however, maintained faith in his plan, which sought to fulfill the promise of Reconstruction in the United States and beyond. In his monumental history *Black Reconstruction in America* (1935), he theorized the centrality of racial exclusion to democracy, and thus the limitations of the political system, in the United States and beyond. He situated this exclusion initially in the fundamental contradiction of the existence of slavery in a putatively democratic society. It was manifested later in the contradictions among commitments to a full extension of democracy "regardless of race and color," the development of an effective system of governance, and the protection of "property and privilege." Moreover, the founding dilemmas of the United States "[remain] with the world as the problem of democracy expands and touches all races and nations."[24] The missed opportunity of Reconstruction — ended by collusion among northern and southern capital and white laborers who chose to be "compensated in part by a sort of public and psychological wage" of whiteness rather than embracing interracial, intraclass solidarity — had world historical implications.[25] "The United States, reenforced by the increased political power of the South based on disenfranchisement of black voters, took its place to reenforce the capitalistic dictatorship of the United States, which became the most powerful in the world, and which backed the new industrial imperialism and degraded colored labor the world over."[26]

Yet, when *Black Reconstruction* looked at African American activism, it was as much forward looking as it was historical. Du Bois wrote of black participation in the Civil War, both through taking up arms and withholding labor, as leading to the defeat of the South. Black people exercising the vote, holding elected office, and engaging in civic activism brought, at least temporarily, a partial realization of democratic promise in the nation during Reconstruction. When black activism dovetailed with the efforts of state-sponsored "abolition-democracy" (the Freedmen's Bureau and aspects of the radical Republican program), Reconstruction represented the possibility of a multiracial, industrial (socialist) democracy.

Du Bois addresses the possibilities of a black reconstruction of democracy in *Dusk of Dawn*. Given the role that both conscious and subconscious desires play in mass ascription to the social order, Du Bois makes clear in the text that the creation of a racial democracy would be accompanied by careful scientific study of the contours of race and racism and "carefully planned and scientific propaganda" by intellectuals like himself. For "not simply knowledge, not simply direct repression of evil, will reform the world."[27] Du Bois's telos in *Dusk of Dawn*, then, is an intellectual/activist orientation, created out of a synthesis of the scientist and the propagandist, now illuminated by a racially attuned Marxian (and to a lesser extent Freudian) scientism, rededicated to historical recovery and sociological investigation, and committed fully to battling racism and understanding race's complex ontology.

We see this orientation put to conceptual work in the often-cited chapters at the center of the autobiography, "The Concept of Race," "The White World," and "The Colored World Within." Therein lies a valuable, more politically and economically savvy rearticulation of his long-standing engagement with, as Eric Sundquist puts it, "the fact that 'Negro' meant nothing that could be measured yet represented a clearly definable historical experience."[28] Or to put it somewhat differently, Du Bois explores what Kate Baldwin describes as an understanding of "the paradox of race as both an impossibility and a fact."[29]

These chapters disrupt and enhance his storytelling in a provocative way. Taking a respite from the chronological narrative of his development as scientist and propagandist, Du Bois "consider[s] the conception which is after all my main subject."[30] He moves the reader again through his various encounters with racial concepts and shifts in his thinking about them. The crucial moment in "The Concept of Race" occurs as he tells a complicated story about his background to comment on the absurdity of race as a determinant of human worth, precisely because of the complicated histories of "intermixture" in the ancestry of every human being. He implies that scientific investigation — perhaps a kind of physical anthropology that could map the complexity of racial mixing — holds the potential to disrupt the categories of racial distinction that have been used to justify the "economic foundation of the modern world." He traces his family history to make the point, carefully noting that both his multi-racial ancestry and his early unfamiliarity with "Africa" call into question the biological basis of racial attribute and affect. His "African racial feeling" was, after all, socially constructed in response to white racism and black communal ritual.[31]

Yet, even if biological race is a fiction, race is no less real in the present, even after "the concept of race has so changed." For the structural, ideological, affective, and institutional legacies of racial exclusion continue to make it real. "Since the fifteenth century these ancestors of mine and their other descendents have had a common history; have suffered a common disaster and have one long memory. . . . Physical bond is least and the badge of color relatively unimportant save as a badge; the real essence of this kinship is its social heritage of slavery; the discrimination and insult; and this heritage binds together not simply the children of Africa, but extends through yellow Asia and into the South Seas. It is this unity that draws me to Africa."[32] The intellectual / activist must also address race's multiplicity. "Perhaps it is wrong to speak of it at all as 'a concept' rather than as a group of contradictory forces, facts and tendencies."[33] And race must be engaged head on, he argues in the chapter "The White World," because of the continued subordination of identifiable groupings of human beings by other identifiable groupings of human beings, regardless of whether the scientific basis of those groupings is logical. "Thus it is easy to see that scientific definition of race is impossible; it is easy to prove that physical characteristics are not so inherited as to make it possible to divide the world into races; . . . all this has nothing to do with the plain fact that throughout the world today organized groups of men by monopoly of economic and physical power, legal enactment and intellectual training are limiting with determination and unflagging zeal the development of other groups; and that the concentration particularly of economic power today puts the majority of mankind into a slavery to the rest."[34]

Still, there remains some ambivalence in Du Bois's narrative about science and propaganda's willingness or ability to take this project on, even as these insights are, in part, framed as a kind of culmination of this thinking now that he has a better grasp of "industrial imperialism." Du Bois knows that the "mark" of his ancestors that "is upon me in color and hair" is "of little meaning." Antiracist science has told him this over the past two decades. "Racial" characteristics cannot explain differences in intelligence, reason, cultural skills, and so on. But these characteristics may remain "important," "as they stand for real and more subtle differences from other men. Whether they do or not, I do not know nor does science know today."[35]

RATIONALIZING THE RACE CONCEPT

Recent work by historians and political theorists has done an excellent job linking Du Bois's scholarly and activist commitments during the 1930s to the conceptual schema laid out in *Dusk of Dawn*.[36] This scholarship puts into play Du Bois's dissatisfaction with the liberalism of the Roosevelt administration and the NAACP; his critique of the black and white lefts' inadequate theorization of race and, in his mind, their naive faith in an interracial labor movement; and his calls for a black reconstruction of democracy in the United States at symbolic (as in *Black Reconstruction*) and practical (as in his plan for an African American consumers movement) levels.

Thomas Holt argues that Du Bois's understanding of race as "a group of contradictory facts, forces, and tendencies" marks the growing sophistication of his understanding of race as social construction rather than biological inheritance as well as his belief, because of his Marxian and Freudian understanding of race's deep imbrications in the social, that democracy cannot be reformed as it exists but rather needs to be reconstructed through black self-activity.[37] Joel Olson similarly asserts that by the 1930s Du Bois had developed an understanding of race as a social construction and, in doing so, offered a "political theory of race" still useful to our present. Du Bois's materialist analysis of the "cross-class alliance" between capital and white labor in *Black Reconstruction* demonstrates the existence of a "bipolar" racial order. This order is intimately connected to but not epiphenomenal to class relations and structures institutions, practices, and ideologies of liberalism.[38] *Black Reconstruction* and *Dusk of Dawn* both suggest, Olson argues, that "the dark world is the democratic antithesis of the white world. The white world is a form of political social power that threatens democracy in the United States and across the globe, while the dark world holds the future of democracy." Du Bois's musings on the race concept in *Dusk of Dawn*, then, provide evidence of a perspective on race that views it as absurd on a certain level but demands that it must be maintained as a tool for analysis and a vehicle or mobilization for the reconstruction of democracy.[39]

Nikhil Pal Singh takes things a step further by situating Du Bois's activist/intellectual project as "a fascinating contribution to the wider re-visions of liberal, democratic (and Marxist) thought underway through-out the North Atlantic intellectual milieu in the 1930s . . . and a response to qualitative changes in the role of racial differentiation in the formation of modern nations, peoples and publics." The New Deal's revision of classic liberalism, with its increasing administration, support of trade unionism, augmentation of consumer purchasing power, and promotion of egalitarianism, had, through a series of "universalizing" practices that worked against regional exclusions, provided tangible benefits to black workers, helped to make civil rights a national rather than a local issue, and facilitated the development of an "emergent black public" in the process. Yet the "unstable mix of urban liberalism and herrenvolk republi-canism," as Singh puts it, perpetuated and to some extent augmented racial inequalities through putatively race-neutral policies that dispropor-tionately benefited whites and, in some cases, through policies that pur-posely excluded blacks.[40]

In order to keep the New Deal coalition intact, Roosevelt had to make compromises with southern politicians over proposed antilynching legis-lation and the Fair Labor Standards Act, which sought to dismantle regional differences in wages and working conditions. Moreover, many of the key national social welfare reforms were racially discriminatory in practice. Social Security protections and National Recovery Administra-tion codes largely did not apply to domestics, agricultural workers, and, in the case of the latter, certain personal service occupations, which com-posed a large percentage of the black workforce. The lack of government attention to the bias in Federal Housing Administration loans, Federal Relief Administration welfare payments, Agricultural Adjustment Ad-ministration crop reduction payments, and Tennessee Valley Authority and Civilian Conservation Corps work programs meant that such bene-fits largely went to whites. Even into the "second New Deal," when other African Americans were celebrating the formation of a "black cabinet," and Du Bois's own public assessment of Roosevelt was improving, he still expressed doubts about specific agencies' commitments to racial justice and the ameliorative capabilities of liberal state projects in general.[41]

Du Bois, then, was invested in complicating naive faiths in both class struggle and state reform as well as in the ways people assumed they would enable race to be transcended. As Singh notes, "He anticipated (correctly) that race and race relations would be the terrain on which a wider array of social and political conflicts were mediated, interpreted, resolved, and displaced." By insisting on black particularity in the struggle for democracy—whether through his formulation of a "Negro proletariat" in *Black Reconstruction* or through his plan for black voluntary segregation—Du Bois tried to call attention to the centrality of race and racial exclusion to modern political discourses and institutions *as well as* to the necessary role of black people in the reconstruction of democracy in spite of, and because of, these exclusions. Singh argues that when Du Bois seeks to "rationalize" the race concept in *Dusk of Dawn*, he is holding on to the idea that "independent, black political activity is intrinsically valuable, an irreducible part of any change in the form of the state on a par with other world-historical social movements, particularly class struggles."[42]

Such valuable accounts linking *Black Reconstruction*'s vision for democracy to the race concept in *Dusk of Dawn* can be productively built upon by shifting the emphasis of the interface of these texts back toward the question of science and to the challenges to democracy posed not just by the multiplicity and persistence of race and racism but also by the ways faith in their dissolution emboldens and transforms them. This, in turn, enables a recasting of *Dusk of Dawn* as a jumping-off point for a new stage of Du Bois's thinking in which long-established ideas, tropes, and rhetorics are reworked and imbued with new meanings in a changing social context.[43] And it allows us to add to a set of ontological-ethical questions animating much scholarship on Du Bois—for example, to what extent must we hold on to race as an analytical and political category even though we know it is fundamentally flawed as a scientific one?—a set of epistemological-ethical questions regarding the necessity of developing knowledge about race's changing foundations and being attuned to the ways refusals of such knowledge enable its reproduction. Accomplishing this requires further engagement with what Du Bois presents as the possibilities and limitations of science in *Dusk of Dawn*, with his ambivalence and uncertainty about the role of the scientist and propagandist in the text, and with the ways such representations resonate with his earlier formulations and his recent experiences as a researcher.

In addition to theorizing race and black political activity, *Black Reconstruction* was also the most significant of Du Bois's rejoinders to the white supremacist historiography of Reconstruction. This intervention went back to "Reconstruction and Its Benefits," his address to the American Historical Association in 1909 that was published the following year in the *American Historical Review*. In *Black Reconstruction*'s final chapter, "The Propaganda of History," he drives home the point that ideology colors the interpretation of data as well as the very framing of the questions that drive an investigation. "Subtract from [political scientist John] Burgess his belief that only white people can rule, and he is in essential agreement with me."[44] Du Bois also rethinks history as science in *Black Reconstruction*. He "want[s] to be fair, objective, and judicial," to recognize and analyze "human frailties and contradiction" when they occur.[45] But he understands that science produces the justificatory framework for explicit white supremacist interpretation as well as a will toward "mechanistic interpretation" that elides the ways individual or group actions or struggles in the past may serve the political needs of the present.[46] Truth, then, must include a degree of propaganda in order to be successfully marshaled against "the propaganda of history." *Black Reconstruction* is predicated, after all, on the proposition Du Bois is obliged to make at the beginning of the volume, "that the Negro in America and in general is an average and ordinary human being, who under given environment develops like other human beings."[47]

This last comment was Du Bois's historiographical version of the principle he had long claimed was necessary to legitimate social-scientific investigation of black lives and to the development of social scientific knowledge more generally. As he noted in "The Study of Negro Problems," originally an address to the American Academy of Political and Social Science in 1897, "the Negro is a member of the human race, and as one who, in the light of history and experience, is capable to a degree of improvement and culture, is entitled to have his interests considered according to his numbers and in all conclusions as to the common weal."[48] Despite the neat narration of his shift from scientist to propagandist in *Dusk of Dawn*, Du Bois sought from the beginning to strike a balance between a commitment to empirical investigation and to reform. Moreover, he argued that a dedication to studying black society held the potential of pushing sociology forward by finding a balance of universalizing theory with detailed empirical observation.

Du Bois's framing of his sociological method was in part a response to "Negro problem" discourse of the late nineteenth century, which criminalized and otherwise pathologized black people, often in social Darwinist terms, via assumptions about their natural racial characteristics and lack of capacity for historical progress. Du Bois, of course, reproduced such discourse in various ways. His essay "The Conservation of Races" (1897), with its biologistic conception of group identity and investment in racial historical destiny, bought into the logic of social Darwinism even as it rejected the assumed outcome of racial competition. And his early sociological work did, in a sense, validate the supremacy of "Western" culture and society as it argued for black inclusion within it. Yet he was also seeking to redefine the "Negro problem" from one of black character to one of American denial of black "humanity."[49] He recognized quite clearly that the racial biases influencing popular behaviors and political discourse were conditioning the practice of social science.[50] Du Bois tried to demonstrate black humanity and push sociology toward an anti-essentialist and antiracist future by demonstrating that "actions" were in part products of "conditions" and that African American societies differed across time and space.[51] Taking on "the brilliant but questionable leadership of Herbert Spencer" directly in a description in 1904 of the Atlanta Conferences, he proposed that a kind of synthesis of grand theory and careful empirical observation — "a real knowledge of natural law as locally manifest — a glimpse and revelation of rhythm beyond this little center and at last careful, cautious generalization and formulation" — might be achieved by interested researchers.[52]

Initially, Du Bois was somewhat circumspect about how one might balance commitments to reform and the quest for truth. In 1897 he stated, "Any attempt to give [science] a double aim, to make social reform the immediate instead of the mediate object of a search for truth, will inevitably tend to defeat both objects."[53] But in the first decade of the twentieth century, as social and institutional pressures called him to question whether he could be a "calm, cool, and detached scientist," he saw with more clarity the mediating role that researchers played in the production of knowledge, as they helped shape the realities they were studying. This realization, in turn, legitimated and compelled an intervention in that reality.[54] Such scholarly activism was particularly important given the ways that racism was already embedded in the production and institutionalization of knowledge. In his unpublished essay "Sociology Hesitant" (1905), oriented largely as a critique of Comtean positivism, Du Bois embarked on an implicit critique of institutionalized racism by showing how putatively "objective" social-scientific method, as well as science more generally, were shaped by politics.[55] Du Bois was, in these pieces, of course, writing at a turn-of-the-century moment that witnessed both the pinnacle of science's obeisance to white supremacy and redefinitions of intellectual life in the United States and Europe, as industrial development, the modern state and university, and imperial apparatuses helped produce a class of knowledge workers who through their deployment of science were committed to analyzing, abetting, and sometimes reforming these institutions.[56] He had, as he recalled in the early chapters of *Dusk of Dawn*, been both implicated in and marginalized by this project.

More recently, however, he had been chastened in other ways. As Du Bois recounts in the final chapter of *Dusk of Dawn*, the previous decade had been one of critical illumination but also great frustration with the politics of knowledge in which he was immersed. As noted, his plans for black economic self-determination and his retention of race as a social analytic earned him the scorn of liberals and radicals alike, within and outside the African American community. His discussion of the self-determination plan in his manuscript "The Negro and Social Reconstruction," a prospective contribution to Alain Locke's series of "Bronze Booklets," was one reason Locke and his corporate sponsors rejected the volume.[57] Locke did, however, publish Ralph Bunche's *A World View of Race*. Bunche's analysis of race as a social construction deployed to enable and justify capitalist exploitation was to some degree consistent with Du Bois's interpretation. Yet Bunche took issue with Du Bois's and others' race-based solutions to inequality, arguing instead that the path forward lay in alliances with white workers.[58]

Black Reconstruction received some surprisingly good press given its political agenda, but liberals criticized Du Bois for his Marxism and left critics took issue with his transformation of Marxism.[59] Du Bois also found himself characterized as nonobjective, even as he argued in *Black Reconstruction* for a more "scientific" history that would transcend the racial biases of its practitioners.[60] More devastating was the failure of his "Encyclopedia of the Negro," a project sponsored through its planning stages by the Phelps-Stokes Fund. Du Bois had for decades been interested in such an endeavor. He assembled editorial and advisory boards in 1909 but could not develop the project further because of limited funding. In the shifting intellectual and social climate of the 1930s, he was cautiously optimistic that such an undertaking might be successful, and he was named principal editor of a new version of the project in 1934. The politics around the encyclopedia, however, were complicated, and

Du Bois was marginalized at different points in the planning process because of perceptions about his personality and politics.[61]

These projects were developing at a moment when black intellectuals claimed and were given increased (albeit limited) authority by the academy, the federal government, the press, and philanthropic organizations as interpreters of the racial order. It was, more specifically, as Jonathan Holloway observes, a period when black social scientists were creating a "bridge from the establishment of modern social science and its technocratic faith in objectivity to the emergence of the social science race relations expert who dominated the academic scene during the modern civil rights movement."[62] Yet black intellectuals were sometimes deemed suspect because of their radical ideas and intelligent presence, and the orientations and relative merits of the interested expert and objective technocrat were often seen at odds with one another, especially when black researchers pressed too hard on questions of racial justice.[63]

Du Bois persevered, maintaining that he could be both "objective" and committed to justice.[64] However, in 1938, in the wake of charges by British social scientists that neither white nor black Americans were capable of objective research on U.S. race relations, calls by other commentators that the focus of social scientific study should be on Negro problems rather than Negro achievement, and criticisms specific to Du Bois for his hastily assembled proposals for the project, the Rockefeller family's General Education Board, the funding source upon which Anson Phelps of the Phelps-Stokes Fund was most dependent, decided to defer support for this project. That same year the Carnegie Corporation, another potential funding source, finalized the deal to fund the Swedish economist Gunnar Myrdal's sweeping study of African American life and U.S. social relations, later published in 1944 as *An American Dilemma*. Not only did funding Myrdal's study address the homegrown objectivity problem but it also put forth, as will be discussed later, a more palatable understanding of the basis for racial injustice in the United States. Du Bois continued to work on the Encyclopedia, publishing a "Preparatory Volume with Reference Lists and Reports" in 1945 and a somewhat longer version of this in 1946, but it was clear by 1941 that Myrdal's project had displaced his. It was not until he took up his work on the *Encyclopedia Africana* in exile in Ghana at the very end of his life that he significantly resumed this commitment.[65]

As the Encyclopedia project became more precarious, Du Bois weighed in on the contemporary politics of racial knowledge. Responding in 1938 to an admirer's praise for *Black Reconstruction*, Du Bois validated the ideal of objective, social scientific research but noted also its potentially damaging, instrumentalist application. He suggested that science needed to be infused with both an ethical commitment to social justice and to a fuller recognition of the lived experience of its marginalized subjects. "I have sympathy," he wrote, "for the ideal of cold, impartial history; but that must not be allowed to degenerate as it has so often into insensibility to human suffering and injustice. The scientific treatment of human ills has got to give evil full weight and vividly realize what it means to be among the world's oppressed."[66] And even as he recognized how antiracist social science had altered academic discourse and was having an increased effect on "intelligent public opinion," he knew prejudices remained. At the end of the decade he still thought it necessary for black scholars to push "certain assumptions concerning Negroes which a number of honest minds still regard as unproven. These assumptions would revolve around the belief that black folk are human beings, with reactions essentially the same as those of other human beings."[67]

Ultimately, Du Bois suggested, the questioning of black scholars' objectivity in light of their commitment to racial uplift and equality was part and parcel of the legacy of white supremacy within scientific institutions and modes of inquiry. Race continued to function insidiously within the scientific community, and this reflected poorly on the ability of science to transcend its racial past. In a contribution in 1939 to a *Journal of Negro Education* symposium, "The Position of the Negro in the American Social Order," Du Bois responded to critics who explicitly or implicitly suggested that his voluntary segregation plan and insistence on the primacy of race in his social analysis reproduced the logic of white supremacy. "[Charles] Johnson and [Ralph] Bunche and myself are working in Negro universities, not because the subject matter which we teach is purely 'racial'; or because science should have a 'racial' tinge; or because ability should be segregated by color; but for the obvious reason that no white university in the United States is going to give us a chance for teaching and research." Regardless of how enlightened social science as a whole was becoming, the structural configuration of the academy and the broader society necessitated that black people (including social scientists) "move in a racial groove."[68]

As a black researcher, Du Bois was working within and against what

David Theo Goldberg identifies as "racist culture." Goldberg demonstrates the centrality of race to modernity and modern subjects, how it has persisted because of the needs of capital and discursively through its own internal logic, and how it conceptually and functionally (via racial identities and racial exclusions) can morph into new, powerful forms, even as modern social and political discourse purports to make it irrelevant. It stands, then, as a paradox of modernity. "As modernity commits itself progressively to idealized principles of liberty, equality, and fraternity, as it increasingly insists upon the moral irrelevance of race, there is a multiplication of racial identities and the sets of exclusions they prompt and rationalize, enable and sustain. Race is irrelevant, but all is race."[69]

Goldberg's analysis specifically calls attention to the role of "racial knowledge" in the creation and perpetuation of racist culture. Racial knowledge is

> dependent upon — it appropriates as its own mode of expression, its premises, and the limits of its determinations — those of established scientific fields of the day, especially anthropology, natural history, and biology. This scientific cloak of racial knowledge, its formal character and seeming universality, imparts authority and legitimation to it. Its authority is identical with, it parasitically maps onto the formal authority of the scientific discipline it mirrors. At the same time, racial knowledge — racial science, to risk excess — is able to do this because it has been historically integral to the emergence of these authoritative scientific fields. Race has been a basic categorical object, in some cases a founding focus of scientific analysis in these various domains.[70]

And during the 1930s, with the coming to fruition of a liberal social science, racial knowledge sustained itself and the social order precisely through its consignment of racism to "premodern prejudice, one that enlightened modern meliorism takes itself to be overcoming through the force of reason." This "liberal meliorism . . . blinds itself to the transformations in racist expressions, in racist culture. It runs from the alterations in the varying forms of racisms, in the contents of their representations, in the modes and implications of their significations, and in their functions and outcomes."[71]

Du Bois saw the perpetuation of race and racism despite scientific advance but also through science at both the theoretical and practical levels, within the realm of research and when social science paradigms informed state policy. Part of the problem was simply that "our casual knowledge always tends to lag behind scientific accomplishment, and it is still possible today to make and reiterate the most reactionary statements concerning Negroes which science has long disproved."[72] But putatively enlightened social scientists were also implicated when their paradigms were unable to comprehend the persistence of racism in its various manifestations. This was the case when they assumed race was an anachronistic concept and that racism would fall by the wayside with the development of democratic citizenship, industrial economies, and urbanization, or when, from a Marxian perspective, they sought to understand race and racism merely as epiphenomena of economic forces. Such paradigms enabled the persistence of race both by cloaking it in other logics and refusing to address its fundamental place in society. Du Bois understood that as it created a frame for dismissing race, science empowered its chameleonic future. It worked in concert with economic interests and semi-autonomous discursive forces as well as through the functioning of the liberal state. We should broadly understand Du Bois as a critic of modernity and, more specifically, as a critic of the discourse of modernization permeating the social scientific approach to race and much Marxist theory as well as the organization of the liberal state circa 1940. His was a perspective grounded in the racial present but anxiously future-oriented as well.

Returning again to *Black Reconstruction*, we can point to some important instances where Du Bois theorizes the ways a kind of universalistic and liberal meliorist faith in statist projects can both enable and transform the racist projects sustaining capitalism. Writing about the limitations of abolition-democracy in light of capital's power and shifting needs, Du Bois calls attention to a familiar ideological conceit: "The American Assumption was that wealth is mainly the result of its owner's effort and that any average worker can by thrift become a capitalist." He suggests that the American Assumption energized abolition-democracy but also defined its limits. The recognition "for the first time in the classic democracy in the United States . . . that the American Assumption was not and could not be universally true" enabled some radical Republicans to recognize that freedom would require political rights, political capital, and governmental mechanism (a "dictatorship of labor over capital and industry") for distributing these resources to black people and protecting their claims to them. Yet the more common objection to slavery rooted in the American Assumption, one that united laborers and capitalists, was the belief that the existence or return of slavery threatened their efforts to accrue wealth. Although abolition-democracy's brokered compromise among social groups led to reforms, it was accompanied by an inadequate amelioration of race-based exclusions and the persistence of faith that the principles of the political-economic system would enable it to right itself in the future. These phenomena, in turn, permitted future exclusions. Speaking of radical Republicans' attempts to launch a reconstructive project immediately after the war, Du Bois writes: "Their theory of democracy led them to risk all, even in the absence of that economic and educational minimum which they knew was next to indispensable. When [Charles] Sumner saw his failure here, he went home and wept. But the belief in the self-resurrection of democracy was strong in these men and lent unconscious power to the American Assumption. They expected that both Northern industry and the South, in sheer self-defense, would have to educate Negro intelligence and depend on Negro political power."[73]

For a time, of course, abolition-democracy's faith in nation and the linkage of its democratic promise to a doctrine of wealth enabled democratic reform, but such meliorism was always at the mercy of the needs of capital, which might offer its support to reform but could just as easily take it away. Speaking of the choice facing the nation in 1867, Du Bois writes: "The decisive battle of Reconstruction looms. Abolition-democracy demands for Negroes physical freedom, civil rights, economic opportunity and education and the right to vote, as a matter of sheer human justice and right. Industry demands profits and is willing to use for this end Negro freedom or Negro slavery, votes for Negroes or Black codes."[74] Such inconsistency is enabled by the ways that the state engages in a hollow championing of market-friendly racial reforms while denying capital's role in racism's intransigence, by a willingness to manipulate racial discourse and the futures of racial subjects at whim in order to advance elite social or economic interests, and by liberalism's general inability to understand the ways race permeates politics. As Du Bois describes Andrew Johnson's granting of amnesty in December 1868 to those participating in the Confederate rebellion: "He declared, in effect, that the dictatorship of labor, attempted in the South under the Reconstruction acts, had led to corruption and bloodshed and, therefore, prevented the rise of industry in the South, which was the real solution of the race problem. . . . Johnson thus illustrated again the way in which the color problem became the Blindspot of American political and social development and made logical argument almost impossible."[75]

These passages suggest an understanding that race and racism persist through multiple processes. Some are clearly committed to denying black humanity or circumscribing the rights to which blacks, even if admitted into the category of human, may be entitled. Yet race and racism are simultaneously products of projects that are ostensibly committed to reforming society, acknowledging black people's humanity, and extending their rights. In the latter case, race and racial inequalities can persist when reforms do not adequately address existing exclusions; when the nation's principles produce a teleological faith that these exclusions will be overcome without a concomitant commitment to investigating fully their causes; and when the failures of such racial reforms stand in metonymic relationship with their "failed" human objects and subsequently become a justificatory frame for a resurgent white supremacy.

As a historian, Du Bois confidently addresses race's multiplicity and chameleonic aspects in *Black Reconstruction*. In *Dusk of Dawn*, however, his autobiographical musings betray more uncertainty about the ability of science to grasp this complex terrain. But this uncertainty also points toward a valuable, critical stance on race and racism. The sense of uncertainty and at times crisis that enters the text and complicates his telos as a "mature" scientist and propagandist speaks to the changing dilemmas regarding racial politics and racial research in which Du Bois found himself embroiled circa 1940. It speaks of a simultaneous investment in and problematization of the assumed inherent progress of modern political theory (whether Marxist or liberal) and social scientific discourse alike. He wanted to draw from both but also believed they needed enrichment to understand the centrality of race to social and political life and the exclusionary place of race in their own epistemologies.

The problem up to this point, unfortunately, was that "both Negro and white thinkers" tended "to minimize and deny the realities of racial difference. The race problem has been rationalized in every way." Even explanations that sought to explain the inferior position of African Americans in terms of poverty, education, or the historical legacy of slavery sometimes failed to take into account the ongoing nature of racial domination, "the fact of a white world which is *today* dominating human culture and working for the *continued* subordination of the colored races."[76] *Dusk of Dawn* suggests, as an alternative, that the researcher must explore the nuances of racial projects, their multiple modes of articulation, and their shifting bases. What was needed was a "rationalizing of the race concept" as a means of further understanding the ways the racist exclusions shaping the world were constantly morphing in form and mode of justification and thus shaping the future.

We can read in Du Bois's positioning of himself as subject and object of racial knowledge an epistemological standpoint from which to apprehend these complex workings of race in the present and the future. Even as he conveys a sense of optimism that racism was under assault, and he journeys toward a kind of revised Marxian, scientific certainty about the foundations of race and racism, he is impelled to revisit his earlier challenge to the ability of grand theory to address the problems of race. Science promised much, as it had for decades, but Du Bois knew from long personal experience that the application and interpretation of science could be selective and that even the best intentioned efforts might do little if not accompanied by an ethical commitment to social justice and a willingness to temper theoretical orthodoxies with a dedication to investigating fully the persistence of racism in various manifestations.

As ambivalent subject and object of scientific knowledge *and* the state, Du Bois places himself in the role of mediating the "truth" of their interface. Such ambivalence in *Dusk of Dawn* propels Du Bois's conceptualization of race in the text as a destabilized concept, the social role of which multiplies as its putative irrelevance is celebrated. The process by which Du Bois arrives at his definition of the "race concept . . . as a group of contradictory forces, facts, and tendencies" is critical. Du Bois bears the mark of race "in color and hair," which should not mean anything significant given what he as a scientist knows, and what liberal opinion knows. But it does. And this personal knowledge as racialized body and professional researcher tests the limits of science. Du Bois does not know whether these markers "stand for real and more subtle differences from other men . . . nor does science know today."[77] And this is the crux of his dilemma. Race as a scientifically legitimate category does not exist, but differences in history, culture, treatment in the labor market and in civil society, and life chances do exist. And the suggestion that science does not know whether subtle differences mean anything should be read not as a retreat into the biological but rather as a commentary on the limitations of understanding, of the uncertainties remaining when theorizing race and racism, their pervasiveness and production in the social, their divergent effects on people inhabiting bodies with different morphological characteristics, and, ultimately, of the way that the fundamental ontological question of the existence of race has served material social processes.

In other words, race can be partially apprehended and explained by existing theoretical apparatuses, investigated by different methods, but none is quite sufficient. A crucial question facing Du Bois as a racialized subject and knowledge worker is whether scientific proof of the insubstantiality of racial categories will fulfill its expected role as a bulwark against racism or whether it somehow participates in the production of new forms of racism. As Du Bois had experienced himself, science, as discourse and array of institutional relationships, continued to remake racial hierarchies even as it announced the insubstantiality of race. Moving into a discussion of white supremacy in the following chapter, "The White World," Du Bois insists further that racial exclusion is a global phenomenon that thwarts the development of human societies. He argues as well that we have not yet developed the political will or languages to fully come to terms with race. "All our present frustration in trying to realize individual equality through communism, fascism, and democracy arises from our continual unwillingness to break the intellectual bonds of group and racial exclusiveness."[78]

When Du Bois seeks to "rationalize the racial concept and its place in the modern world," he is not merely justifying the use of the term and political organizing around it but proposing that there is a need for further phenomenological work to better understand both the social bases of race and racism as well as the conceptual bases and assumptions that enable their survival. Du Bois believes scientific inquiry remains necessary and he hopes that careful study will produce insights into race's and racism's mutability and their future manifestations and applications. Debunking the legacies of nineteenth-century pseudoscience is crucial. So are a Marxian understanding of political economy, a hardheaded analysis of social policy, and Freudian insights into unconscious urges driving human behavior. But none fully suffices. An antiracist scientist/propagandist must also commit to changing his or her perspective of what race is, how it is produced in shifting social contexts, by shifting bodies of knowledge, and how it positions and reproduces human beings in constantly changing ways. And a fundamental challenge persists: even as one theorizes race's complicated, shifting, destabilized life, one must keep in mind the common, prosaic effects of race on racial bodies that stand at the center of their social experiences and very existence. We see this, for example, when Du Bois emerges from a meditation on the ways his multiracial background confounds any essentialist definition of race: "Race is a cultural, sometimes an historical fact, . . . I recognize it quite easily and with full legal sanction; the black man is a person who must ride 'Jim Crow' in Georgia."[79]

MORE APOLOGIES

Du Bois built upon this analytical project in his journal *Phylon*, which he edited from 1940 until his dismissal from Atlanta University in 1944. He pursued it as well through the short-lived Phylon Institute, an update of the Atlanta Conferences that he hoped would systematically address "the Economic Condition of the American Negro and his future possibilities" by bringing together scholars from various black colleges and universities for extensive collaborative research projects.[80] Du Bois started planning for both projects upon his return to Atlanta University in the mid-1930s. Although somewhat constrained from the start by tepid support from his school and a lack of cooperation from other black educational institutions, Du Bois was at least briefly, if not completely, vindicated in his goal to reestablish himself as an activist scientist and propagandist.[81] And in both *Phylon* and the Phylon Insitute we see the limitations of his mediating intervention as an interested black researcher and an important step forward in mapping the contradictory and shifting conceptual terrain of race locally and globally during the early 1940s.

Du Bois thought *Phylon* could be a vehicle for reimagining social science, its applications, and its scope at midcentury. It followed, to some degree, the agenda of the failed Encyclopedia, with its planned synthesis of empirical facts and portraits of black achievement and its commitment to "restor[ing] to the American Negro his rightful hegemony of scientific investigation and guidance of the Negro problem."[82] He positioned himself as both intellectual forbear and peer of young social scientists who had recently criticized him for his deployment of the race concept. Du Bois saw *Phylon*, which took its name from the Greek for "race," as a complement to publications like the *Journal of Negro Education* and the *Journal of Negro History*. But he also hoped to chart a method that eschewed what he considered the failed promise of objectivity in a society structured by racism. His approach began instead with a political commitment and epistemological orientation he imagined he shared with other black researchers but which also transcended "the internal study of racial groups" and moved toward "a general view of that progress of human beings which takes place through the instrumentality and activity of group culture."[83]

As launched in the 1940s, the Phylon Institute was designed to reconfigure a black reconstruction for democracy. Du Bois would refer to it later as "a New Deal for Negroes."[84] He now looked not to a consumer's movement but to Negro colleges for a plan of action. In various statements seeking funds and institutional support for the project, Du Bois put forth a plan for extensive, coordinated sociological work by researchers affiliated with these colleges. This knowledge would, in turn, be used to promote "social uplift" in the areas of education, social services, recreation, and health. It would engage specifically "the problems of earning a living among Negroes since these are fundamental to practically all other efforts."[85] This project can be seen as addressing, again, the failures of the U.S. government's New Deal, as well as an attempt to institutionalize a response to the multiplicity of ways that racial inequality was manifest and reproduced through state action and inaction. Du Bois was also attuned to changes brought by World War II. As he put it, "The war had upset conventional economy, exacerbated racial consciousness, and already led to bitter clashes. The developments after the war were bound to add to these difficulties. There is one and only one fundamental and definitive way to meet this situation and that is to begin a systematic study of the essential facts of the present condition of the Negro race and to establish a way of continuing and making more complete and effective such a study."[86]

One such area of scholarly investigation was the realm of culture. At this moment when culture's role as an instrument of and weapon against racial distinction was being transformed, it remained for Du Bois, as it had been for decades, a mode for negotiating dilemmas regarding both race and science and a kind of shorthand for understanding differences in both treatment and circumstance of different human groupings. In the inaugural issue of *Phylon*, he penned another "Apology," justifying again his retention of the race concept. In keeping with the journal's subtitle, "The Atlanta University Review of Race and Culture," Du Bois explained that the terms "race" and "culture" were used "more or less interchangeably," given his and others' understanding of race as "cultural and historical in essence, rather than primarily biological and psychological." Yet he retained the signifier "race" precisely "because of the reality back of it" as its ontological status changed. The "greater groups of human kind" that racial science had erroneously sought to narrowly define did, in fact, share experiences and orientations precisely because of these taxonomies and the political-economic uses of racial categories.[87] Such differences, then, must be acknowledged, studied, and, when appropriate, developed culturally and politically as a means of both group advancement and, ultimately, the creation of a global humanism rooted in a cosmopolitan ethos. "Here if anywhere the leadership of science is demanded not to obliterate all race and group distinctions, but to know and study them, to see and appreciate them at their true values, to emphasize the use and place of human differences as tool and method of progress; to make straight the path to a common world humanity through the development of cultural gifts to their highest possibilities."[88]

The growing understanding of race through the prism of culture was a fundamental component of the complicated ontological grounding of race circa 1940. Scholars grappled with the question of whether an embrace of cultural difference would be a step forward or would simply reproduce racial logics established in the past. The problems and possibilities of both particularist and universalistic embraces of culture at this moment are evident in the well-known debate between E. Franklin Frazier, author of *The Negro Family in the United States* (1939), and Melville Herskovits, who wrote *The Myth of the Negro Past* (1941), over the extent to which black culture in the United States was a product of African retentions or represented assimilation into the fabric of U.S. society. Frazier's argument, downplaying African retentions and using assimilation as a gauge of the health of black society, sought to counter the notion that black people's values and practices were incompatible with those of modern white Americans. Herskovits, on the other hand, promoted African retentions and their influence on white society as a pluralist rejoinder to the devaluation of black culture and its African past as well as to the assumption that assimilation to the white norm provided the proper means to black advancement. Both assumed the other's analysis played into the racial logics they were trying to challenge, and their debate illustrates the dilemmas involved when trying to understand the relationship between culture and race at a moment when the former was gaining capital as a means of understanding human difference. Herskovits assumed the Boasian view that substituting race for culture and understanding the intrinsic worth of different cultures would challenge scientific racism. Frazier, on the other hand, saw culture more instrumentally, less as a self-affirming set of group practices and beliefs than as a mode of social differentiation, intimately related to class, that followed the logic of racial difference.[89]

Both of these thinkers negotiated but did not fully grasp the process by which a culture-based racism involving elements of both the particularist and universalistic was taking shape at this moment. We can see here the alchemical beginnings of what would come to fruition during the postcolonial era: a "differentialist racism," which, as Etienne Balibar argues, "is a racism whose dominant theme is not biological heredity but the insurmountability of cultural differences, a racism which, at first sight, does not postulate the superiority of certain groups or peoples in relation to others but 'only' the harmfulness of abolishing frontiers, the incompatibility of life-styles and traditions." Yet, as he continues, there is often an assumption that human cultures can be "divided into two main groups, the one assumed to be universalistic and progressive, the other supposed irremediably particularistic and primitive."[90]

We can readily identify in Du Bois's formulation elements of both universalistic and particularist elements of this discourse, both of which have in subsequent years informed modes of cultural distinction that have shored up race in the wake of its biological discrediting. However, we can also see that by cobbling together race and culture he called attention to the process by which the racial ordering of society proceeded through a culturalist logic. What remains valuable in Du Bois's deployment of culture as a mode of understanding race is the way it helps him map race's complicated and chameleonic existence. And it simultaneously moves toward a pluralist stance that was implicated in but nonetheless responded to and illuminated the scientifically grounded, modernizing, and universalizing antiracist discourse standing at the center of U.S. statecraft during and after the 1940s.

Du Bois maps the changing contours of race in "A Chronicle of Race Relations," a feature he edited in every issue of the journal from its inception until he left Atlanta University in 1944. Averaging eighteen pages in length over the course of its publication, this feature consisted of Du Bois's commentary on various phenomena pertaining to race, defined broadly, supported by often-lengthy quotes from public officials, government declarations, and passages pulled from newspapers, academic journals, and recent books. Du Bois organized this commentary into bulleted passages, collected under a series of headings that sought to describe the life of race historically, geographically, culturally, methodologically, and conceptually.[91]

Du Bois begins the second iteration of the Chronicle by setting forth two fundamental challenges to making sense of race relations in the 1940s. First, he raises the issue of the complicated, ever-shifting conceptual basis of race. Rather than evade the category, one must instead understand its changing material and ideological life, its different manifestations, and the ways that other social processes are sometimes misidentified as race. "This chronicle, therefore, will treat the matter of race in the broadest sense as contact between biological races so far as such races are indicated; as contacts between cultural and national groups; as contacts between economic classes especially when economic differences accentuates and emphasizes the racial snarl." The second challenge is to come to terms with the simultaneous invisibility and hypervisibility of race in public discourse. Work on "racial and cultural groups," particularly regarding social inequalities they face, is seldom reported, unless such reporting is cast in "sensational" terms. "Despite all this," he claims, "Phylon is going to try to give a reliable and so far as possible even a scientific picture of race facts and relations which can be compared from quarter to quarter and will be consolidated and reviewed once a year."[92]

Du Bois then uses the Chronicle to reexamine the "race concept," which he described in *Dusk of Dawn* "as a group of contradictory forces, facts, and tendencies." He encourages thinking about different ways that race might be conceptualized, addressing, for example, how various structural processes and differently conceived modes of human differentiation and cohesion work in concert with one another. Du Bois examines relations between national governments and their subjects as well as among human groupings, cultural formations, and processes that develop across national borders. Although he maintains a Marxian perspective on labor, economic developments, and imperialism, his mapping also seeks to locate race as a semi-autonomous phenomenon within juridical, political, cultural, and academic realms of endeavor and knowledge. In this second installment of the Chronicle, for example, his subheadings cover geographical regions (Europe, Africa, West Africa, South Africa, Asia, India, the West Indies, the South) as well as spheres of activity and conceptual questions ("objects and methods," "racism," "art," "peace," "economic classes," "intercultural"). He also notes the differing contours of racism across the globe, as when discussing recent scholarship on the racisms emanating from German and Italian fascisms.

As Du Bois promotes this expanded frame for making sense of the complex life of race, he engages the possibilities and pitfalls of science and propaganda. In various issues of the journal he points to the role of science in supporting colonial administration and white supremacy more generally. Thus he recognizes the importance of research projects and statements by professional academic organizations debunking the biologistic foundations of race that began to appear in the late 1930s and 1940s. But he is also aware of the ways that science, through its recent liberal interrogation of the biologistic basis of race, serves a paradoxical function, both illuminating and obfuscating as well as challenging and supporting the racial order.[93] In an entry titled "Race in Theory" in 1943, Du Bois refers to recent *Scientific Monthly* articles by W. M. Krogman and Robert Redfield that quite valuably undermined biologistic thinking about race yet acknowledged it as a social "fact." Du Bois follows this with an entry, "Race in Practice," which complicates such scientific optimism. "Despite the increasing unanimity of science on the subject of race," he argues, "it is astonishing how the older racial theory dominates practical governmental and social action."[94]

Objective, scientific inquiry is valuable so long as it can serve black society (as well as the broader population of colored people across the globe) by sanctioning racial reform and so long as it can fundamentally affirm the moral status of racial minorities as human beings. Yet even these projects are limited by the small numbers of black researchers associated with them. Responding in 1944 to a suggestion that *Phylon* "make up its mind to be either an organ of science or of propaganda," Du Bois cautions against the development of "a Negro science in a segregated Negro field." Yet he argues for the validity of black social scientists working from the perspective of, as he described it a few years earlier, "a racial groove." Du Bois argues further that in a Herrenvolk democracy, built through deep historical process upon black labor and attendant ideas about blackness, a kind of interested science was precisely what was needed. Black "immigration" from the fifteenth through the nineteenth centuries was the greatest social event of modern history. It founded modern capitalism in industry; it tested, challenged and thrust forward, modern democracy; and has been and still is the greatest controlled laboratory test of the science of human action in the world. . . . No group of facts is so worth scientific study, despite the desperate endeavor to distort, lose and belittle it. If the pursuit of this aim be propaganda, then Propaganda we welcome and embrace. . . . There are certain things PHYLON assumes without any attempt at proof; among these are the equal humanity of persons of Negro descent; and the capability of Negroes to progress and develop along essentially the same lines as other folk. If now this initial attitude is propaganda, we cheerfully plead guilty.

The job of the scientist/propagandist, as in the nineteenth century, is still to help unmoor democracy from its racially exclusionary past and, as part and parcel of this project, affirm the humanity of black people.[95] And in keeping with his long-established practice of interrogating the potentially racist outcomes of putatively empirical science, he continues to demand that a science of human sameness not shy away from the questions of the interestedness of investigators and the question of the historical foundations of racism.

In other words, as he moved into the 1940s, Du Bois continued to ambivalently champion an antiracist science as a means of both demonstrating the common humanity of people across the planet and documenting the experiences and life chances of people across the globe. Doing so helped him craft an increasingly nuanced understanding of how European colonialism, U.S. imperialism, and white supremacy in general were maintained through a complex yet complementary system of affirmations and disavowals of race through a multitude of social structures and different modes of racial knowledge. As this ambivalence toward science informs the Chronicle's survey, it helps shape his account of the ways various institutions, modes of analysis, political formations, and ideas could both produce or dismantle racial modes of social organization and knowledge production. What the Chronicle encourages, then, complementing the analysis in *Dusk of Dawn*, is a perspective on the ways in which various social entities may simultaneously enable and challenge racism either by affirming or disaffirming the existence of race, and how this may be understood on a global scale.

Also propelling the study of race into the future in Du Bois's work circa 1940 was his exploration of its moral scene. Not only did he call into question the self-righteousness of American hegemony at a moment when U.S. empire was being expanded; he also began to address how its augmentation proceeded through the enabling and incorporation of black politics. This, in turn, suggested to him a need for black subjects to consider carefully how the moral economy of liberal reform perpetuates racism nationally and globally *and* how they must contend with the ways they were implicated in it.

Gunnar Myrdal's *An American Dilemma* ultimately became the most visible expression of a political and moral demand for a fully realized universal citizenship rooted in science in the U.S. public sphere at midcentury. Although the full impact of Myrdal's influence on race relations was not felt until the Cold War era, we can see in *Dusk of Dawn* the beginnings of a parallel, alternative consideration of the alchemy of race, rights, science, and empire that Du Bois would voice throughout the 1940s. Du Bois gestured toward such a framing in a curt response in 1940 to an invitation from Ralph Bunche, in his capacity of researcher for the Myrdal project, to answer a brief questionnaire regarding race, knowledge, and his own social experience. Du Bois declined, referring Bunche to the autobiography being published that fall, adding, "I think you will find in that all the data you need."[96]

Du Bois was disappointed that Myrdal's study, not his, would become the touchstone for understanding and negotiating race at midcentury. He remained publicly respectful and supportive of Myrdal's project and encouraged somewhat by its direct acknowledgment of the persistence of white racist beliefs at a moment when other social scientists were assuming their disappearance and its analysis of the socioeconomic impact of de jure segregation in the South. Yet Du Bois could not have been pleased with Myrdal's downplaying of political economy and the shift in emphasis, when compared to plans for the Encyclopedia, from the black subject of history to the black object of racism and moral redemption. As Myrdal put it: "Though our study includes economic, social, and political race relations, at bottom our problem is the moral dilemma of the American — the conflict between his moral valuations on various levels of consciousness and generality."[97]

As others have noted, Myrdal's moral imperative based on the scientific proof of human sameness played a critical role in changing conceptions of race and struggles to secure rights into the 1950s. The NAACP's Legal Defense Fund and its allies cited it in briefs for a series of landmark desegregation cases culminating in 1954 in *Brown v. Board of Education* (Chief Justice Earl Warren also referred to it in his opinion on the *Brown* decision itself). This call to action based on common biology was also found in UNESCO's statements on race in 1950 and 1951, which were the result of a UN Economic and Social Council resolution "to consider the desirability of initiating and recommending the general adoption of a programme of disseminating scientific facts designed to remove what is generally known as racial prejudice."[98]

However, as Myrdal and his colleagues drew upon science debunking race (and an Enlightenment faith in rational analysis and reform) they did so in a way that rejected historical materialist understandings of racism in the contemporary world.[99] Myrdal's emphasis on modernization also located within the United States and its stated commitment to extend universal rights a certainty of overcoming its racial history. The implication of such a proposal in the domestic sphere was a stated imperative toward a national homogeneity against which both racist exclusions and black color consciousness were deemed contrary to national ideals. Moreover, by explaining persistent racial hierarchies as products of a cycle of racial discrimination and black social pathology, Myrdal's study was predicated on the legitimacy of the U.S. nation — and, by extension, the broader fabric of white society — as the arbiters of racial justice, as well as on the goal of assimilation for blacks into American society (and by extension, Western "civilization") as the most legitimate solution to their demands for equality. As Lee Baker notes, "Myrdal's theme appealed to the American public because he fashioned the Negro problem into a moral dilemma for Whites and a formidable [moral] task for Blacks, to assimilate and work themselves out of poverty."[100]

Myrdal's deployment of science against race also linked the struggle for civil rights in the domestic sphere to the struggle for human rights in a global context. But again it did so in a way that emphasized the primacy of the "American Creed" and narrowed the field of vision with which race and racism might be perceived. It worked in concert with other celebrations of modernization in promoting U.S. interests and righteousness during World War II and the early Cold War years.[101] By arguing that the

United States' successes in the revamping of the global order would be predicated on the successful inclusion of African Americans in the U.S. body politic, Myrdal vindicated the goals of black activists and intellectuals during the 1940s. However, he also helped establish the more narrow political and discursive terrain within which civil rights leaders and supporters would eventually operate, for his study implicitly positioned the United States as heir apparent to the "civilizing mission" of the European imperial powers while presenting the promise of black inclusion within its borders as the moral justification for the expansion of U.S. hegemony.[102]

Du Bois presciently counters Myrdal in the *Dusk of Dawn* chapter "The Colored World Within," positing that the "task" for African Americans is not assimilation into an ultimately just, national project but rather a black-led reconstruction of democracy at home and abroad. This would be accomplished through intellectual projects like his own and through a "*third* path" of activism (a consumer movement), situated between demands for inclusion and nationalism: one that would permit autonomous group economic development *and* "co-operation and incorporation into the white group on the best possible terms."[103]

Yet it is in the chapter "The White World" where Du Bois levels his most biting critique of the moral framing of projects such as Myrdal's, a kind of anticipatory rejoinder to the dematerialized, nationalist, and assimilationist account in them. Here Du Bois addresses the predictable question of whether his collective aspersions toward "the white world" are either unfair or reductionist. He points out that American principles do pose a challenge to white supremacy in theory, but white supremacy persists, despite "the philosophy of [Thomas] Jefferson, . . . the crusade of [William Lloyd] Garrison, . . . the reason of [Charles] Sumner." Thus the assumed antiracist elements of the universality of the American project are called into question.[104]

Du Bois addresses the matter of race and social responsibility further in two dialogues with imagined white interlocutors. He engages his fictional "white friend," Roger Van Dieman, in a debate over the merits of different groups, and in doing so he calls attention to the ways purportedly racial attributes (beauty, intelligence, cultural development, and so on) constitute the relative moral worth of human beings in societies structured by racism. He accomplishes more as he surveys the ways another "friend," an "average reasonable, conscientious, and fairly intelligent white American[,] faces continuing paradox" because of race.[105] The "dilemma," at root, is that different codes by which this person lives — as a Christian, as a gentleman, as an American, and as a white man — are at odds with one another because of the way race corrupts the principles upon which such identities are founded and because the identities themselves are forged in a white supremacist context.[106] Although his "logical" friend agonizes over the paradoxes he faces,

> Other folk are deliciously impervious to reason. They are pacifists with the help of the police and backed by careful preparation for war. They are filled with Good Will for all men, provided these men are in their places and certain of them kept there by severe discountenance. In that case courtesy smooths human relations. They certainly aim to treat others as they want to be treated themselves, so far as this is consistent with their own necessarily exclusive position. This position must be maintained by propaganda inculcating a perfectly defensible contempt for inferiors and suspicion of strangers and radicals. They believe in liberty under a firm police system backed by patriotism and an organization of work which will yield profit to capital. And, of course, they believe in poverty so long as they have sufficient wealth. This they are certain is the way to make America the greatest country on earth for white supremacy.[107]

When racial exclusion is fundamentally and contradictorily woven into the fabric of society, "the democracy which the white world seeks to defend does not exist. It has been splendidly conceived and discussed, but not realized." Nor does the solution remain entirely within the black community in the United States and its reconstruction of democracy, although that project remains central. Du Bois moves instead toward an interracial and global notion of collective responsibility. "If [democracy] ever is to grow strong enough for self-defense and for embracing the world and developing human culture to the highest, it must include not simply the lower classes among the whites now excluded from voice in the control of industry; but in addition to that it must include the colored peoples of Asia and Africa, now hopelessly imprisoned by poverty and ignorance. Unless these latter are included and in so far as they are not, democracy is a mockery and contains within itself the seeds of its own destruction."[108]

The challenge for African Americans in particular does not simply stem from their history of racist exclusion. It also emerges from the privileges and responsibilities of citizenship (however compromised) in a state increasingly exercising its political, economic, and military power abroad.[109] In response to Van Dieman's suggestion that if things are so bad in the United States he should consider leaving, Du Bois, as a symbolic black U.S. citizen, points out that the incorporative dimensions of imperialism in its past (European) and emergent (U.S.) manifestations mean that escape from imperialism's political and ideological systems is difficult. And this brings with it responsibility. Du Bois thus expresses his own dilemma: "I am as bad as they are. In fact, I am related to them. They have much that belongs to me—this land, for instance, for which my fathers starved and fought; I share their sins; in fine, I am related to them."[110] He is also, of course, an intellectual. And as he implicates himself in empire, he bespeaks the paradoxical positionality that Abdul-Karim Mustapha, following Gramsci, ascribes to Du Bois later in the 1940s, as a "Negro intellectual" in the context of empire: he serves the project of empire through the analytical frameworks he helps reproduce, yet, "at the same time, because of his (moral) philosophical concerns and commitments—which are primarily residual—he understands that his function is to produce a fissure in that framework."[111]

If Du Bois's science offers promise within this moral scene, it will not come from merely debunking the race concept and assimilating into the universal promise of Western society. It will involve intervening more radically in the global racial order. "Negroes in Africa, Indians in Asia, mulattoes and mestizoes in the West Indies, Central and South America, all explain the attitude of the white world as sheer malevolence; while the white people of the leading European countries honestly regard themselves as among the great benefactors of mankind and especially of colored mankind." The challenge for black intellectualism and politics is to develop social analyses and activism that transcend both of these self-righteous visions and instead seek to understand both the "rational and conscious" as well as the "subconscious and irrational" aspects of white supremacy, linked as they are to the subjugation of workers and minority populations in national and global contexts. This is the path for dismantling "industrial imperialism," for bringing "the great racial groups of the world . . . into normal and helpful relation to each other," and for understanding "the colored world," in particular, "as existing not simply for itself but as a group whose insistent cry may yet become the warning which awakens the world to its truer self and its wider destiny."[112]

THE FUTURE WORLD

Dusk of Dawn and *Phylon* suggest we continue to think carefully about the centrality of race and racism to modernity and more specifically to the ways that they have been fundamentally intertwined with capitalism and with the development of liberalism, in the United States and elsewhere. Although these components of modernity have been transformed in dramatic ways since the 1940s, Du Bois's own attention to world historical process and to the particulars of the present as well as his willingness to engage with and transform theory point to ways that we might draw on his work while remaining attentive to recent transformations regarding race, capitalism, and liberalism.

Du Bois in the 1940s instructs us to retain our suspicions about the universal progress and promise of current regimes of power and of the older narratives of liberation often invoked to counter them. And, through his complicated engagement with race and science in particular, Du Bois suggests an ethos that contemporary investigators can deploy when looking at race and racisms in all their complex manifestations, even as popular and political common sense argues that science impels us to move on to other subjects. Du Bois's project signals the way that an antiracist intellectual project must be attuned to the potential racist power of both affirmations and disaffirmations of racial difference in various aspects of social and political life, as well as through different kinds of institutional configurations. In other words, it is not merely that discourses of colorblindness and racial transcendence mask the existence of racial hierarchies. Rather, these orientations are potentially the ideological mechanisms upholding white supremacy.

We face such challenges when confronting the belief that the United States has become a colorblind society which no longer requires racial redress. While this view is supported by very real economic and educational gains by some immigrants and middle-class, U.S.–born people of color, evidence shows persistent inequalities among whites and blacks (and, to varying degrees, other racial minorities) in family income, wages, wealth, health, incarceration, home ownership, and the like.[113]

We also face such challenges when trying to address the ways race is simultaneously made visible and invisible by our present political economic regime of neoliberalism, which David Harvey defines as based on a theory that "human well-being can best be advanced by liberating individual entrepreneurial freedoms and skills within an institutional framework characterized by strong private property rights, free markets, and free trade."[114] Neoliberalism has, as a general rule, tended to further concentrate wealth among the already rich individuals, nations, and corporations in the global community. The logic of small government that (often disingenuously) informs the practice of neoliberalism dovetails with the neoliberal state's approach to racial inequalities. What David Theo Goldberg calls "racial Americanization is produced by a mix of doing nothing special, nothing beyond being guided by the presumptive laws of the market, the determinations of the majority's personal preferences, and the silencing of all racial reference, with the exception especially of racial profiling for purported purposes of crime and terror control."[115] As Vijay Prashad provocatively paraphrases Du Bois, "The problem of the twenty-first century, then, is the problem of the color blind. This problem is simple: it believes that to redress racism, we need to *not* consider race in social practice, notably in the sphere of governmental action. The state, we are told, must be *above* race."[116] This is a phenomenon deeply enmeshed within the international and transnational development of capitalism. "Color blindness as an international ideology neglects, in bad faith, the *production* of inequality in our world by the manipulation of the finance markets to benefit those who already have wealth."[117]

Yet intimately connected to neoliberal colorblindness are affirmative articulations of racial identity, like multiculturalism's celebration and recognition of cultural and racial difference. The global exchange of commodities and movement of human beings that go hand in hand with the neoliberal project enhance intercultural sharing, hybrid identities, and a sense of familiarity. Such exchanges are often seen as evidence that the era of race is over. They support a view upholding the benevolence of the corporate practices that facilitate such exchanges, as well as the sense that official interventions into the racial order are no longer necessary. Yet such cultural visibilities and exchanges are also markers of profoundly unequal social relations across and between the overdeveloped and underdeveloped worlds. George Lipsitz demonstrates this in his compelling account of the differential relationships to Disney's figure of Pocahontas of the Haitian women workers who sew pajamas with her likeness in sweatshops, of elite consumers who buy these products for their children, of the CEO of the Disney Corporation, and of Native American activists contending with the genocidal legacies that the Pocahontas myth has helped to ameliorate.[118]

Moreover, we must contend with the ways multiculturalism forms the terrain through which new forms of racism emerge. Responding to Slavoj Žižek's analysis of multiculturalism as "hegemonic," Sara Ahmed characterizes multiculturalism as a political discourse that "conceals forms of racism, violence and inequality," as it imagines liberal societies as being "beyond racism." By being presented by liberal societies as a hegemonic position, it then permits and encourages new forms of racism "as a refusal of [its] orthodoxy" and as a corrective to its excesses. "The best description of today's hegemony is 'liberal monoculturalism' in which common values are read as under threat by the support for the other's difference, as a form of support that supports the fantasy of the nation as being respectful at the same time as it allows the withdrawal of this so-called respect. The speech act that declares liberal multiculturalism as hegemonic is the hegemonic position."[119]

Reading Du Bois's consideration of the problem of the "future world" in this light suggests that we can consider the relationship between his present and anticipated future during the middle of the twentieth century and our own present and future. Writing at the beginning of what we can identify as a historical cycle that began with the ascendancy of U.S. imperial power, a ramping up of economic productivity, an enshrinement of the welfare state, and a liberal racial discourse accompanying it, Du Bois was operating in a different moment from ours, given the neoliberal political-economic order, new forms of imperial sovereignty, a more pervasive and explicit commitment to colorblindness and multiculturalism alike, and the failures of the socialist and nationalist movements he thought would solve the problems of his present.

However, Du Bois did witness some of the specific genealogies in which we are currently still immersed. His work points to a moment of beginnings for the ways our lives continue to be structured by the coalescence of the decline in biological racist discourse *and* political economic racial analysis, by the popularization of psychological and cultural understandings of the race concept, by the interface of liberal meliorism and state policy, and by a nationalist discourse of freedom and democracy with righteous universal application. His engagement with the scientific, political, and moral imperative to move beyond racial thinking at the moment these phenomena coalesced points, on the one hand, to the ways they might still ideologically function to occlude the persistence of racialized inequalities stemming from historical circumstance and more recent economic development. But Du Bois's work also encourages us to consider how these inequalities are perpetuated domestically, internationally, and transnationally in insidious ways through our righteous performance of a democracy we do not admit is unrealized. And, as his comments about his own implication in this system suggest, the figure of the African American intellectual (and, by extension, ordinary thinking person) continues to bear responsibility and promise for intervening in this state of affairs.

I must stress here that Du Bois's mediation into the realm of race and science implicated him in the reproduction of a masculinist intellectualism as well as an exclusionary racial analysis and politics vis-à-vis categories of gender and sexuality. Even as he spoke passionately about the ways racism and economic oppression coincided to structure the lives and life chances of colonized subjects and racial minorities, like most of his contemporaries he paid almost no sustained attention in his late 1930s or 1940s writings to the categories of sex or gender or to the particular challenges facing women of color and sexual minorities. Occasionally he addressed the specific social position of black women, but such comments were typically supplementary to more general thoughts about labor or race relations.[120] Moreover, we can identify in Du Bois's narration of his career as scientist/propagandist in *Dusk of Dawn* a series of conflicts that, as Keith Byerman observes, position him as "the wronged son resisting arbitrary or self-aggrandizing father figures."[121] His twinned commitments to inquiry and agitation in the face of such power is, following Hazel Carby, an articulation of a gendered intellectual practice consistent with his earlier, masculinist examples of self-representation.[122] In these ways he was implicated in the reproduction of incomplete modes of racial analyses that feminist scholars and activists would have to revise a generation later.

Still, we can extract from Du Bois's ambivalence with science in *Dusk of Dawn* an orientation that can be put in dialogue with feminist theorizing. Gender remains an undertheorized category in *Dusk of Dawn*, but given the ways that science has also been implicated in gendered hierarchies and often articulated via a masculinist politics of knowledge, we can think about the gender-critical perspectives that might be drawn from Du Bois's critique of science's supposed neutrality and lack of bias and his attention to the ways it reproduced the (racial) social order at both the discursive and institutional levels. Keeping in mind Ange-Marie Hancock's assertion, discussed in the introduction, that Du Bois's work anticipates feminist intersectionality theory's attention to the mutually constitutive aspects of multiple social categories, I also propose that his understanding of the multiplicity of race and his attention to the future in *Dusk of Dawn* encourage that his ideas be put in dialogue with work that has been more attentive to emergent social formations and ideological projects through which race is articulated with gender and sexuality.[123] Over the remaining chapters I will call attention to some of the gendered exclusions in Du Bois's work and reference as well as some possibilities in his formulations.

Among the central issues Du Bois commented on in *Phylon* and elsewhere during the early and mid-1940s were World War II and postwar peace plans. In short, war and peace critically informed his understanding of race and racism as phenomena deeply linked to imperial histories and intertwined with the intellectual and moral challenges of social justice in his present. We, in turn, may use his insights to gain purchase on the interface of race, war, and imperial pasts in our present.

My analysis of Du Bois's thoughts on such matters is informed by accounts of wars as products of imperial sovereignty and of present-day wars as rooted in the colonial past. After surveying a handful of influential accounts, I turn to Du Bois. I address his long-established concerns about the violence of imperialism, the centrality of war to modernity, and the limitations of liberal democracies. I then explore how he reconfigured these concerns in response to the imminent global conflict. I discuss how his equanimity about the rise of Nazi Germany and imperial Japan expressed the moral inconsistencies of what Marianna Torgovnick describes as an emerging "war complex" yet still provided a platform for launching an insightful critique of how racial formations of the colonial past were being rearticulated. I explore how Du Bois, like other black activists, saw the principles ostensibly guiding the Allied war effort, as well as black participation in that effort, potentially enabling a reconstruction of democracy across the planet. But I also take into account Du Bois's attention to hypocrisy in the war effort. For complicating his faith in democracy's reconstruction was a fear that the United States' ascendant power during the war, the articulation of this power with other forms of imperial sovereignty, and opportunistic rhetoric about the nation's virtue would perpetuate racial exclusions.

Du Bois also wondered what the end of the war would mean for colonial subjects and racial minorities. He saw Allied peace plans as exclusionary in their imagination and application, enabling of neoimperial military and economic relationships, and thus guaranteeing legacies of violence against and among racialized people across the planet. I show how Du Bois put forth an alternative, antiracist vision for peace in speeches, newspaper columns, *Phylon*, statements on behalf of the NAACP, his book *Color and Democracy*, and his lobbying efforts with the United Nations.

Du Bois's analysis of World War II and the "peace" that followed gives greater illumination of his understanding of race as a destabilized but still-powerful concept and of the continuing life of racism in the first postracial moment. By addressing how a colonial past was rearticulated through war in the present of the 1940s, Du Bois also illuminates the beginnings of a complex economy of sovereign power that shapes our own present. He demonstrates both the meaning and meaninglessness of "peace" as rhetorical frame and as geopolitical ideal. Moreover, he exposes an ethical calculus that has accompanied the economic, military, and political actions that shape our present, one that purports to be against race but which can permit exclusionary treatment of people made racial by long legacies of imperialism. Finally, Du Bois's work in the 1940s helps us understand how such exclusions are perpetuated in the present through our memories of the virtues of this decade.

PERMANENT WAR

As wars across the planet increasingly constitute a permanent state of affairs, they provide a constant threat to the very existence of millions of targeted and "collateral" human beings whose circumstances bring them closer and closer to the conflicts. They also shape the basic conditions of human life — at the levels of political economy, culture, biopower, and so on — even for those physically far removed from battlefields. A fundamental question facing us is how race and racism are produced by and serve to justify this state of war.

Michael Hardt and Antonio Negri argue that the permanent state of war is fundamentally linked to new forms of imperial sovereignty. Although some powers — the United States, for example — clearly play a more central role than others, Hardt and Negri argue that we should no longer understand imperial power in the world simply as that expressed by sovereign nation-states. Instead, they emphasize the emergence of "'network power,' a new form of sovereignty [that] . . . includes as its primary elements, or nodes, the dominant nation-states along with supranational institutions, major capitalist corporations, and other powers." The embodiment of this power, "Empire," uses war "as an instrument of rule," with periods of war and peace becoming less and less distinguishable. "Today's imperial peace, *Pax Imperii*, like that in the times of ancient Rome, is a false pretense of peace that really presides over a state of constant war." The system of perpetual war, they insist, represents the "primary obstacle to democracy" while making struggles for democracy more necessary than ever.[1]

Like others addressing the global state of war, Hardt and Negri invoke the notion of "the state of exception" to understand the political, legal, and ethical frameworks through which perpetual war is maintained and human life destroyed with relative impunity. They argue that we can understand war today in light of two exceptions: "one Germanic and the other American in origin." War as a limited state of exception to the functioning of sovereign power — a concept in the German legal tradition — has now become "permanent and general." This legal concept coalesces with two definitions of the exceptionalism of the United States, which plays a central role in the creation of the networked power of Empire. There is the long-standing definition of the United States as *"an exception from the corruption* of the European forms of sovereignty, and in this sense it has served as the beacon of republican virtue in the world." This view today provides a basis for the nation's presumed privileged status as promoter of democratic principles and the rule of law. "U.S. exceptionalism also means — and this is a relatively new meaning — *exception from the law,"* as evidenced by recent disregard for international agreements on the environment, human rights, arms control, and the treatment of prisoners of war.[2]

Hardt and Negri recognize the rhetorical use of the first U.S. state of exception in justifying the second, but they downplay its role in structuring policy and belief in the twenty-first century. Although they valuably point to World War II and the early Cold War as crucial moments in the development of war as potentially absolute and central to human experience, where the production and protection of life go hand in hand with the destruction of it, they gloss over a process through which these twinned U.S. exceptionalisms helped reshape both the contours of imperial power and its meaning.[3] Discussing this in detail would require something else largely missing from their analysis: a consideration of how the racial projects of old forms of imperial sovereignty have been transposed, albeit in different forms, into the present of Empire. In order to understand this, we need to keep in mind the more affirmative, but no less racial, political projects upon which contemporary expressions of sovereignty are based. For the ascension of the United States as an imperial power in the middle of the twentieth century, justified and enacted through a rejection of established colonialisms and their racist scaffolding, as well as through a commitment to human rights, perpetuated old forms and created new forms of sovereignty that continue to define (racially) a world at war. In other words, we need to keep in mind the ways American exceptionalism, reconfigured in this context at midcentury, continues to define the states of exception that abet and are produced by global war.

Hardt and Negri are not alone in undertheorizing the connections between present-day wars and the imperial past. We need to better understand how racial and racist legacies are brought to the "postracial" moment through permanent states of war. Pushing us in a useful direction are analyses of expressions of sovereignty refined in the colonies, "whose central project is," in the words of Achille Mbembe, *the generalized instrumentalization of human existence and the material destruction of human bodies and populations*."[4] Equally helpful are accounts that consider the long half-lives of the colonial past's narrative strategies and recent manifestations of justificatory frameworks built upon the race concept. Derek Gregory, for example, demonstrates how such practices and narratives are manifest in the imperial strategies of the United States and its allies in the Middle East:

> "Locating" mobilized a largely technical register, in which opponents were reduced to objects in a purely visual field . . . that produced an abstraction of other people as "the other." . . . "Opposing" mobilized a largely cultural registrar, in which antagonism was reduced to a conflict between a unitary Civilization and multiple barbarisms. . . . "Casting out" mobilized a largely political-juridical register, in which not only armed opponents . . . but also civilians and refugees were reduced to

the status of *homines sacri*. Their lives did not matter. The sovereign powers of the American, British, and Israeli states disavowed or suspended the law so that men, women, and children were made outcasts, placed beyond the pale and beyond the privileges and protections of the Modern.[5]

Gregory notes as well how such projects are enacted through different modes of historical erasure: most notably, a refusal of a colonial past shaping the political and economic landscape of the region and a selective memory of recent alliances and interventions. Such erasure has enabled the United States, for example, to present itself as a virtuous, innocent, and universal nation, a guarantor of freedom rather than, say, an erstwhile ally of Saddam Hussein with long strategic interests in Iraq.[6]

RACE WAR COMPLEXES

Du Bois had long been ambivalent about the idea that war could improve the conditions of black and brown people. His essay "The African Roots of the War" (1915) not only anticipated Lenin's discussion in 1916 of imperial colonialism as the highest stage of capitalism but also augmented it by highlighting colonialism's violence.[7] Du Bois also in that essay and a revision published in *Darkwater* redefined the meanings of war and peace, situating the former as a global and enduring process in the age of imperialism and pointing out the largely illusory aspects of the latter for colonial subjects and racial minorities. He theorized the interrelationship among foreign and domestic racisms that developed hand in hand with war, and making these connections enabled him to call into question the supposed moral authority of the United States on the global stage.[8] In 1918 Du Bois, in his controversial *Crisis* editorial "Close Ranks," had advised African American men to temporarily put aside their "special grievances" and join a war effort that could help democratize a significantly colonized world through an assertion of U.S. power and, in the process, advance black citizenship claims in the United States.[9] But World War I ultimately demonstrated to him the horrors of modern warfare, the persistence of imperialism, and a peace process, even with U.S. participation, that was fundamentally unconcerned with the political autonomy or even basic rights of colonized peoples or racial minorities.[10]

With war again on the horizon, as he indicated in an essay in 1936, "Social Planning for the Negro, Past and Present," there remained grave

dangers for black Americans and significant hypocrisy in the violent teleologies of Marxian revolution, fascist militarism, and Euro-American
imperialism alike. He anticipated much capacity for "cruelty and unnec-
essary bloodshed," which by definition would involve the killing of the
"innocent" and position black Americans in the roles of "buffer and victim, pawn and peon." He advocated an African American position on the
coming conflict: "We black men say, therefore, we do not believe in
violence. Our object is justice not violence, and we will fight only when
there is no better way." He referenced his plan for an African American
consumer's movement, presented here as a nonviolent, socialistic alternative to the dangerous militarism of other political projects.[11]

Given these views, it is striking that during this period Du Bois also
exhibited a fair amount of equanimity toward the increasing aggression
of Nazi Germany and imperial Japan. His commentary during and following a four-month visit in 1936 to Germany funded by the Oberlander
Trust did address the Nazis' catastrophic anti-Semitism, equating it with
past horrors such as the Spanish Inquisition and African slave trade, and
he called attention to the regime's hostility toward women. However,
Du Bois also expressed ambivalence toward the Third Reich, as when he
looked to the Nazis' state intervention in the market as a potential, quasi-
socialist solution to the economic woes facing other nations or when he
favorably compared his treatment as a black man while traveling in Germany to his reception in the United States. Such commentary ultimately
earned him significant criticism and played no small role in the precarious
position in which he found himself as an intellectual and race leader
during the decade.[12]

Accusations that he was invested in a naive and shortsighted racialism,
or perhaps was even an agent of Japanese fascism, followed his outspoken
support for Japan and downplaying of Japanese aggression in China during and following a trip to Asia in late 1937. Du Bois, of course, had
looked to Japanese power as a challenge to the "color line" since the
Russo-Japanese war, which fit into, as Bill Mullen points out, a larger
discursive practice of "propos[ing] Afro-Asian mutuality and recognition as a cornerstone of global liberation."[13] Earlier in the 1930s he wrote
of the hostilities between China and Japan in a neutral fashion, concerned
with how both nations were playing into the hand of European power by
turning their backs on an opportunity to help "the yellow and brown
race, nine hundred million strong take their rightful leadership of man-

kind."[14] But as the conflict progressed, Du Bois expressed growing sympathy for the Japanese cause, even after some aspects of the atrocities in Nanjing in the winter of 1937–38 began to be publicized in the United States. Du Bois went so far as to suggest that Japanese imperialism was a more benign form than that of European powers because it was not predicated on white supremacy. He said as well that Japan's rise to power continued to serve as inspiration to colored peoples across the globe and might prove to be a positive turn in world history. Justifying his position to a troubled NAACP supporter, he pointed to Chinese complicity in European colonialism (thus impeding "Asiatic freedom") and called attention to the ulterior motives of China's defenders, who, he argued, had their own designs on the country's resources.[15]

Du Bois made such comments at a time when other African Americans and colonial subjects were weighing in on what they saw as opportunism or hypocrisy on the part of Western powers in their calls for intervention or nonintervention in the "colored world." The United States' neutrality in the Italo-Ethiopian conflict and Great Britain's appeasement of Italy during its conquest of the African nation were particularly galling and helped energize a diasporic, anticolonial politics in the United States, black Britain, and elsewhere. When it came to the conflict between China and Japan, other African Americans were also suspicious of anti-Japanese rhetoric emanating from U.S. sources, which they suspected might be geared more to supporting British interests in China than to real concerns with Chinese freedoms and security. And Britain, for many blacks, was already suspect given its colonial past in the United States and more recent activities in the Caribbean. Some saw value in Japan standing up to European imperial powers and thought that such action could, in revolutionary terms, spell the end of racism. Although the dangers of Nazi Germany were quite apparent to most blacks in the United States, the recognition of fascist tendencies in the United States created some measure of ambivalence about the Nazi project as well.[16]

Such views about the Nazi war machine and Japanese imperialism, informed as they were by a commitment to black uplift, have been roundly criticized by Du Bois scholars and others. On the one hand, they clearly indicate a limited modality of racial thought. David Levering Lewis describes Du Bois's thoughts on Japan in particular as an expression of a troubling "belief system, which was now capable of abiding the immoral and inhumane for the sake of ultimate racial and economic justice."[17] And

Vijay Prashad notes that views like Du Bois's about Japan bespeak the fact that at a moment when the fascist states of the 1920s and 1930s deployed imperialism's "racist system of political domination and economic exploitation, not just against those in the distant colonies, but also against domestic difference," activists from the periphery or those made peripheral in the core by race often remained trapped in the logic of racism when putting forth nationalist, cosmopolitan, or socialist projects. "Resistance to racist imperialism came, then, both on the terrain of racism and in opposition to it."[18]

Yet with states exhibiting growing disregard for the safety of and increasing willingness to target civilian populations, such commentary also points to a kind of qualitative shift in the ways some people thought through race and developed ethical understandings of economies of violence involving populations marked by difference. Marianna Torgovnick remarks that World War II, in particular, helped establish a "war complex" in political imaginations in the United States. At a moment when civilian death became "commonplace, and even expected in strategies used by modern, 'civilized nations,'" and when "world war use[d] the structures of modernity (law, nation-states, technology), the recognizable and necessary structures of our lives, to enforce the brutality of combat" on bodies often specifically targeted as religious, ethnic, or racial, there emerged "an unresolved and perhaps unresolvable attitude toward mass death," which simultaneously sought to acknowledge and deflect the human cost of war.[19]

My contention is that this war complex resonated in specific ways with many African Americans, most of whom did not need to be reminded about the centrality of violence to and the human costs of modernity. That they were, in a sense, locked into race as a mode of analysis and critique is not surprising given its centrality to capitalism, imperialism, and herrenvolk democracies. But the critique emanating from what we might call a "black war complex" involved a distinct engagement with the violence of history brought to the present. On the side of deflection, we can, of course, see opportunistic readings of geopolitics that would consign, at the rhetorical level at least, populations (for example, civilians in Nanjing) to conditions of "bare life" to make a point about the hypocrisy of their defenders. On the side of acknowledgment, we can see coming out of what scholars sometimes term "the black popular front," and continuing through World War II, a recognition that war was linked inextricably to imperial projects and that the persistent possibility of mass civilian death required and provided the conditions for an emergent political critique. This enabled various thinkers to theorize as central to modern sovereignty both the violence directed to racialized populations and the selective ethics that justified this violence. It also provided an opportunity to explore the linked power of exceptionalist rhetoric of and willingness to create states of exception by the United States and its allies.[20]

Du Bois's comments about Japan, Nazi Germany, and the Soviet Union demonstrate that he was often trapped in a deflective discourse but that he also developed a growing understanding of a new constellation of race and racism emerging in the modern world, produced out of the rhetoric of war and peace and through acts of military aggression. Writing of the Soviet Union in an *Amsterdam News* column in 1940, he expressed some disdain for "the tyrant Stalin." However, he also "care[d] not if in the face of this accomplishment [socialistic, industrial, agricultural, intellectual developments], they have murdered, suppressed thought and made ruthless war. With all they have accomplished more than they have destroyed." Turning to Japan in the same column, he took the opportunity to respond to a letter he had received from the former secretary of state Henry L. Stimson, requesting support for an ongoing "pacific and evolutionary" U.S. policy in Asia that revolved around support for China in its conflict with Japan. Du Bois saw such support as a clear path toward war with Japan. His response to Stimson, then, was to refuse cooperation and instead point out that a history of Chinese "exclusion" in the United States suggested that the nation was not so much interested in Chinese political autonomy as it was in "low wages, cheap raw materials and increased private profit." He concluded by wondering why Stimson had not raised a similar alarm regarding the Italian attack on Ethiopia a few years earlier.[21] Thus, even as he rehearsed the utopian, ends-justify-the-means racial and economic logics used to justify all manners of oppressive and even genocidal imperial, anti-imperial, and neo-imperial projects in the years since, he pointed to how the violence of the imperial past was being unleashed in the present and would continue to structure the future world.

Du Bois's negotiation of the war complex was also intertwined with his attempt to understand not just the imperial past manifest in the present and future but also the linked and changing ontologies of race and racism during this first postracial moment. As discussed in chapter 1, Du Bois was inspired by scientific proof of the fictiveness of race, hanging onto outdated modes of racial thought and drawing on both as he tried to make sense of the power of race as an unstable, morphing, and always powerful force. At times Du Bois saw Japan's and Germany's collective rise to power as potentially destabilizing the global racial order. In 1940 he wrote in *Phylon* that "the outcome of the present war is bound to have large effect upon the theory of races and the relations of the larger cultural groups of mankind." This might stem from a changing political-economic order, the application of Nazi racial theory, or both. Though he was horrified at the obvious racial animus that Hitler directed toward Jews, the fact that the Japanese were positioned as Aryan in the Nazi racial order suggested that race was being destabilized. Nazi racial theory, he suggested, was slippery enough that in their interest of global domination and practical pursuit of this, the Nazis may end up promoting a kind of "racial accommodation," through which black people might become allies and secure more rights than under present colonial powers.[22] Although his prognostication was clearly wrong, it still suggests that we keep in mind that wars do indeed alter the terrain of racial knowledge and racial formations in often unexpected and accelerated ways. Later, Du Bois reprinted in *Phylon* a poem from the socialist magazine *Common Sense* by Granville Hicks, who pointed out both the absurdity of racial categories and the ways that racial affinities and formations were in flux during the war: "The Nazis, who are clever chaps, / Make Aryans of friendly Japs, / But Hearst, who's cleverer by far, / Propounds a theory of the war / That makes Chinese our racial kin / And yellows every German skin. / The cult of race, by such inventions, / Attains Einsteinian dimensions."[23]

TOWARD A UNIVERSAL RECONSTRUCTION?

Allied policy initiatives, international agreements, and idealistic statements about war aims just prior to and early in the conflict provided a mechanism for black activists and intellectuals to ponder questions regarding race, democracy, and the future global order. Roosevelt's Executive Order 8802 theoretically forbade discrimination by government agencies involved in defense production and by private defense firms operating under government contract. Issued in June 1941 in response to a threatened protest in the nation's capital by the March on Washington

Movement, the order (like the movement that inspired it) linked struggles for civil rights at home to the battle for political freedoms abroad. So did the Pittsburgh *Courier*'s "Double V" (double victory) campaign, connecting the defeat of the Axis to the end of racial prejudice in the United States.

Among the crucial issues for many African Americans were the extent to which the United States would inherent the mantle of imperialism from the European and Asian powers, how the principles guiding U.S. political cultures would abet or challenge that rise to power, and the roles that African Americans and colonial subjects might play in the ensuing world order. Nikhil Singh identifies competing universalisms that informed such questions. These were symbolized by the debate between publisher Henry Luce and Roosevelt's vice president Henry Wallace. In his pamphlet "The American Century" (1941), Luce proposed that the future of U.S. prosperity and global security depended on scaling back New Deal reforms on the domestic front and the exercise of military power abroad as a means of supplanting collapsing colonial systems of governance. Wallace, on the other hand, in his address "Century of the Common Man" (1942), argued for greater social reforms, a multilateral global order, and a fuller extension of rights around the world.[24]

Most politically active African Americans sided with Wallace, although even he came in for his share of critique from those who thought his vision was constrained by the assumption that the United States was the primary source of freedoms. Yet African Americans were potentially implicated in the vision (Luce's) that would emerge triumphant. For they occupied a special position in wartime struggles over moral authority and over the extent to which democratic principles would be extended during and after the conflict. Even as African Americans posed a dilemma for the United States as a potentially disruptive political bloc, their prospective liberation also constituted an issue upon which the United States could stake its claims for global domination.[25] Given the threat that enduring racism at home posed to the vision of national righteousness guiding both the war effort and larger imperial designs, African Americans were uniquely positioned to make civil and human rights demands. However, to the extent they were successful, they might enable U.S. global hegemony, because their inclusion could be seen as evidence of the nation's commitments to civil and human rights, its anti-imperialism, and its transcendence of its own racial history.[26]

Du Bois used the issue of stated war aims early in the conflict to comment on the problem of power and rights in the coming postwar world. He insisted on the necessity of a lasting peace at the conclusion of the war while articulating fears that a negotiated peace between major powers might lead to racial exclusions. There were practical questions regarding how any negotiated peace would impact state policies, economic relations, and international laws, which in turn structured the lives of racial minorities and colonial subjects. There was also the issue of how peace for the United States and the old colonial powers might mean perpetual war for colonized subjects and racial minorities. He noted in the pages of *Phylon* in early 1940 that various peace proposals being bandied about did not include in their definitions of peace an end to the violence of colonial exploitation or the granting of rights to colonized people. Some proposals, he feared, simply assumed that a fairer division of the colonized world among the major powers would solve the current conflict.[27]

In a column in the *Amsterdam News* in February 1941, in which he offered what Franklin Roosevelt "ought to have said" in his recent third-term inaugural address, Du Bois posed as the major challenge facing the world not the defeat of Hitler or support of England but "the absolute stoppage of war as weapon of civilization." Challenging Anglo-American exceptionalism, Du Bois laid blame for the current state of war equally on England and Germany, in England's case because of its role in the slave trade and colonial imperialism. Proposing an internationalist and egalitarian role for the United States based upon its well-rehearsed democratic principles, Du Bois idealistically announced: "We solemnly renounce as we gird ourselves to fight to the death, all desire for territory, dominion over others, increased wealth, trade or power, and hereby declare our object simply and solely, the settlement of disputes and differences; of oppressions, hurts and insults, by peaceful conference, argument, investigation and appeal."[28]

Like many in African America and the colonial world, Du Bois joined the discussion about the Atlantic Charter. Entered into by Winston Churchill and Roosevelt in August of 1941, the Charter was agreed to by twenty-six allied nations on January 1, 1942, in a "Declaration of United Nations." The Charter and Declaration defined the goals of the war beyond the defeat of the Axis nations, and they established the framework for the creation of the United Nations in 1945. The Atlantic Charter's eight points included commitments to give up designs on territorial expansion; to refuse changes in geopolitical boundaries without the consent of peoples affected by them; to support the self-determination of peoples to choose their own government and to restore self-government to those for whom it had been denied; to grant equal access to raw materials; to lower trade barriers and improve conditions of labor; to establish lasting peace and achieve freedom from want and fear; to establish freedom of the seas; and to disarm aggressor nations and establish a "permanent system of general security." The Charter represented a concerted attempt by Churchill and Roosevelt to juxtapose Anglo-American values with those of the fascist powers and, on the part of the Roosevelt administration, as Elizabeth Borgwardt argues, "to internationalize the New Deal."[29]

Yet, questions about how these agreements might facilitate a just postwar future were made more urgent for certain populations by Stalin's assertions that the Charter might not apply to Eastern Europe and Churchill's statement to the House of Commons, shortly after the agreement was signed, that the right to self-determination would apply to those living under Nazi occupation but not to Britain's colonial subjects still in need of "progressive evolution" toward self-government. Roosevelt pushed Churchill on this point in February 1942, arguing that the right to self-determination applied to all peoples. His insistence echoed his "Four Freedoms" speech of January 1941, some of the principles of which made it into the Charter. In addition to voicing a liberal social agenda in the domestic sphere, Roosevelt argued that the future of global security depended on "freedom of speech and expression," "freedom of . . . worship," "freedom from want," and "freedom from fear." Churchill, however, was unrepentant. In November 1942, in response to "One World" advocate Wendell Willkie's insistence that the Charter applied to all human beings, Churchill stated that the existence of the Atlantic Charter did not compel him "to preside over the liquidation of the British empire."[30]

These principles as well as the controversies about them provided an opportunity for black activists to press governments for clarification on their commitments to democracy in the postwar future. In late 1943, for example, an array of African American individuals and groups associated with left, labor, civil rights, and spiritual causes signed onto "A Declaration by Negro Voters." Among other issues, this statement expressed the desire "that this war bring to an end imperialism and colonial exploitation. We believe that political and economic democracy must displace the present system of exploitation in Africa, the West Indies, India and all other colonial areas."[31]

The question of whether Africans, in particular, would get to enjoy the Four Freedoms became a pressing issue in anticolonial politics. As will be discussed in chapter 3, a Phelps-Stokes Fund–sponsored report, *The Atlantic Charter and Africa from an American Standpoint* (1942), written by the Committee on Africa, the War, and Peace Aims, of which Du Bois was a member, argued that the Charter's principles, particularly that of self-determination, should be applied to the continent. The NAACP lobbied Roosevelt to make good on his interpretation that the Atlantic Charter applied to the colonized world, while L. D. Reddick's essay in 1943 in the *Crisis* defined "Africa" as the "test of the Atlantic Charter." That same year a group of West African newspaper editors, led by Dr. Nnamdi Azikiwe, future president of Nigeria, published a memorandum titled "The Atlantic Charter and British West Africa," which drew on the Charter's affirmation of self-determination.[32] In response to what she perceived as the limitations of the Charter, Amy Jacque Garvey, widow of Marcus Garvey and leader of the African Communities League, approached black leaders throughout the diaspora, including Du Bois, about the possibility of drafting an African Freedom Charter that would supplement the Anglo-American document.[33]

Even before Churchill's narrow interpretation of the Atlantic Charter to the House of Commons, Du Bois worried that it was racially exclusionary. Not only might principles of self-determination be enforced selectively but admonitions against territorial changes could preserve existing colonial relationships. He was concerned that the promise of free trade and access to raw materials "means the right of white peoples to exploit and enslave the colored peoples." Ultimately, the problem was that this agreement did not acknowledge the extent to which imperialism defined world affairs and was not appropriately proactive in addressing its legacy. So Du Bois proposed an alternative: "The first step to reform, uplift and peace, is not merely to seek the end of war among European nations, but to revise and control and rationalize the fundamental attitude of the white toward the colored world. When men of all races and colors are recognized as equal in the rights and aspirations, then the beginnings of world peace are in sight!"[34]

In 1942 Du Bois suggested that the Charter might even augment imperialism. The "defense of smaller nations" and "self-determination in all nations" proposed in the agreement might be relatively noble legacies of the League of Nations, but "add[ing] higher wage and freedom from want for Europe and America; . . . 'Freedom' for 'our way of life,' meant continuance of the established system of private profit without essential change." In the future, the world might even witness "Disarmament and World Police by white folk."[35] He made similar comments the following year in a *Foreign Affairs* article, where even as he praised Roosevelt for challenging Churchill's narrow interpretation of the Charter, he suggested that the president "did not seem to be thinking of Africa when he mentioned freedom of speech, freedom from want and freedom from fear."[36]

Despite such criticisms, Du Bois, like other African Americans, was generally resolute about the inevitability and importance of an Allied victory once the United States entered the war.[37] However, he warned against a naive faith in the Allies' stated war aims. In a Valentine's Day column in the *Amsterdam News* in 1942, Du Bois pondered his call made in 1918 to "close ranks" with white Americans and support the war effort. He supported the sentiment of the earlier column, though his call to arms was now somewhat dispirited and bitingly conditional: "We may sadly admit today that the First World War did not bring us democracy. Nor will the second. . . . We close ranks again but only, now as then, to fight for democracy and democracy not only for white folk but for yellow, brown and black."[38] A month later he opined, "We fight not in joy but in sorrow with no feeling of uplift; but under the sad weight of duty and in part, as we know to our sorrow, because of the inheritance of slave psychology which makes it easier to submit and obey rather than rebel. Whatever our mixed reasons are, we are going to play the game; but listen, Fellow Americans, for Christ's sake stop squawking about democracy and freedom. After all, we are black men and we live in America."[39] He similarly warned in *Phylon* that same year of the dangers in an "unconscious" mass belief that the war was being waged for "race equality." Although he provided examples of noble attempts to define it as such, he also noted the hypocrisy in other statements. He suggested that a lack of critical engagement with the ways that racial hierarchies persisted in spite of and sometimes as a result of such enlightened struggle would merely ensure their further entrenchment.[40]

Du Bois was thus still compelled to highlight the limitations of the democracy for which the Allies were fighting. Another Chronicle entry in

Phylon in 1942 titled "The Changing Face of War" used Japan's attempted conquest of Asia in the guise of anti-imperialism to contemplate complex ways that race and racism informed the conflict. The very processes by which war was waged in Asia, the shape of the societies involved, the often ambivalent attitudes of their citizenry to both Axis and Allied powers reflected legacies of imperialism. The fact that imperial Japan's slogan "Asia for the Asiatics" swayed some people in Asian colonies can be seen as evidence of the nostalgic racialism informing politics in the periphery. It also, Du Bois asserted, was an indictment of the profound ways in which the European nations had failed miserably in their democratic promise, which was nowhere more clear than in their colonies.[41]

Du Bois also pointed to the failures of democracy in the United States at a moment when it was trying to distinguish itself through its anti-fascism and anticolonialism. Du Bois suggested that the U.S. racist project was not so much being overthrown as reconstituted in an insidious, no less powerful and destructive form as the nation established itself as a protector of freedoms. In 1942 he pointed out that Luce's "American Century" proposed "domination of the world by English-speaking peoples, that is, by the peoples who have led in fostering the slave trade and color caste."[42] "With all our tumult and shouting and pious rage against Hitler," he suggested, "we are perfectly aware that his race philosophy and methods are but extreme development and application of our own save that he is drawing his race lines in somewhat different places. . . . Democracy cannot have a rebirth in the world unless it firmly establishes itself in America. . . . otherwise they are setting before the world a vision of continual struggle, of continual recurrence of war after war, the end of which no living man can see."[43] In other words, unless the nation lived up to its democratic principles, the righteous (and necessary) fight against the Nazis or Japanese might ultimately reproduce old forms and engender new forms of racial exclusion.

One must also keep in mind, Du Bois noted, that the stated goal of global racial equality could easily be relegated to the margins if it interfered with more pressing economic or strategic interests. Not only did the unequal distribution of wealth cause wars; the profit motive ensured their longevity and the exclusions that defined their termination. Du Bois noted increased U.S. capital investment in Africa that was now "nearly equal to British investment." Yet Africa was more or less invisible in articulations of Allied war aims and preliminary plans for postwar reconstruction.[44]

He discussed in *Phylon* the economist and New Deal official Robert A. Brady's recent book *Business as a System of Power*, quoting Brady's contention that more dangerous to democracy than Hitler was the "organized economic power backing the Hitlers in nation after nation throughout the industrialized world as a device for shoring up for yet a while longer a disintegrating economic system."[45] One must understand as well how race was constitutive of this system, Du Bois indicated later that year: "The merging of the race problem into a problem of the distribution of wealth is more and more indicated as this war goes on."[46]

The celebration of democratic principles might even be used to enact new forms of racial exclusion in the context of world war, as the imperial "civilizing mission" was reworked through the Allied role as guarantor of human freedoms in the face of other militarisms. In early 1943 Du Bois described "four speeches" by world leaders, all defining global democracy quite differently. He noted the telling irony of the South African leader Jan Christian Smuts labeling the war a "crusade . . . for man's rights and liberties and for the personal ideals of man's ethical and spiritual life." Implicit in this civilizationalist discourse coming from a leader of a nation at that moment consolidating its white supremacist identity and legal system, Du Bois suggested, was both an exclusionary approach to democracy's application and an erasure of economic concerns and needs. Such a vision, he implied, was increasingly overshadowing calls like Wallace's for "ethnic democracy," in which "the different races and minority groups must be given equality of economic opportunity."[47] This concern about augmented racial exclusion undercutting democratic rhetoric applied to the home front as well. Du Bois had, of course, voiced strong critiques of the New Deal project during the 1930s because of its inability to fundamentally address economic inequality and legacies of racism. Yet he was more recently troubled by the growing "contempt" for New Deal liberalism and attempts to temper its commitments. Worse yet were outright attacks on established government programs that provided benefits and protections for racial minorities. Du Bois was especially concerned with attacks on Federal Employment Practices Commission protections for black workers, engineered in part by southern members of Congress.[48]

Du Bois, however, did not just limit himself to antiracist anti-imperial critique. He used it as a foundation for a wartime re-articulation of his vision for a reconstruction of democracy. Such a practice could be partially sustained and enabled by the rhetoric and practice of the U.S. nation-state, but only if the war aims themselves were transformed by the actions of people of color, in alternative spheres of political activity, in the United States and elsewhere. Du Bois was inspired by self-activity of colonized people in various parts of the world and saw them potentially redefining the meaning of the war.[49] Quoting his own *Darkwater* in May 1942, Du Bois said, "A belief in humanity is a belief in colored men. If the uplift of mankind must be done by men, then the destinies of this world will rest ultimately in the hands of darker nations."[50] Around the same time he called on African America, and Atlanta University in particular, to take a clear role in the "admission into the ranks of democracy of the darker peoples of the world," a project he described as "universal reconstruction."[51]

May 1942 also witnessed Du Bois proposing unsuccessfully to the editors of *Fortune* magazine an essay that can be read, especially given that Henry Luce was the magazine's editor-in-chief, as a rejoinder to the imperial doctrine embedded in the idea of an "American Century." Du Bois hoped to discuss World War II as perhaps the first step in an inevitable struggle for racial democracy across the globe: "Just as the Civil War in the United States began as a war for federal union and became a war against slavery, which gave it the necessary ethical slogan, so the present war which began as a struggle against Germany changed to a plea for the domination of the world by English-speaking nations but cannot achieve ethical sanctions without becoming a war for the political and social equality for the great races of man."[52] The following year he invoked the ongoing challenge of the reconstruction of democracy as he looked toward the end of the war: "The problem of the reconstruction of the United States, 1876, is the problem of the reconstruction of the world in 1943."[53] Yet, as before, reconstruction would not be an ameliorative activity, correcting aberrations in a generally sound democratic project. Rather, it would involve a fundamental interrogation of societal values, economic practices, and the ways they were linked to global systems of racial domination: "If we want to realize humanity and world peace, this can only be done at the cost of so thorough and drastic an overturning of our inherited fixations and cultural patterns as will shake the Western World."[54]

Yet, in keeping with comments made in *Dusk of Dawn*, Du Bois kept an eye on the ways African Americans might be implicated in the imperial project. In an article in the Chicago *Defender* in September 1942, crafted in response to the newspaper's suggestion that he write about "interracial good will," Du Bois asked his readers to move beyond the logic of the Double V and its ultimately national subject-serving reading of global politics. He asked, when contemplating interracial unity, "What races shall we have in mind? The whites and blacks of America, or the whites, blacks, yellows, and browns of the world?" He stated emphatically that African Americans must not integrate a national political-economic project that would by definition exploit colored people elsewhere. The struggle, he continued, was "against all race hate and caste, whether in America, England, Japan, or Germany." Moreover, he cautioned, invoking Gandhi, African Americans must not merely give lip service to protecting human freedoms while condoning mass civilian casualties: "We are not trying to exterminate anybody, least of all the Germans or the Japanese." Ultimately, he concluded, "We are fighting against false ideas and noisome prejudices, within or without our own nation or race and we are fighting side by side with every free soul who wants to abolish slavery from this earth; the slavery of poverty, the slavery of color, the slavery of nation."[55]

"PACIFISM FOR WHITE PEOPLE ONLY"?

With the war turning in the Allies' favor in 1943 and with victory almost certain in 1944, Du Bois turned more and more to the coming postwar order. Although he remained suspicious of U.S. state and corporate goals, there still seemed cause for believing that the United States would eventually support some measure of domestic civil rights reform and decolonization abroad. Moreover, Du Bois soon found himself in a position to more actively intervene in official planning for peace.

In late 1943, following increasing tensions with President Rufus Clement over his planned Phylon Institute, Du Bois was notified that he would be terminated from Atlanta University in June 1944. He accepted the NAACP board's request that he return to the organization as director of special research. The NAACP was a different entity from the one he had left ten years earlier. Black mass activity during the 1940s had radicalized the organization and helped intensify its legal and political struggle for domestic civil rights reforms and its commitments to anticolonialism. The organization was larger, more powerful, and more efficient. It had also in

1942 and 1943 turned significant attention to the problem of a just and lasting peace following World War II.[56] Although Executive Secretary Walter White and other NAACP officials saw Du Bois's appointment primarily as a chance to generate favorable publicity and aid one of its founders, Du Bois assumed he would be working actively to ensure that the interests of people throughout the African diaspora were adequately represented in "post-war planning" efforts and to facilitate the "collection of facts concerning colored peoples, in war and peace, and the relation of these facts to democracy and peace in the future."[57] During his first fourteen months in this new position, he wrote extensively, published a new book, *Color and Democracy*, represented the NAACP (along with Walter White and Mary McLeod Bethune) as a consulting body to the U.S. delegation at the United Nations founding conference, and participated in the fifth Pan-African Congress, held in Manchester, England.

In "Prospects of a World without Race Conflict," an essay in the *American Journal of Sociology* in 1944, Du Bois explained that racial exclusions compromised visions for postwar reconstruction. "The supertragedy of this war[,] . . . the treatment of the Jews in Germany," did not seem to him to be sinking in as a lesson for the future. Rather, it appeared to be a particularly horrific outgrowth of a still entrenched "racial philosophy" that would color an Anglo-American dominated postwar world. Plans for improving health, education, and labor were, for the most part, concerned with whites in Europe and the United States. Particularly galling was the refusal to address the problem of poverty in a systematic, equitable way: "Our attitude toward poverty represents the constant lesion of race thinking. We have with difficulty reached a place in the modern white world where we can contemplate the abolition of poverty. . . . But this conception is confined almost entirely to the white race. Not only do we refuse to think of similar possibilities for the colored races but we are convinced that, even though it were possible, it would be a bad thing for the world." In other words, "inherited prejudice and unconscious celebration" coalesced with the needs of capital to create a series of exclusions that would position poor people, the majority of whom had darker skins, as potentially deserving of freedom and more or less welcome in the world community but also to a degree disposable.[58]

What was needed, then, was an expanded definition of peace. In a paper delivered in Haiti in the summer of 1944, Du Bois asked, "What has Democracy to do with Colonies and what has skin-color to do with

Peace?" The answer, he suggested in another paper delivered in the island nation, must be grounded in an understanding that "universal peace" would not be achieved until democracy was more fully extended: "Peace in the long run must be based on contentment and the world is not content with the colonial status." The solution, Du Bois claimed, lay in a decoupling of Western culture, science, and technology from regimes of economic and administrative exploitation as well as from the discursive framework holding "that everything European was right and progressive, and everything Asiatic and African was decadent and barbaric." Human progress, the salvation of democracy, and global peace were now to be the work of colonized subjects and racial minorities working in more productive, just ways with the intellectual, cultural, and technological legacies of the West.[59]

Du Bois scrutinized the conference at Dumbarton Oaks that fall, at which major global powers began negotiations over the specifics of the formation of the United Nations. Du Bois saw in the agreements sketched out at the conference a willingness to defer freedoms for colonial and racial subjects. He was troubled by the overrepresentation on the Security Council by "white folk" and was disappointed that participants failed to address in any significant way the status of colonies and the rights of their subjects. He was also alarmed that Chinese participation was delayed until the United States, Soviet Union, and Great Britain had come to agreement over major issues and that these nations rejected a Chinese resolution opposing racial discrimination — albeit one that was not put forth forcefully — and adopted instead a principle of "sovereign equality of peace loving states." He raised these concerns publicly at Undersecretary of State Edward Stettinius's postconference briefing in October and at other forums.[60]

In the meantime, Du Bois penned an NAACP board of directors resolution to Roosevelt on September 11. It petitioned "the President of the United States to make clear now that the United States Government will not be a party to the perpetuation of colonial exploitation of any nation" and will oppose "any policy which means freedom for white people or any part of the white people of the earth on the one hand, and continued exploitation of colored peoples, on the other."[61] Stettinius's response affirmed the government's commitment to "fundamental principles of equitable and just treatment of all peoples," though such application was, to some degree, paternalistically conditional. Quoting a radio address given in 1942 by Secretary of State Cordell Hull, Stettinius wrote, "It has been our purpose in the past—and will remain our purpose in the future—to use the full measure of our influence to support attainment of freedom by all peoples who, by their acts, show themselves worthy of it and ready for it." He pointed to Cuba and the Philippines as examples where such purpose was successful.[62]

In December Du Bois wrote an essay for *New Leader*, in which he again responded to the discussions at Dumbarton Oaks. He worried about the concentration of power among the members of the Security Council and the presumed lack of power of the UN Economic and Social Council, which was the part of the body charged with "promot[ing] respect for human rights and fundamental freedoms" but given no power to protect or support these rights. He was concerned also that the United Nations would not adequately counter an emergent imperialism, forged less through occupation than through a web of transnational business relationships and the concomitant limitations of local and national political reforms. In addition to the problem of the colonies, there were other nations, "nominally independent, which by reason of accumulated debt owed creditor nations and current control of their labor and industry by absentee capital, will be in no position to act independently or speak freely, even if admitted to seats in the Assembly."[63] And he foresaw a situation wherein democratic struggles in the North would be compromised by the Faustian bargain participants would make with imperial power as they sought to better their own economic foundations: "The disposition of parties on the left, liberal parties and philanthropists to press for colonial improvement will be lessened by the bribe of vastly increased help of government to better their conditions. The working people of the civilized world will thus largely be induced to put their political power behind imperialism, and democracy in Europe may continue to impede and nullify democracy in Asia and Africa. This is the danger. What are we going to do about it?"[64]

On February 28, 1945, Du Bois attended a briefing on the United Nations Monetary and Financial Conference held in Bretton Woods, New Hampshire, in July 1944. The conference had been organized to remake the global economy via the nascent International Monetary Fund and venues for international investment and exchange. At the briefing Du Bois cautioned against the immorality and social costs of a postwar U.S. economic imperialism, given the inattention at the conference to structural inequalities governing financial investments in colonies: "There is in the Bretton Woods proposals so far as I can gather no reference to colonies or colonial conditions. Yet colonies are economic rather than solely political problems. Seven hundred and fifty millions of people, a third of mankind, live in colonies. Cheap colonial labor and materials are basic to post-war industry and finance. Was this matter mentioned in any form at Bretton Woods?"[65]

Du Bois would address these connections in more detail in his book *Color and Democracy: Colonies and Peace*. He proposed the volume to the publisher in November 1944, and it was released on May 25, 1945, a few weeks after the German surrender.[66] Du Bois framed this generally well-received book as a rejoinder to the narrow vision of the representatives at Dumbarton Oaks. He delivered wide-ranging, biting commentary on the status of colonies and a critique of racism and colonial subjection, while putting forth an alternative plan for postwar reconstruction. The title of this book also made its way onto Du Bois's NAACP letterhead for a time, demonstrating how closely he viewed his agenda as director of special research to the anticolonial vision therein.[67] Although Du Bois addressed various issues related to the future of all of the keywords in the volume's title, I emphasize here the ways he gestured toward an understanding of new and shifting contours of race and imperial power emergent at this moment.

In the book's opening paragraph, Du Bois avers that "the present war has made it clear" that "the majority of inhabitants of earth who happen for the most part to be colored, must be regarded as having the right and the capacity to share in human progress and to become copartners in that democracy which alone can ensure peace among men, by the abolition of poverty, the education of the masses, protection from disease, and the scientific treatment of crime."[68] Such a view is in part possible, he tells us later, because race as a conceptual category and justification for exploitation has been transformed. Ideologies holding that white people "were the natural rulers of the world" and the majority of black, brown, and yellow people "were naturally so inferior that . . . they would be [in]capable of self-government" have been largely discredited.[69] Yet the history of imperialism that this racial mythos supported in the past survives: "These facts [the debunking of the race concept] do not affect our actions today, because government and economic organization have already built a tremendous financial structure upon the nineteenth-century conception of race inferiority. This is what the imperialism of our day means."[70] Imperialism "also affects the situation of the working classes and the minorities in civilized countries."[71] On the one hand, the racial project of colonialism has been brought to bear on minority groups in Western democracies. This includes "the treatment of the Jewish minority in Germany," a "calamity almost beyond comprehension."[72] On the other hand, given that political and economic relations with the colonized world can augment "standards of living" for working-class and minority populations in Europe and the United States, as when the tax burden for social programs is paid for by returns on investments in the colonized world, these populations are impelled "to put their political power behind imperialism." Thus, the pursuit of "democracy in Europe and America will continue to impede and nullify democracy in Asia and Africa."[73]

What, then, are the alternatives? At the beginning of his centerpiece chapter, "Democracy and Color," Du Bois asks, "How far are we working for a world where the peoples who are ruled are going to have effective voice in their governments?"[74] Part of the problem is the poverty produced by an unequal distribution of wealth, which has left masses of people uneducated, economically illiterate, and otherwise unprepared to effectively participate in democracies. For a brief moment, Germany seemed to represent the possibilities of modernizing democratic reform and the empowerment of workers, until its political culture was corrupted by Hitler's racist project and the consolidation of "newly organized business and industrial interests under state direction."[75] With the defeat and dissolution of the Axis powers imminent, however, Du Bois argues that the greatest threat to "popular demand for democratic methods . . . is not Fascism, whose extravagance has brought its own overthrow, but rather imperial colonialism, where the disenfranchisement of the mass of people has reduced millions to tyrannical control without any vestige of democracy."[76] Solutions to the democracy deficit must be attentive to emergent constellations of power that are protected by "legal sanction," legislation, propagandistic media, educational institutions, and the "production and distribution of wealth" more generally.[77]

Du Bois looks to the United States, given its own history of racial exclusion and its perceived central place in the postwar global order. "The attitude of the United States in this development puzzles the observing world of liberalism," Du Bois writes, "Intelligence and high wages in this land are linked with an extraordinary development of the rule of wealth and sympathy with imperial ambition in other lands, as well as steps toward greater American imperialism."[78] He again looks to two fundamental factors linking a compromised democracy in the United States to its abiding of older and emergent imperialisms: (1) the overrepresentation via congressional representatives of voters residing in western and southern states with small populations, which is an arrangement that "springs from colonial America before the nation had become democratic"; and (2) the disenfranchisement of black voters, which not only denies them a fundamental civil right but augments the provincialism of the electoral system. In other words, "the race problem has been deliberately intermixed with state particularism to thwart democracy." The exception that defines political culture at home not only "gives rein and legal recognition to race hate, which the Nazis copied in their campaign against the Jews"; it also enables, through the election of officials with investments in the racial status quo, like southern members of Congress, a general rightward thrust in the political sphere. Ultimately, these phenomena "[force] the United States to abdicate its natural leadership of democracy in the world and to acquiesce in a domination of organized wealth which exceeds anything elsewhere in the world."[79]

The situation is complicated, according to Du Bois's analysis. On the one hand, the political project of U.S. liberalism enables the United States' ascension as a global power as it defines itself against the old colonial nations. Yet it was precisely the championing of its liberal values that helps the United States to adopt the imperialist mantle. This compromised democracy—this championing of democratic principles and then the partial abandonment of this project because of the needs of capital, existing frames of racial exclusion, and refusals to fully remediate them—permits a neoimperialist extension across the globe that is virtuous in appearance but racially exclusive in its own way.

Du Bois also seeks to understand the complex relationship of the state to corporations, which further limits democracy through their articulated power. Although there is not adequate "scientific study" to comprehend fully this relationship, there must be attention to the way that the state is "controlled by organized wealth." This arrangement is not straightforward, for "wealth today is centered in the hands of certain powerful corporations . . . by chance, power, and intrigue." And during a war cast in Manichaean terms as a struggle for democracy, the fact "that international cartels have kept their organization and their profits even in time of war and across the lines of warring nations" speaks of a trans-national organization of wealth that is intertwined with yet supersedes national sovereignty.[80]

Du Bois points to the ways that war may constitute a permanent state of affairs in the putatively postwar period, with the growing imperial power of the United States and an international system of war profiteering rear-ticulating the colonial past. He argues that the constellation of military power and formal and informal financial and political arrangements that constitute and exceed the United States' sovereign power at this moment builds upon a racial logic stemming from both its own history of slavery and segregation and the broader history of imperialism. He points to wars as defining characteristics of modernity and outgrowths of racial inequali-ties and the systems that produce and are justified by them. "In the rifts of race," he writes, are "many and multiplying causes of war."[81] And the Bretton Woods conference, he laments in the chapter "Peace and Colo-nies," "gave no attention at all to colonies and investments in colonial cheap labor and raw materials. Yet here more than elsewhere, lurk the main causes of modern war."[82] He lists 133 armed conflicts between 1792 and 1939, which he argues generally enacted or stemmed from imperial-ism and territorial conquest. And to the extent that many of these wars were waged during "an era dominated largely by organized pacifism," it becomes clear that we have a "pacifism designed 'for white people only.' "[83] In this sense, then, peace is a relative term, defined through a racial logic forged in the colonial past. It is a noble goal, but as its realization is celebrated, black and brown bodies continue to be destroyed.

Du Bois's penultimate chapter examines "the riddle of Russia," sug-gesting that its socialist vision and "racial tolerance" may hold the key to creating a more peaceful and just world, as long as it does not emerge from the war as an imperial power.[84] Yet there is still hope for U.S. stewardship in the postwar world, so long as it is dedicated to a more antiracist and socialistic reconstruction of democracy:

> If the United States really wishes to seize leadership in the present world, it will attempt to make the beneficiaries of the new economic order not simply a group, a race or any form of oligarchy but, taking advantage of its own wealth and intelligence, will try to put democracy in control of the new economy. This will call for vital, gigantic effort; real education for the broadest intelligence and for evoking talent and

genius on a scale never before attempted in the world, and putting to shame our present educational camouflage. With that program the sympathy and interest of the majority of the people of the world, particularly of the emerging darker peoples, will make the triumph of American industrial democracy over the oligarchical technocracy of Neuropa [Nazi Europe] inevitable.[85]

Du Bois thus presents World War II as a test case for liberal democracy as well as a potential laboratory for reconstructing it, to some extent for and by subjects in Western democracies, in large part for and by colonized peoples. World War II also presents a test case for the race concept as both a signifier of a racialized social order and a conceptual framework for understanding how the world operates, in part through the practice of war. There is hope for the future, but Du Bois still fears that an emergent racial project of U.S. imperial sovereignty is being worked out at this moment. "So long as the colonial system persists and expands" in disguise under the stewardship of the United States, he argues, "theories of race inferiority will help to continue it," and therein will always lie the seeds of violent struggle.[86] The new imperial order throws down the gauntlet to the racisms of fascism and old colonialisms, but it is also predicated on a continuation of a series of racial exclusions, precisely through its refusal to recognize the extent to which the race concept organizes the world. Such presentation not only serves the needs of capital, deflecting attention from the racially exploitative relationships that follow imperialist interventions and the racially inflected wars that support them; it is also necessary to the systems of representations through which the universal nation is produced and through which its actions are justified.

THE POLITICS OF PEACE AND HUMAN RIGHTS

Color and Democracy ends with a consideration of postwar peace plans, calls to maintain Western alliances with the Soviet Union, and an evaluation of the United Nations. A global commitment to human rights, which would by definition address the situation facing colonial and racial subjects, did not seem likely but might be feasible through the United Nations, though only so long as there were adequate representation of colonial peoples in the General Assembly and sufficient mechanisms to check imperial power in its old and new forms. Du Bois calls for the creation of a new Mandates Commission under the auspices of the UN's Economic and Social Council. Such a committee would correct the failures of the original mandates system established by the League of Nations, which put some possessions of Germany and the Ottoman Empire under the control of Allied nations. He also calls for a statement by each "imperial power" of their intent "to raise the peoples of colonies to a condition of complete political and economic equality with the peoples of the master nations, and eventually either to incorporate them into the polity of the master nations or to allow them to become independent free peoples."[87]

The question of how most effectively to represent colonial subjects was also addressed at the NAACP–sponsored Conference on Colonialism, held at the Schomburg Library in Harlem on April 6, 1945. There Du Bois brought together prominent African Americans and anticolonial activists from Africa and the Caribbean. Conference goers ultimately did not follow Du Bois's lead in calling for a new Mandates Commission, however. Some, like Kwame Nkrumah, thought that the retention of the term "mandate" "implie[d] sell-out to the colonial powers."[88] But their adopted resolution—the centerpiece of which was a call for a "colonial commission" that would be "composed of representatives of all permanent members of the UN Security Council, additional representatives elected by the General Assembly, and members who represent directly the several broad groups of colonial peoples"—showed a shared commitment to liberation via international representation, even if it insufficiently smoothed over disagreements about the ideal pace of decolonization. The delegates also agreed that the commission should have a staff with indigenous representation from the colonies. It would establish and enforce consistent "economic, social, and political standards" in the colonies; determine specific dates for the eventual political self-determination for each colonial territory; and build international cooperation for "the industrialization; economic advancement; improvement of education, health, and other social services; transportation; communication; and other similar matters in all colonial areas."[89]

Du Bois and conference attendees were not alone in their belief that international effort to solve the problems of colonialism were necessary. Black people of varying ideological and political orientations hoped the United Nations would link civil rights and antiracism at home to human rights and decolonization across the globe. They looked expectantly to its founding conference in San Francisco in the spring and summer of 1945. Although there were disagreements among activists, many found common ground, along with representatives of small nations and political groups, in efforts to shape the organization into one at least as concerned with securing and monitoring human rights and economic and social justice as it was for maintaining peace and security. Du Bois, along with fellow NAACP officials Walter White and Mary McLeod Bethune, served as consultant to the U.S. delegation at the founding conference.[90]

Many interested parties would be profoundly disappointed with the UN's early development. Du Bois, White, and Bethune realized that they were little more than window dressing for the U.S. delegation. They and other consultants confronted Stettinius about the fact that human rights were not being more vigorously supported, particularly as they would apply to colonized peoples. However, the NAACP had no success in convincing the U.S. delegation to support the statement they had crafted, which called for "a declaration at San Francisco of the racial equality of the great groups of mankind in international law" and recognition that colonialism "has been and still is a frequent and repeated cause of war and oppression" and should be the object of collective international reform. And while there was a significant shift from the vision of postwar security and sovereignty outlined at Dumbarton Oaks — namely in Article I of the UN Charter's commitment to rights and freedoms for all human beings "without distinction as to race, sex, language, or religion" — anticolonialists, civil rights activists, and representatives of smaller nations found their vision at odds with Western powers' economic, strategic, and political goals. Many were disappointed that there was not a more explicit endorsement of racial equality and rights for colonial subjects in the founding documents and that the charter did not provide a mechanism for redress for human rights violations.[91]

The United States did its part in making sure these elements were not included. As Du Bois's analysis of its "abdicat[ion of] its natural leadership of democracy" anticipated, U.S. diplomats feared that a more meaningful statement on human rights or condemnation of racism would never win support from U.S. senators whose constituencies were invested in the racial status quo. The UN petition did come, after all, at a critical historical juncture, with racisms and antiracisms informing an emergent conflict between a "traditionalist" orientation toward human rights and sovereignty, which preserved local and national authority, and a more cosmopolitan orientation that called for some measure of international protection and enforcement.[92] The United States' potential support for interventions in colonial affairs and human rights guarantees in the face of racial, gendered, and economic exclusions was also compromised by the perceived need of Western European support in an emerging bipolar world, the desire to prevent new power centers from emerging, aspirations for economic integration among capitalist powers and access to raw materials and markets for U.S. businesses, the desire to maintain strategic possessions (particularly in the Pacific Islands), and a fear that ameliorating rights violations along one axis of exclusion (for example, sexism) would open the door to those claiming exclusion along other axes (for example, racism, class oppression). The United States' compromised support for human rights is perhaps best exemplified by John Foster Dulles's addition of an amendment to the charter's anti-discrimination language, guaranteeing that "nothing in the Charter shall authorize . . . intervention in matters which are essentially within the domestic jurisdiction of the State concerned."[93]

Still, black activists continued to link domestic civil rights struggles to a broader global campaign for human rights and economic empowerment and tried to get support for such efforts from the United Nations. African American activists presented a series of petitions to the United Nations to protest and ideally rectify the oppression of African Americans. The first was sponsored by the National Negro Congress (NNC) and drafted by the historian Herbert Aptheker. The "Petition to the United Nations on Behalf of Thirteen Million Oppressed Negro Citizens of the United States of America" was presented to the NNC national convention on June 1, 1946, and submitted to the UN secretary general's office five days later. From there it went to the UN Economic and Social Council, although the United States did its best to prevent serious discussion of the matter. The UN's request to the NNC for additional information led to a vibrant year of grassroots organizing, research, and "People's Tribunals"; however, a lack of resources, internal conflicts, and growing anticommunist hysteria led to the organization's demise in 1947 and its absorption by the Civil Rights Congress. As the NNC was gathering information, however, an NAACP team led by Du Bois was already expanding and redrafting the petition. Eventually titled *An Appeal to the World: A Statement on the Denial of Human Rights to Minorities in the Case of Citizens of Negro Descent in the United States of America and an Appeal to the United Nations for Redress,* the petition consisted of an introduction by Du Bois, in which he rehearsed the claims that the United States' failure of leadership on the world stage was a product of domestic racial exclusions. The six chapters that followed, written by different scholars and activists, addressed the legal and social status of African Americans and explored questions of human rights in the past and present.[94]

The reception of Du Bois's petition was shaped by the growing geopolitical conflict between the United States and the Soviet Union. As the report was being completed, it was unclear whether the United Nations would even accept it because of its Commission on Human Rights' uncertainty about, and great debate over, whether it could acknowledge or act upon such complaints. Eventually, at the urging of General Carlos Romulo, a commission member from the Philippines, a subcommittee was established to review such petitions. After much political maneuvering, the UN agreed to receive the petition in October 1947 but merely passed it along as reference material to a subcommittee drafting the Universal Declaration on Human Rights. The NAACP pushed on, hoping to receive a hearing on its grievances, and was told it must secure the sponsorship of a member state to continue. After the United States and India declined to bring the petition forward, the NAACP found itself in the awkward position of receiving Soviet support in an early Cold War maneuver intended to embarrass the United States. Not unexpectedly, the United States blocked the United Nations' consideration of *An Appeal to the World* at the end of 1947, in large part because of the Soviet Union's support for it. Adding insult to injury was erstwhile ally and Human Rights commissioner Eleanor Roosevelt's lack of support for the petition and her subsequent resignation from the NAACP's board of directors.[95]

The politics around the petition also illuminates how the liberal/left consensus among black intellectuals and activists began to unravel during the early Cold War, at a moment when, as Thomas Borstelmann writes, "the essential strategy of American Cold Warriors was to try to manage and control the efforts of racial reformers at home and abroad, thereby minimizing provocations to the forces of white supremacy and colonialism while encouraging gradual change."[96] Du Bois and White clashed over strategies for bringing the petition to the United Nations. Eventually White distanced himself from the *Appeal* and instead accepted Eleanor Roosevelt's invitation to back her own covenant on human rights created under the auspices of Truman's President's Committee on Civil

Rights. The published version of this, *To Secure These Rights*, released the same month the NAACP had its petition heard at the UN, called for various civil rights reforms in U.S. society (voting rights laws, antilynching legislation, the desegregation of the armed forces, and so on) that the Truman administration would pursue. It drew upon the logic of Myrdal's *An American Dilemma*, defining the United States again as an exemplary universal and interventionist nation. After some wrangling with White, Du Bois released the *Appeal* to the public in January 1948, but the document's thunder had already been stolen.[97]

White's changing position exemplified the NAACP's retreat during the Cold War from the expansive vision of human rights and commitment to anticolonialism that helped define its agenda for the first half of the decade. NAACP leaders did not abandon the agenda immediately and were, for a time at least, willing to voice criticisms of Cold War rhetoric and practice. White, for example, stated his belief that Churchill's "Iron Curtain" speech in March 1946 exaggerated the Soviet threat in order to justify the perpetuation of Britain's imperial ambitions and the development of those of the United States.[98] Yet the process by which the organization distanced itself from radical anticolonialism and gravitated toward Cold War liberalism was already under way. In late 1945 and early 1946 organization leaders determined that the growing conflict between the United States and Soviet Union made alliances with visible left-wing figures like Paul Robeson and William Patterson and radical political organizations like the National Negro Congress and Council of African Affairs into liabilities. This was especially apparent when the press began to examine these relationships — for example, Arthur Schlesinger Jr.'s suggestion, in a *Life* magazine article in July 1946, that the Communist Party was "sinking tentacles" into the NAACP — or when southern members of Congress continued their opposition to civil rights reforms by linking black activism with communism. It was even more the case in 1947, when HUAC hearings brought additional attention to domestic subversions and the Truman Doctrine's announcement of a global state of emergency because of the Soviet threat defined critiques of U.S. foreign policy beyond the pale of legitimate dissent.[99] Moreover, an upsurge in racist violence during the immediate postwar period cautioned some black activists to take more moderate positions. For others, leaders and laypeople alike, wartime migrations, economic gains in the war economy, and new opportunities within the "welfare-warfare" state made it more realistic to think about integrating culturally and economically into U.S. society.[100] White and other civil rights leaders eventually saw the strategic value of supporting Truman's policies. They recognized that the administration's domestic and foreign policy aims in the early Cold War era were compromised by the persistence of racism in the United States and thus it was willing to undertake limited domestic reforms. With growing pressure from the administration, and in exchange for concessions on domestic civil rights issues, the NAACP leadership separated domestic and international rights issues, chastened critics of U.S. foreign policy, and put the organization's support behind anticommunism.[101]

As the NAACP urged political caution among its members, however, Du Bois moved forward with his critique of U.S. imperialism and domestic political repression. This after personality conflicts with White and other NAACP leaders and major disagreements over procedural issues in the organization had already caused some to rethink their decision to invite Du Bois back into the fold in 1944. Du Bois's friendships and alliances also continued to be problems for the NAACP. He caused great consternation by giving the keynote address at the communist-led Southern Negro Youth Congress's Southeastern conference in 1946, the text of which would be published by the Marxist journal *New Masses* as the pamphlet "Behold the Land." He produced similar sentiments when he joined Paul Robeson's Crusade against Lynching, after the NAACP itself had declined an invitation. Working on the *Appeal* and his growing relationship with Shirley Graham (whom he would marry in 1951) also put Du Bois in greater and visible contact with people in the Communist Party and other left organizations.[102]

Shortly after Schlesinger's piece appeared, Du Bois criticized the Soviet dictatorship but argued that it needed to try to achieve its goals, as it was the only nation earnestly trying to address the problem of poverty created by capitalism. Later, he was vocally critical of the Truman Doctrine and joined Paul Robeson and Henry Wallace in opposing the Marshall Plan. And he angered White again in 1948 when, after deciding that the growing political crisis (not to mention the organization's obvious support for Truman) made the NAACP's proscription against partisan politics moot, he supported Wallace's presidential campaign. The support for Wallace also led to Du Bois losing his Chicago *Defender* column. The final straw for the NAACP was a *New York Times* story documenting a supposedly leaked Du Bois memorandum, in which he critiqued the organization's retreat from its leadership on anticolonial and human rights issues as it forged an alliance with the Truman administration. Du Bois claimed that the NAACP was not only "loaded on the Truman bandwagon" but was serving "the reactionary, warmongering colonial imperialism of the present administration." Upset with Du Bois's insubordination and worried about his political cost to the organization nationally and his influence on its branches, the NAACP Board terminated Du Bois's appointment in September 1948.[103]

THE GREATEST GENERATION?

We can think through Du Bois's attempts to address the colonial past shaping his 1940s for purposes of understanding how that racial past and present are embedded in our twenty-first century. For the perpetual conflicts of Cold War and post–Cold War era proxy wars, interventions of various kinds, and the global war on terror have been based on and have produced a racial logic that Du Bois showed emerging in somewhat different terms in the practice of violence and plans for peace during and after World War II.

It is important to point out that Du Bois made his comments at a moment of ascendancy of U.S. power. We stand now at a moment of declining U.S. hegemony, although U.S. power is still central to various transnational and international systems of political, military, and economic domination. Immanuel Wallerstein has valuably defined this period from 1945 to the present as a "cycle of the capitalist world-economy," with an economic expansion from 1945 to around 1970 and a contraction from that period to the present.[104] Moreover, the political-economic foundations of this ascendant imperial democracy in the late 1940s were still predicated on a Fordist industrial economic order, a "centrist liberalism" vis-à-vis the welfare state, and commitments, albeit unequal ones, to "developmentalism" abroad in hopes of ensuring both political loyalties and markets for U.S. goods.

The world more recently has been shaped by a shift from producer-centered to finance-centered economy, higher unemployment, and movement of production from higher- to lower-wage areas. Such changes helped produce and were abetted by the neoliberal revolution beginning in the 1970s, which championed, among other things, privatization, deregulation, private property rights, and a state less accountable to social welfare and oriented instead to private capital accumulation. The form and function of financial NGOs, most notably the IMF and World Bank, have changed from providing stability of free trade via fixed exchange rates and the like to spreading neoliberalism globally through structural adjustment programs in which nations exchange debt rescheduling for agreements to cut social welfare programs, increase privatization, and so on.[105] Moreover, in 1945 about one third of human beings on the planet were still living either as colonial subjects or as minorities lacking basic rights in independent nations. The solution to the political crisis facing the world, Du Bois and others assumed, was national(ist) liberation struggles or socialist state-building projects that would lead to fundamental transformations of societies and increased standards of living. Since then, the colonies have become independent and most minority populations have secured their rights, at least on paper.

Still, struggles for minority rights continue, and many people in relatively new independent states continue to live under deplorable, often worsening, conditions, as a result of intersecting mixes of "neocolonial" political repressions, failed nationalizing initiatives, neoliberal structural adjustment policies, declining access to health care and education, stealth arrangements of forced labor, falling wages, mass incarceration, and other factors. Moreover, the struggle against fascist militarism and the burgeoning conflict between the United States and the Soviet Union, manifested in a series of interventions, coups, and proxy wars, have now been replaced. With the Soviet Union and its satellite states gone capitalist, our system of perpetual war is defined by the United States' willingness to act more aggressively in shaping the global order *and* by numerous, increasingly deadly, and drawn-out systems of political violence occurring in approximately one-third of the countries in the world.

Much of this violence and the economic relationships that sustain it occur under the radar, but like more apparent activities they, too, are linked to the colonial past. Carolyn Nordstrom argues that the legal and illicit ("shadow") financial networks that profit from and fund small-scale wars and the political violence that persists during times of "peace" fuel both underground economies and "key power, financial, and development grids of the world," to such an extent that "the modern state is configured around both the formalization and the informalization of economic and political power." "In many ways," she continues, "these non-formal market(eer)s parallel, and even make use of, colonial-style market systems: simple extractions of labor and resources channeled along equally simple routes to cosmopolitan centers around the world."[106]

So the problem of color and democracy remains at a moment of global war, and Du Bois is valuable to the present because of the ways he examined mechanisms put in place at the beginning of the cycle Wallerstein identifies, which continue to structure racial hierarchies and the meaning of race on a global scale. World War II brought home the historical links between war, imperialism, and race. It is clear, as many have remarked, that the Allied fight against fascism, the horrors of the Holocaust, and the participation of racial subjects in the Allied military and as workers on their domestic fronts helped usher in a period of racial reform. But the war also solidified old racial exclusions and enabled new ones to develop. Du Bois drew from past experience that modern war simply took a deeper toll on poor people, many of whom were racial subjects in a world that had been fundamentally organized through the slave trade, imperialism, and racially exclusionary democracies. Past experience and events he witnessed in the 1940s showed him that these social costs might continue into the future, with war becoming even more fundamental to modernity if democratic societies did not adequately attend to the racial exclusions of the past or sufficiently ameliorate (let alone expand) the violence of capitalism. He saw the various ways that the United States in particular would take on the mantle of old colonialisms, reformulating their projects in profound ways but, again given the needs of capital and the colonial outcomes of social organization across the globe, reproducing to some degree their racial exclusions. As he puzzled through the implications of ascendant U.S. power, Bretton Woods, Dumbarton Oaks, and transnational war profiteering, he also began to make sense of a new constellation of power that would reproduce such racisms.[107]

Although this constellation of power has changed dramatically in the years since — as the colonial has given way to the neo- and postcolonial — racial exclusions persist. The inability of policymakers to take race into account adequately and transcend their own racial myopia during the midcentury moment of war and global reconstruction was an act of exception that not only enacted racial exclusions in Du Bois's present but laid the groundwork for future exclusions at the level of politics, economics, culture, and the physical endangerment and destruction of human bodies. Du Bois also understood how the pursuit of "peace" without a commitment to addressing legacies of colonialisms and their articulation with new imperialisms would mean perpetual war and destruction for those already deemed racial subjects and might create new categories of "homines sacri."

Moreover, Du Bois's perseverance at midcentury in uncovering the racial logic governing strategic initiatives in war and peace, supported as they were by erasures of legacies of racism and imperialism, calls attention to the ways our colonial present is served by a justificatory framework (with its simultaneous denials of Western culpability and colored humanity) developed during World War II and the Cold War. For it is precisely through its veil of virtue, as a guarantor of freedom and democracy, that U.S. and U.S.–influenced sovereign projects make race invisible, allow old racial exclusions to be reproduced, and enable new ones to arise. Comparing NATO's relative action in the Balkans and inaction in Rwanda and Sierra Leone during the 1990s, a Zambian journalist put it bluntly: "The irony of the Kosovo crisis is that it was caused by racism (at the ethnic level) and it was saved by racism (at the international level)."[108]

Of course, as that observation suggests, the relationship between race and war is profoundly complicated. The imperial ambitions of the United States and nations of the global North explain only some of the violence occurring on earth. Countries across the globe are riven by ethnic, religious, political, and class-based wars that put into conflict political identities that precede, are products of, and emerge later than the imperial epoch to which Du Bois paid close attention. Much conflict stems in no insignificant ways from the very struggles for independence in which Du Bois and others of his generation put so much faith. Yet Du Bois's linked comments about the multifaceted nature of rearticulated imperial power, his warnings of escalating and unending violence, and his attention to the profit motive guiding the practice of war push us to think carefully about scenarios where the legacies of imperial relations reemerge in civil wars in places like Darfur and Iraq; where long-standing beliefs about which human beings matter and which do not drive decisions to intervene, how to intervene, or not to intervene in places like Darfur and Iraq; and where colonial-style extractions of resources and war profiteering funneling capital to metropolitan centers shape human lives in places like Darfur and Iraq.

When Du Bois chose to consider these issues in light of domestic political cultures and everyday acts of consumption, he provided a mechanism for thinking about how the lives of ordinary Americans are connected to those racialized subjects in societies where war is woven into the fabric of life in more immediate ways. Du Bois's insistence in *Color and Democracy* and elsewhere that the status of people elsewhere was linked to the lives of working people and racial minorities in the global North reminds us that global war shapes our lives by, among other things, diverting resources away from education and other forms of social spending, augmenting the penal system and security apparatus, and constraining possibilities of democratic culture. His analysis also suggests the complicity of ordinary people in war projects in both past and present. Du Bois shows us, in other words, how a triumphant, neoimperialism, whose global democratic promise has been inconsistent and exclusive, is linked to aggressive political, economic, and military activity, as well as to political quiescence and consumerism in the developed world.

Finally, Du Bois not only helps us understand that an ethical calculus was put in place that continues to enable racial exclusions through the enactment of militaristic virtue during World War II. His disruption of that virtue at its genesis calls attention to the selective memory of the conflict. Marianna Torgovnick makes it clear that the war complex's economy of acknowledgment and deflection links our present to the past of the World War II period. She notes that we have quite often understood the September 11 attacks on the United States and subsequent war on terrorism through the rhetoric and images of World War II that have been used instrumentally. She considers why certain events or images are invoked again and again to promote the idea of the United States as a "virtuous, heroic," and otherwise exemplary nation: "D-Day, 'the greatest generation,' citizen soldiers fighting against the forces of totalitarianism, the effectiveness of trials for war crimes and crimes against humanity, the Holocaust as an evil inflicted by Nazis upon Jews, genocide as something that should never happen again." All the while, other images, which might support a contrary view, are acknowledged somewhat less, at least in official discourse: "internment camps for Japanese and Japanese Americans; incendiary bombings of cities in Germany and Japan; the atomic bombings at Hiroshima and Nagasaki; and, . . . the vital Soviet role [at great cost to its civilian population] in defeating the Nazis."[109] Thus we can also think about how the state of perpetual war today, taking a particular toll on poor people of color, may be enabled by the ambivalence toward mass civilian deaths established during World War II, a refusal to attend to a full historical analysis of how and why certain kinds of civilians tend to be indiscriminately killed in times of crisis, and a selective memory of World War II that enables that refusal. Bringing Du Bois to the present enables us not only to see the practice of global race war as a political trajectory defining the American century but also to glimpse the roots of its justificatory mechanisms. His analysis refuses selective memory of the conflict by calling attention to the racial exclusions of the "good war" and disrupting the moral certitudes that followed.

Africa, the *New York Times* announced in 2006, although "rife with disease, famine, poverty and civil war — is suddenly 'hot.'" Surveying calls to action by celebrities, increases in charitable donations, aid tourism, and the representation of Africa in fashion, the *Times* points out that in a complicated world, with animus toward the United States rising, many Americans are drawn to the continent "by what they see as a clarity — both political and moral — in Africa's problems." The article adds that these problems tend more and more to be perceived at a continental rather than national level. And, referencing a recent editorial by Paul Theroux, it suggests that many see Africa as an "unfinished" project through which they can ennoble themselves by acting upon it.[1]

Such continental projection is part of a long genealogy, in V. Y. Mudimbe's words, of "discourses on African societies, cultures, and peoples as signs of something else."[2] Achille Mbembe reminds us how such concerns may replicate the inability to understand "African human experience" through anything other than a "negative interpretation," in which its "elementariness and primitiveness . . . makes Africa the world par excellence of all that is incomplete, mutilated, and unfinished, its history reduced to a series of setbacks of nature in its quest for humankind."[3] We should also consider how projecting upon Africa has accompanied geopolitical projects that have greatly affected the lives of Africans, such as exploration, trade, slave-raiding, colonialism, and, more recently, neo-imperialist mineral extractions, structural adjustment plans, and NGO- and government-sponsored aid work.

Yet as problematic as imagining Africa and Africans has been, it may provide an opening for rethinking Africa's relationship to the rest of the world. Those concerned with global justice face a conundrum. As James Ferguson notes, the construction of "a place-in-the-world called 'Africa'" as "a problem" because of wars, poverty, failed states, the AIDS pandemic, and the like reproduces colonial modes of denigration. Yet these problems are real for people who live there, as social conditions deteriorate under a "worldwide capitalist restructuring . . . [that] has left little or no place for Africa outside of its old colonial role as provider of raw materials (especially mineral wealth)."[4] Moreover, the orientation toward independence that energized anticolonial activism, postcolonial development, and anthropological investigation is now mobilized to emphasize African's responsibility for its own problems. It is thus time, Ferguson argues, to put forth the "claim of worldly connection and membership, the claim that explicitly contests the separation and segmentation that have so far been the principal fruit of 'globalization' for Africa."[5]

W. E. B. Du Bois wrote about the place of Africa in the world for much of his career. He devoted significant attention to African history in four books published before 1940 — *The Negro* (1915); *Africa: Its Geography, People and Products* (1930); *Africa — Its Place in Modern History* (1930); and *Black Folk Then and Now* (1939) — and in numerous shorter writings. Informing his analysis were Hegelian dialectics; Herderian folk nationalism; a genealogy of Ethiopianism linking members of the African diaspora spiritually, culturally, and politically while anticipating a redemptive, collective liberation; more prosaic Pan-Africanist writings, such as those of Joseph Ephraim Casely-Hayford of the Gold Coast; and, increasingly, the influence of Marxian political economy. He was from the beginning invested in challenging white supremacist and Eurocentric scholarship that ignored Africa or presented it as a conundrum. He emphasized Africa's contributions to world culture and civilization throughout history while positioning Africa as a challenge for the global community in the present. Africa was both a symbol of a world in crisis — of the continuing problems of colonial imperialism and racism — and its hope for a more democratic future.[6] In his essay "The African Roots of the War" (1915), for example, he argued that the end of colonialism and some measure of self-determination in Africa was a necessary step toward global peace and the empowerment of labor.[7]

Du Bois developed such ideas in conjunction with his participation in the Pan-Africanist movement. He served as secretary to the 1900 Pan-African Conference organized by Henry Sylvester Williams and Alexander Walters in London. There he first publicly spoke the words "the problem of the twentieth century is the problem of the color line." Du Bois was the central figure in the Pan-African Congress movement of the early decades of the twentieth century, which held gatherings in 1919, 1921, 1923, and 1927. And he played no small part in the movement's elitism and the high representation in it of English-speaking people of African descent from the Americas.

But during the 1940s and 1950s Du Bois addressed Africa's place in the world in a more radical fashion. As discussed earlier, Africa figured prominently in his critique of war and exclusionary peace plans during and after World War II. After he returned to the NAACP in 1944 and subsequently grew closer to anticolonial and left activists, concern for Africa's place in the world was central to his internationalist politics. Key activities related to Africa during his second career with the NAACP included planning and participating in the fifth Pan-African Congress, held in Manchester; drafting a petition to the United Nations seeking representation for colonized subjects in Africa; and writing his volume *The World and Africa: An Inquiry into the Part Which Africa Has Played in World History* (1947), which incorporated material from his previous works on the continent.

After being forced to resign from the NAACP, Du Bois began working more closely with the Council of African Affairs (CAA), a group founded in 1937 by Paul Robeson and Max Yergan as the International Committee on African Affairs. The CAA was radicalized early in the war years and thereafter played a crucial role in developing an anticolonialist perspective in the U.S. civil rights community. After the war it maintained its internationalist and Marxist orientation (eventually running afoul of authorities because of it) as other civil rights activists adopted a Cold War liberal perspective.[8] Over the course of the 1950s, under the auspices of the CAA until it disbanded in 1955 and independently, Du Bois wrote about and sometimes was in dialogue with participants in independence movements in Africa. He spent the last few years of his life in Ghana, working on his long-deferred encyclopedia project.

Throughout this period Du Bois rearticulated the idea, voiced in the essay "The African Roots of the War" and elsewhere, that African liberation was a necessary step in the creation of a more democratic world. As an activist, he sought collaboration among anticolonial activists, labor groups, Western powers, the Soviet Union, and the United Nations. As a scholar and opinion maker, he sought to identify and then reimagine the place of Africa in the world — historically, politically, culturally, and economically. Africa presented perhaps *the* ethical challenge for the world at a moment when questions about the scope of human rights reforms were paramount. Du Bois averred that writing Africa into world history, as both land of civilizational achievement and object of Western terror, might make the case for a fuller extension of human rights. He hoped as well to explore the possibilities of political organization and affective belonging that might draw Africans further within the global community. Du Bois's attempts to reimagine Africa and the world must be understood with the critiques of Mudimbe and Mbembe in mind. When Du Bois looked to Africa, he was often talking about "something else" and he was fully capable of reproducing ethnocentric and elitist sentiments that have often accompanied outsiders' assessments of the continent. However, despite and in some ways because of its contradictions, his project, especially at the end of the 1940s, suggests an alternative, more inclusive global imaginary and a more focused, or at least differently focused, moral concern for Africa and therefore a more substantial challenge to the global racial order in our "colonial present."

AFRICA IN THE WORLD

In an *Amsterdam News* column in 1940 Du Bois proposed a revival of the Pan-African Congress movement, suggesting that a fifth congress be held in Haiti in 1942.[9] He recognized there was increasing interest in Africa because of its status as a southern front of World War II, the role its colonial lands had played in international conflicts leading to the war, and questions about how colonies would figure into postwar power relations. Yet further investigations of Africa's place in the world were potentially stymied by a racist discourse about it and a scholarly funding apparatus still inclined to support research projects in service to colonialism before those attendant to African freedoms.[10] Du Bois himself had unsuccessfully tried to obtain funding from the Carnegie Corporation to bring an alternative, "Negro" perspective to the study of South and West Africa.[11] Nonetheless, in the fall of 1941 Du Bois proposed to *Atlantic Monthly* two articles that offered a "complete restatement of the so-called Negro problems" by considering Africa's place in the world. Although the magazine rejected them, Du Bois delivered the unpublished essays as lectures at Vassar College and Yale University the following April. "The Future of

Africa in America" and "The Future of Europe in Africa" linked the questions of colonialism in Africa and civil rights throughout the Americas to the development of the future world.[12]

In the essay presented at Yale, "The Future of Europe in Africa," Du Bois made points that were central to his writings on Africa for the next decade. Greater clarity was needed on the issues facing Africa and better information was required about its diverse peoples and regions, its economy, its colonial administrations, and so on. A more rigorous analysis of Africa must also respect Africans' own interpretations of their continent's relationship to modernity. It would involve responding, as it were, to the "indictment which Africa has against the modern world." Understanding Africa thus required coming to terms with how the "two great world movements" of slavery and colonialism had largely defined "the relation of Africa to the rest of the world." Surveying its history would then challenge a colonial discourse holding that Europeans' relationships with Africa were primarily philanthropic and would refuse its subordinate inclusion in the hegemonic global order projected for the end of the war. Du Bois also raised the issue of whether the United States would supplant, via different means, the European project of empire, as it sought to increase its own capital investments in and political and military power on the continent.[13]

As he rethought the relationship of the world and Africa, Du Bois engaged in a conceptual balancing act. He described Africa as a differentiated place, as a means of subverting the essentializing stereotypes about the continent and its peoples and developing a more rigorous analysis of African history and contemporary political economy. Du Bois had previously cited the influence of the Africanist anthroplogist Melville Herskovits on his understanding of regional variation in Africa.[14] In "The Future of Europe in Africa," Du Bois similarly argued that there were "at least ten Africas," defined by geography, culture, economic development, colonial administration, and varying systems of local self-government.[15] Du Bois may be seen as responding to Hegel, who had divided Africa into three geographies. Hegel viewed two of them (North Africa and Northeast Africa) as products of European and Asian influence, while the third, "Africa proper," remained "the land of childhood, which lying beyond the day of conscious history is enveloped in the dark mantle of night."[16] Rejecting such racist, civilizationalist conceptions of Africa, Du Bois tried to present it as dynamic and complicated. Yet Du Bois also theorized Africa as a continent, at a symbolic and world historical level, as a means of engaging in geopolitical analysis and critique.

Du Bois revisited several of these points in a *Foreign Affairs* article in 1943 where he more explicitly argued that the future of the race and racism would be determined, in part, by the relationship of Africa to the world and, more specifically, by the economic relations that structured that relationship.

> As long as there is in the world a reservoir of cheap labor that can raise necessary raw materials, and as long as arrangements can be made to transport these raw materials to manufacturing countries, this body of cheap labor will compete directly or indirectly with European labor and will be often substituted for European labor. This situation will increase the power of investors and employers over the political organization of the state, leading to agitation and revolt within the state on the part of the laboring classes and to wars between states which are competing for domination over these sources of profit. And if the fiction of inferiority is maintained, there will be added to all this the revolt of the suppressed races themselves, who, because of their low wages, are the basic cause of the whole situation.[17]

In other words, for the good of the Africans and non-Africans, the world had a responsibility to attend to the place of Africa in the world and the racial and political-economic order of which it was part and parcel.

If the larger context for rethinking Africa's relationship with the world was the struggle for some measure of democratic socialism, an immediate issue was the question of Africa's place in postwar reconstruction plans. Du Bois delivered his Vassar and Yale addresses while he was assisting with the preparation of the Phelps-Stokes Fund–sponsored report *The Atlantic Charter and Africa from an American Standpoint*, released under the authorship of the Committee on Africa, the War, and Peace Aims. As a member of the general committee advising Anson Phelps Stokes and a smaller executive committee, Du Bois had over the previous months submitted memoranda to the group, worked on an appendix of key dates in African history, and commented on drafts of the report. At an executive committee meeting on April 25, 1942, held while he was in the Northeast for the Yale and Vassar talks, Du Bois argued that the report needed to pay more attention to the United States' responsibility for African affairs given its growing investments on the continent. He further asserted that the draft report did not adequately address the problems of modern imperial exploitation and histories of the slave trade and colonialism.[18] He followed these comments with a long letter offering revisions, in which he addressed what he perceived as rather benign assessments of the slave trade and colonialisms and the volume's lack of sustained analysis of how these regimes depended on racism. He was uncomfortable as well with the report's praise for recent reforms instituted by colonial powers.[19]

The report was presented publicly in June 1942.[20] It was notable for its rejection of ideas about Africans' racial inferiority and argument for their capacity for self-government and modernization. The report demanded an end of colonialism, an equitable application to Africa of Atlantic Charter principles, basic human rights for African peoples, and that those rights had to be taken seriously when planning for a postwar future. It argued that without "the wise settlement of Africa's problems[,] . . . there can be no enduring basis for world peace," and it advocated that "representative" African Americans attend the postwar peace conferences to lobby on behalf of the rights of Africans.[21] Yet even as it addressed these issues, the report paternalistically stressed the dangers "if complete self-government is provided before the people are qualified through education and experience to make use of it wisely and effectively." And despite the critique of colonialism, the report consigned most of its evils to the past and, contrary to Du Bois's suggestion, noted its "appreciation of the progressive steps forward which have been taken in recent decades by various Colonial Powers."[22]

As part of its search for a potential mechanism for postwar planning, the report addressed the vexing question of how a version of the League of Nations mandate system might be implemented following the present war. Created in 1919, this system ceded control of territories held by vanquished Germany and the Ottoman Empire to the international body, which put them temporarily under the control of individual Allied nations.[23] The report stressed that "the Mandate ideals of the vital importance of native rights, welfare, and development should be applied in all African territory controlled by European powers" and would be a step toward eventual self-government. The case for independence, however, was cautious. The word "guardianship," the report argued, was better suited to describe mandate relationships than the commonly used "trusteeship," "as it rightly implies that the relationship is not permanent but has as its purpose the fitting of the ward for self-government as soon as his education and experience permit."[24]

Du Bois tempered some of his criticisms when he reviewed the published version of the report in *Phylon* later that year. He did, after all, attend the committee's final meeting at the end of May, at which members reviewed the galleys. There, Du Bois helped broker a compromise on the language about mandates and successfully inserted a point pertaining to land rights for "permanent residents" of Africa.[25] In his review, Du Bois concluded that the report was "by far the best thing on the African problems which has been published in recent years" and marked an important shift in thinking about the continent. Americans had moved beyond "the purely missionary and philanthropic standpoint . . . [of] a generation ago . . . to a place where we can now contemplate the possibility of an autonomous self-governing Africa." He also thought it symbolic that twelve of the forty members of the committee "were of Negro descent," given that "Africans" had seldom been present in discussions of its future occurring outside of the continent.[26]

Still, he said the report did not go far enough in situating the continent's problems in an imperialist context or stressing the urgency of their resolution. It also "contained a good deal of compromise" by virtue of the competing interests represented on the committee. His "chief criticism," was that the British colonial system was represented too favorably, suggesting again his discomfort with the presumed ethical supremacy of the Anglo-American alliance. The moral legitimacy of these nations engendered by the fight against fascism provided the ideological cover for the "economic exploitation of Africa for the benefit of white nations." Du Bois reproduced comments in the review that he had sent to the executive committee after reading an earlier draft of the report, urging them to make a more emphatic statement about the potential problems with American capital investment in Africa without adequate safeguards of wages, child labor, and so on, and in the absence of mechanisms by which adequate resources would be dedicated to public infrastructures. To apply the principles of the Atlantic Charter to Africa without taking such political-economic issues into consideration, he added, "would leave us open to blame either for a lack of knowledge or lack of courage."[27]

Du Bois included in "The Future of Europe in Africa" an alternative, eight-point program for the postwar era that he had forwarded to the executive committee. As did the report, he emphasized that ideas about race that "fix forever" human relations "and indicate their possibilities" must be discarded. Yet what must not be discarded was an understanding of "the relation between European capital and colored labor involving high profit, low wages and cheap raw material." What Africa should mean to the world in the postwar order was "wide contact of human cultures and mutually beneficent intercourse of human beings as will gradually by inspiration, comparison and wise selection, evolve the best civilization for the largest number of human beings." This move could be facilitated, first, by a kind of global New Deal and then by some measure of workers' control of the means of production, which Du Bois argued was more likely to emerge in the colonies and the quasi-colonies than among "misled people of Europe whose conception of democracy has been industrial anarchy with the spirit of man in chains."[28]

Despite these radical views, Du Bois's investment in Africa remained, in some ways, defined by its elitism, paternalism, and ethnocentrism.[29] Du Bois had done his part as the "father of Pan-Africanism" in defining the movement along these lines during the 1910s and 1920s. He had, in fact, proposed something like the mandates system eventually adopted by the League of Nations to President Woodrow Wilson in late 1918.[30] He and other delegates to the early Congress meetings were less invested in an immediate end to colonialism than they were in reforming the colonial system as a necessary first step in securing freedom for colonial subjects. Du Bois's Pan-Africanism also assumed a "talented tenth" vision of uplift by intellectuals, particularly African Americans, who would play a special leadership role given their relatively privileged access to modern education and their familiarity with, if not full access to, liberal political institutions. Although Marcus Garvey's Universal Negro Improvement Association would make Pan-Africanism more of a mass concern in the 1920s and 1930s, it did little to displace the notion that African Americans and blacks from the Caribbean would be leaders in a diasporic political project.[31] And as Cedric Robinson demonstrates, Du Bois's service for the U.S. State Department in the 1920s as minister plenipotentiary to Liberia, as well as subsequent commentary on the African nation, betrayed an "elitism characteristic of his class perspective" while being insufficiently critical of the Americo-Liberian ruling class's oppressive economic practices (including forced labor) and of the U.S. government's and U.S.–based corporations' involvement in them.[32]

Even as Du Bois countered *The Atlantic Charter and Africa from an*

American Standpoint's paternalistic treatment of Africans by stressing African autonomy, he tipped his own paternalistic hand. At the April 25 committee meeting he differed with Ralph Bunche on the question of whether native Liberians needed to be better integrated into the nation's state administration. Du Bois asserted that it would simply be accomplished through intermarriage with the country's African American–descended elite.[33] When Du Bois suggested in his *Phylon* review that membership on the Committee on Africa, the War, and Peace Aims represented a significant step forward in securing African opinion on African affairs, he was essentially referring to a group of African Americans. Although several Africans living in the United States, including the future leader of Ghana, Francis (Kwame) Nkrumah, were invited to deliver comments and memoranda to a committee meeting during the drafting of the report, none of the twelve people of "Negro descent" whom Du Bois noted were on the committee itself was from Africa.[34]

In "The Future of Europe in Africa" Du Bois quoted his own *Darkwater* that "a belief in humanity is a belief in colored men," but he also said that while he did not doubt "the capabilities of native Africans," Africans must work toward their freedom collaboratively with others given "all the problems of new inexperienced social leadership."[35] Elsewhere, he demonstrated that his more explicitly Marxist analysis could also be framed in paternalistic terms: "I am convinced that the development of backward races and lands cannot be left in the unguided and uncontrolled power of private investors. Private investment should be welcomed; but it should be under control in Africa even more than it is in England."[36]

PAN-AFRICANISM, HUMAN RIGHTS, AND REPRESENTATION

Yet Du Bois's Pan-Africanism was soon energized and transformed by anticolonial and human rights work occurring across the diaspora. And in the contradictions of his changing vision—his paternalistic championing of African self-determination, the ways an investment in Western modernization informed his radical take on African labor and anticolonialism, his gendered representations of Africa—we find a perspective valuable to the present.

In early 1944 Du Bois was contacted by Amy Jacques-Garvey of the African Communities League and Harold Moody of the London-based League of Coloured Peoples (LCP). They broached the idea of creating an African Freedom Charter modeled on the Atlantic Charter and an

African Regional Council to represent the continent at the United Nations. Du Bois proposed in response a meeting of the Pan-African Congress, ideally to be held in Paris, Dakar, or Liberia after the war. He asked Garvey, Moody, and Paul Robeson and Max Yergan of the CAA to be his co-conveners, and he received broad support for the Congress from U.S.–based civil rights organizations. After returning to the NAACP that September, Du Bois won approval from its board to establish a committee to plan for the conference.[37]

Du Bois's vision for the meeting was initially consistent with those put forth for earlier Congresses. He gave lip service to African representation, assumed leadership would be provided by diasporans, and saw the Congress not as an opportunity to generate specific anticolonial demands but as a chance to gather information and begin consultations about the most prudent path for Africa's future. In their correspondence in spring 1944, Garvey gently pushed Du Bois on his paternalism. She asked that he not refer to Africans as "natives" because of the offense it would cause and urged him to consult more widely with African organizations and add a "born African"—she suggested Dr. Nnamdi Azikiwe—as a co-convener.[38]

Pan-Africanism, meanwhile, was being infused with energy from anticolonial, antiracist, and labor organizations and activists based in Great Britain. Prominent groups included the LCP, the West African Student's Union (WASU), and the International African Service Bureau (IASB). The IASB was formed in London in 1937 by a group that included the Trinidadian Marxists George Padmore (the nephew of the 1900 Pan–African Conference convener Henry Sylvester Williams) and C. L. R. James; the future Kenyan leader Johnstone (Jomo) Kenyatta; the student leader I. T. A. Wallace-Johnson from Sierra Leone; and the British Guianan Pan-Africanist T. Ras Makonnen. The IASB was the galvanizing force for the creation of the Pan-African Federation (PAF) in 1944, which provided a "united front" infrastructure for bringing together labor, anticolonial, and student organizations (with the notable exceptions of the WASU and LCP) from Britain and British-held Africa and which eventually played a key role in shifting Pan-Africanism's institutional and ideological gravity from United States and West Indian civil rights and economic uplift organizations to British and African anticolonial and labor groups.[39]

At the World Trade Union Conference in London in February 1945, members of the PAF and black delegates from left and labor organizations in the West Indies, British Guiana, Africa, and Europe demanded a universal application of the self-determination clause of the Atlantic Charter, reforms in the colonies, an increased role for labor in postwar planning, and representation at the United Nations. After reconvening for a weekend meeting in Manchester, site of much black and anticolonial activism, conference delegates, members of the IASB, and others called for a Pan-African Congress, coinciding with a second World Trade Union Conference in Paris that September. They hoped their efforts could be coordinated with the NAACP's and Du Bois's. Yet this group stressed the need for more African and labor representation. They also planned to invite to the conference "fraternal delegates from Asia and the Middle East," as well as "sympathetic whites" as nonvoting delegates. IASB founders Padmore, Kenyatta, and Wallace-Johnson were on the "special international conference secretariat," under the direction of Dr. Peter Milliard, which was also given the task of producing a manifesto to present to the United Nations. Joining them was Nkrumah, still based in the United States.[40]

Padmore included excerpts from a draft of the manifesto in a Chicago *Defender* article on March 17, in which he also announced plans for the fall Pan-African Congress and reproduced portions of a draft of the "manifesto."[41] Padmore's "call to action" noted that "the rapid economic development, industrialization and the advancement of the social standards of Africa must form an integral part of any plan of world prosperity." Therefore, it was incumbent on the United Nations to extend the Allies' struggle against fascism and racism (incomplete as the latter may have been) and the principles of the Atlantic Charter into efforts to incorporate Africa into the world community. Padmore called on the UN to intervene in the development of African peoples; to allow Africans to participate in the administration of a postwar world "guided by the principle of equal rights for all men"; to make Africans the principal beneficiaries of the wealth produced on the continent; to move toward "self-government within a definite time limit"; to eliminate illiteracy, poverty, and disease in Africa; and rather than turning over Italian colonies in Africa to Great Britain through the mandate system, to work toward the eventual realization of their independence.[42]

After reading his statement, Du Bois wrote to Padmore, offering support but also advice. He expressed concern about committing to the time and place of the Paris meeting and about an agenda established by the organizers before the delegates arrived. One line of reasoning was that a later meeting, six months after the end of the war, would permit broader representation from the colonies. Although he did not directly challenge Padmore's leadership or that of non–U.S. labor or anticolonial groups, Du Bois's correspondence during this period reflected the persistence of his proprietary interest in Pan-Africanism and some discomfort with what Padmore described later as the "democratic decentralization" of the movement. A few months later, Du Bois saw the need to correct Padmore's reference that he was the nephew of Henry Sylvester Williams, who had initiated the "Pan-African movement" in 1900. Du Bois reminded him that Williams organized a Pan-African "Conference" in 1900 but that Du Bois had created the "Congress" movement.[43]

Yet communications from activists in England, conversations with Henry Lee Moon of the CIO and Alphaeus Hunton Jr. of the CAA, and encounters at the NAACP-sponsored Conference on Colonialism in April 1945 were simultaneously convincing Du Bois that labor would play an important role in defining Pan-Africanism's future. The conference brought together at Harlem's Schomburg Library civil rights leaders and anticolonialist activists from the United States, Africa, and the Caribbean to discuss varying paths for colonial independence. Early in the planning process, Hunton encouraged Du Bois to invite "executive members of labor organizations" and suggested that, among other contemporary events, the upcoming World Labor Congress in London was an "index" of how labor would be shaping international affairs.[44] While he would continue in the coming months to fear that the upcoming Pan-African Congress would be too specifically focused on the goal of national liberation, and while he maintained an African American proprietary right to represent Africans, Du Bois wrote to Padmore and Moody several days after the Harlem conference, indicating his approval of the Paris meeting coinciding with the labor conference and stating explicitly to the suspicious Moody "that the intellectual leaders of the Negro throughout the world must in the future make close alliance and work in cooperation with the leaders of labor."[45]

Although the September Paris meeting did not materialize, the Congress was eventually held in October in Manchester. Du Bois and Henry Moon were the only two African Americans in attendance. This limited representation seems the result of the short notice of the final date and location, postwar travel restrictions, the NAACP's dwindling support over the course of 1945 for Pan-Africanism and the left politics energizing it, and conflicts between communist members of the CAA and Padmore, who broke from the party in 1934.[46] Du Bois also played a fairly limited role planning the event, for much of his attention in the late spring and summer was directed to activities associated with the formation of the United Nations. Still, he was introduced at the gathering as the "father of Pan-Africanism," elected president of the Congress, and played an active and influential role in discussions at the conference, even as others, such as Kenyatta and Nkrumah, came into their own as political figures. Thereafter, Du Bois served as liaison between the PAF and African American organizations.

Moreover, even as the Manchester conference marked a transitional moment, when Pan-Africanism was being defined more and more as a vehicle for unity among African states working toward independence, there was great consistency among the conference's final resolutions and Du Bois's own, long-standing commitments. The delegates foregrounded their belief in "Peace," albeit with the condition that Africans might have to use force as a "last resort" in their quest for freedom. They also expressed a sense that independence must dovetail with global cooperation: "We demand for Black Africa autonomy and independence so far and no further than it is possible in this 'One World' for groups and peoples to rule themselves subject to inevitable World Unity and Federation."[47] For his part, Du Bois indicated in remarks at the conference a growing commitment to self-determination in whatever form circumstance demanded, despite a recognition that such a political project may be imperfect: "It is perfectly clear from hearing all the gentlemen have said as to what the African peoples want. They want the right to govern themselves. . . . Any people who have been deprived of self-government for a long time and then have it returned to them are liable to make mistakes. That is only human, and we are saying we have a right to make mistakes as that is how people learn, so we are asserting that we must have self-government even if we make mistakes."[48]

Meanwhile, efforts continued to try to get the UN to redefine Africa's relationship to the world. The PAF organized the All Colonial Peoples' Conference in London in June 1945 to coincide with and respond to the UN founding conference in San Francisco. Attendees put out another manifesto there, arguing again for the extension of Atlantic Charter principles and calling on the UN to create a World Colonial Council that would work toward the abolition of racially discriminatory laws, the extension of citizenship rights in the colonies, and eventually the dismantling of colonial systems of sovereignty.[49]

The fundamental limitations of the UN and of the agendas of the global powers that shaped its policy were soon made clear, however. Du Bois and others had already witnessed largely ignored resolutions and requests pertaining to human rights in Africa in the run-up to the founding conference. In December 1944 Du Bois signed on to a CAA petition to President Roosevelt and Undersecretary of State Edward Stettinius that called for the United States to raise African standards of living and help support African industrialization in ways that would benefit Africans more so than foreign investors. This followed the group's unsuccessful attempt to lobby the State Department to bring equitable African development to the Dumbarton Oaks table and to the day-to-day operations of the State Department's newly created Division of African Affairs. Their argument was based on the idea that equitable development would be good not just for Africa's masses but also for the global economy when Africans' purchasing power and productive autonomy increased.[50]

As discussed in chapter 2, Du Bois was ultimately disappointed in the UN charter. Not only did it fail to guarantee colonial independence; it left most colonial subjects unrepresented. Although the charter included a plan for colonial trusteeships, Du Bois thought it was not adequately committed to eventual independence, was predicated on the paternalistic superiority of Western powers, and was limited in scope. Under Article 77, the organization would, in the end, assume responsibility for about 3 percent of the colonial population, as the plan only applied to current "mandates" (that is, the several colonies that the League of Nations had put under the control of other nations at the close of World War I), those territories currently under Axis control, and those colonies European powers voluntarily placed in this category for administration. Du Bois was among those who expressed dismay when the South African leader Jan Smuts, who helped create the League of Nations mandate system, used his position as chair of the Committee on the General Assembly at the UN founding conference as a platform for promoting his plans to annex the mandated territory of mineral rich South-West Africa (later Namibia), a former German possession that South Africa had administered since the close of World War I. More infuriating was the United States' tacit approval for the proposal by preventing UN opposition to it.[51]

If the UN was a disappointment in its current configuration, perhaps the solution lay in African American representation of Africans' needs to the global body, as the Committee of Africa, the War, and Peace Aims and others had suggested earlier. In March 1946, Walter White asked Du Bois what recommendations the NAACP should make at the upcoming UN organizing conference at Hunter College. Du Bois argued that the civil rights organization should demand that trusteeships extend to all colonies and that the United Nations intercede in the South-West Africa matter. The NAACP should also claim the right to "represent the peoples of Africa before the UNO and to speak for their interests." This was required, he argued, because colonized subjects could not represent themselves under the auspices of the UN Charter and because colonial powers could not be trusted to do so fairly.[52] In addition to being influenced by previous discussions of African American representation of Africans at the United Nations, Du Bois may also have been inspired by India's provocative attempt to represent South African Indians, who lacked representation by the Union of South Africa's white supremacist government, at the opening session of the United Nations.[53] White had doubts about this plan, for such claims begged the question of whether "colored peoples of Africa, West Indies, or any part of the world had authorized or requested us to do so." Du Bois insisted, demonstrating the persistence of African American duty and entitlement for intervening in African affairs but also a shifting perspective that any such intervention be done with the cooperation and approval of a revived and recentered Pan-Africanist movement.[54]

Du Bois correctly doubted much would come of the March meeting in New York. But over the coming months, simultaneously with his work on *An Appeal to the World*, he worked on a petition to present to the United Nations at the September meeting of its General Assembly that would allow a consortium of black activists to represent colonized Africans at the world body.[55] He told Padmore that he hoped a group of black Americans could "speak as friends of the colonies of Africa," indicating as well that there might come a point when the "Pan-African Congress" itself could serve as "observer or consultant." He requested and received (in terms of a statement and information) support from the PAF for his petition.[56] Du Bois also contacted a number of other individuals and institutions, in the United States and elsewhere, seeking feedback on his document and plans for presenting it.[57]

Du Bois hoped the petition would mark a "logical first step" toward a fuller extension of human rights to African peoples and "peace and progress for all mankind." Although officials with the colonial powers and the United States might object to such representation because it would be "an invasion of national sovereignty" or because they believed black people did not have adequate intelligence for self-representation, the "argument [could] be countered by close and intelligent cooperation among the African peoples, their descendents and their friends, and by insistence on the obvious fact that the countries profiting from the ownership of colonies are not the best judges of the interests of colonial people; and that there is no human group incapable of voicing at least in some degree its distress, if the world is willing to hear and makes reasonable effort to know the truth."[58]

Du Bois framed the petition as initiated by the Pan-African Congress. In it, he charged that the continuing existence of "poverty, ignorance and disease in colonies, especially those in Africa," represented a threat to the world community. There was "great need of the world today" for "intelligent citizenship capable of controlling the actions of men by democratic methods of government." The problem was not innate African character but rather the "assumption" that Africans could not represent themselves. He said the solution was the "participation of designated representatives of the African colonial peoples" so that they were represented "to the maximum extent possible under the present charter of the United Nations." Although he admitted that the Pan-African Congress was not "wholly representative," he argued that it did serve the important function of forging links among African Americans and "their African brethren." Through its auspices, he concluded, African Americans and blacks from the Caribbean learned that they should not so much lead but "should share in the responsibility for the liberation and modern development of Africa."[59]

On September 4 Du Bois notified Secretary General Trygve Lie of his intent to present the petition to the UN. Two weeks later Du Bois sent a draft of his petition to and subsequently received endorsement of it from civil rights, anticolonial, Pan-African, left, black women's, black labor, church, professional, and pan-Hellenic organizations. A few weeks after that, he convened a meeting of representatives from twenty civil rights organizations to discuss the petition and further work that might be done on the question of African representation.[60] Two regional NAACP chapters were among the groups endorsing the petition. Walter White and the national branch did not. Indeed, Du Bois worked on the petition largely on his own over the course of the year and expressed great frustration to Padmore about the NAACP's lack of support, and White's in particular.[61] White and others were already ambivalent about Pan-Africanism in 1945, and during the summer of 1946, when Arthur Schlesinger Jr.'s *Life* piece suggested undue Communist Party influence on the NAACP, the organization was increasingly hesitant to commit further to radical anticolonialism. Matters would only get worse as Cold War lines were drawn and the national organization was increasingly obliged to scale back its support of radical causes and its critique of U.S. foreign policy in exchange for concessions on civil rights concerns. In the end, Du Bois "did not go further than word the petition" and by the end of the year he had largely abandoned his efforts through the NAACP to secure African American or Pan-African representation of colonial Africa at the UN. He explained to Padmore in December that the fact that "practically all visitors" were able to attend General Assembly sessions meant that the demand to be present without voting rights "was not worth contending for." The larger problem was that the UN Charter and the politics around it offered little hope for anticolonial groups to provoke meaningful action on the part of the organization.[62]

Still, there were other avenues for reconceptualizing the place of Africa in the world. Despite the limitations of U.S. Cold War policy and UN actions, the continent had increased visibility in domestic political discourse. In a letter to the *New York Times* in November 1946, Du Bois wrote that Africa's appeal "to the world for hearing and redress" might finally be heard because "the silence of the Press and of Liberal thought on Africa and its problems has broken briefly." This was critical for both Africa and the world, which were endangered by a collective effort "to separate African colonialism from Asiatic and perpetuate in Africa that slavery, serfdom and exploitation of labor and materials which the wiser world is trying to abolish as the one and only path to democracy." "Is it possible," he continued, "to build One World, free and Democratic, on the foundation of a continually enslaved Africa?"[63] The answer, of course, was no, and in an earlier, unpublished version of the letter, Du Bois turned to history to explore the roots of this dilemma and the unrealized possibilities offered in the past. He surveyed as well the present horrors that stemmed from its irresolution:

> Remember that it was five hundred years ago almost to a day, when in the midst of the Renaissance of European culture, the Spanish peninsula came into direct contact with West Africa; an Africa whose art and social organization are among the great accomplishments of mankind. This contact, which might have merged with the vast Sudanese cultures to unite a re-born Europe and an ancient Africa, degenerated, in the slow course of two hundred and fifty years, into a horror which forged fetters of slavery on the wrists of modern toil; implemented it with race hate, and made the Industrial revolution found its empire on colonial slavery even more than on free democratic labor. The contradiction and paradox grew and festered until it flamed in the conflagration of two world wars and exploded at Hiroshima. What shall we do today in this desperate effort to save civilization? Shall we again ignore and despise Africa, in an attempt to rebuild the world?[64]

Du Bois also linked African and African American freedom in the letter, worrying that both were in danger of being sacrificed to the needs of the Cold War.[65] But Africa was also a challenge to African Americans, as they pondered their relationship to the imagined nation and to the Cold War state. Expressing his frustration in a memorandum to White about the NAACP's lack of attention to African affairs, Du Bois wrote, "In its relations to Africa and the social problems there, this organization is facing a problem similar to that of the whole United States, in the question of the relationship of this country to other countries of the world."[66] The implication, of course, was that the NAACP must choose whether it would help reproduce existing imperial relationships or seek to ameliorate them. One way of choosing, Du Bois argued, would be for the organization to renew its commitment to Pan-Africanism and to collect and disseminate further information on the continent, particularly regarding indigenous freedom struggles. He suggested to White that the NAACP begin issuing pamphlets describing African social movements; providing information on labor conditions and trade-union movements; offering biographical information on African leaders; and presenting "data concerning African organizations during the twentieth century."[67]

On January 17, 1945, the day after returning the corrected manuscript of *Color and Democracy* to his publisher, Du Bois proposed to Viking Press a book tentatively titled "The Africas."[68] By the end of the year Du Bois had solidified plans to write about "the new meaning of Africa to the modern world which I think most people and thinking people of today are missing."[69] He devoted much of the first six months of 1946 to "an attempt to rewrite world history and integrate the Negro into it." *The World and Africa* was published the following January.[70]

Du Bois offers in *The World and Africa* a historiographic and imaginative approach to race, rights, and human connectivity. He calls it "a history of the world written from the African point of view; or better, a history of the Negro as part of the world which now lies about us in ruins." As it ameliorates the erasure of Africa and its people from history, the volume also seeks to show "that black Africans are men in the same sense as white European and yellow Asiatics."[71] This move, of course, follows his long-standing, interventionist academic project of demonstrating black humanity and also of centering that claim as a fundamental premise from which any legitimate scholarly inquiry about black people begins. And also, as in *Black Reconstruction* and other texts, he "appeals[s] to the past in order to explain the present."[72]

Du Bois theorizes this exclusion of Africans from world history as both an ideological framework justifying the operation of racial capitalism and as a cause and symptom of the political crisis facing the world during the postwar moment. The process "of forgetting and detracting from the thought and acts of the people of Africa, is not only a direct cause of our present plight, but will continue to cause trouble until we face the facts."[73] He describes a postwar world in political and moral crisis. Europe and European civilization have collapsed in the wake of global war and the horrific racial projects (Auschwitz, Hiroshima) accompanying it. He explicitly links the crisis in Europe to imperialism and its legacies: "There was no Nazi atrocity — concentration camps, wholesale maiming and murder, defilement of women or ghastly blasphemy of childhood — which the Christian civilization of Europe had not long been practicing against colored folk in all parts of the world in the name of and for the defense of a Superior Race born to rule the world."[74] Moving west, the United States, which takes pride in its diversity, opportunities, and commitment to democracy, remains limited by its contradictions. Government intervention in the economy upholds unequal distributions of wealth and the degradation of labor, particularly those employed in "personal service" positions often occupied by women and racial minorities. Also troubling are a decline of political dissent, an increase in the propagandistic function of the press, growing racial animus directed at Jews and African Americans at a moment when they seek greater social inclusion, a university system and strata of intellectuals increasingly dedicated to securing profit for corporations, a less radicalized labor movement, and a popular culture supporting the "idea that private profit rather than social welfare is the end and aim of man."[75]

Racism, an outgrowth of imperialism and slavery, stands at the center of the various paradoxes creating these crises of civilization. Du Bois revises arguments from *Dusk of Dawn* about the moral scene of race and global culture. He notes the "contradiction between the Golden Rule and the use of force to keep human beings in their appointed places." Related paradoxes include the prevalence of famine and poverty in imperial systems justified by the "White Man's Burden" and religious uplift; "lip service . . . paid to the idea of the rule of the people[,] but at the same time the mass of people were kept so poor, and through their poverty so diseased and ignorant, that they could not carry on successfully a modern state or modern industry"; a situation where peace between European nations is contradicted by increased militarism and the subjugation of colonized subjects; and the general degradation of labor, philosophy, and moral behavior.[76]

Capitalist ideology and an attendant lack of knowledge of (racial) political economy create an inordinate fixation on consumer goods as well as a climate of blamelessness that enables modes of exploitation. Du Bois offers the example of a young woman of some means in England and asks: "How far is such a person responsible for the crimes of colonialism? . . . The frightful paradox that is the indictment of modern civilization and the cause of its moral collapse is that a blameless, cultured, beautiful young woman in a London suburb may be the foundation on which is built the poverty and degradation of the world. For this someone is guilty as hell. Who? This is the modern paradox of Sin before which the Puritan stands open-mouthed and mute. A group, a nation, or a race commits murder and rape, steals and destroys, yet no individual is guilty, no one is to blame, no one can be punished!"[77] Such practices in the present echo the imperial processes of the past. Writing about the great human, not to mention elephant, costs of the nineteenth-century British ivory trade in the chapter "The Rape of Africa," Du Bois describes a "characteristic drama of capitalistic exploitation," "where neither the society darling nor the great artist saw blood on the piano keys."[78]

Moreover, such ideological occlusion of the racial and political-economic order structures the politics of human rights at this moment. The decidedly "American" phrase "So what!" signifies the unwillingness of most citizens to interrogate the political rhetoric of figures such as Churchill, Jan Smuts, and the South Carolinian secretary of state James F. Byrnes, who argue passionately for the necessity of freedom and democracy on the world stage while making it clear from statements and actions that, in the interest of capital, they need not be extended to racialized populations.[79]

African history, then, becomes a mode for better understanding the political economy of race and interrogating the ideological screen that upholds it in the present. Du Bois illustrates the role of slavery and colonialism in the making of the modern world and the paradoxes before it as its inhabitants debate the particulars of freedoms, security, and rights in the postwar world. But writing African history for Du Bois is also to insist on African inclusion in the modern world, to counter the ways "Africa and the Negro have been read almost out of the bounds of humanity."[80] As Mahmood Mamdani notes, Du Bois calls into question the historiographical logic on which European superiority is founded by describing African accomplishments that either parallel or predate those of ancient Greece, Renaissance Europe, and the Industrial Revolution.[81] Yet Du Bois also showcases cultural practices that present alternatives to contemporary Western ones. In his chapter on West African peoples, he argues that they not only developed metallurgical skills prior to Europeans but also engaged in "perhaps the greatest attempt in human history before the twentieth century to build a culture based on peace and beauty, to establish a communism of industry and of distribution of goods and services according to human need."[82] Here we see not only an inflated civilizationalist response to the civilizationalist argument that a lack of black contribution to world culture justifies Africa's historical subjugation but also a rejoinder to the claim that a lack of African development in the present justifies the limited extension of human rights.

Du Bois again balances an attention to the diversity of Africa with a consideration of the meaning of Africa as a continent, as a means of writing against its denigration and exploitation. In a chapter on the "peopling of Africa," exploring African difference helps him deconstruct the ideological power of the undifferentiated, "'genuine' Negro," the sign of racial inferiority that justifies the expropriation and exploitation of black lands and bodies. He juxtaposes the "hideous," "tobacco-shop" Negro with the various peoples who populate the continent: "There is no one African race and no one Negro type. Africa has as great a physical and cultural variety as Europe or Asia."[83] But Du Bois does hold on to the category of "the Negro" when challenging those who, following a different logic of white supremacy, write "the Negro" out of narratives about, for example, the political or cultural accomplishments of classical Egypt or early modern Zimbabwe. In such cases, Du Bois insists on "Negroid" presence and agency. He admits readily that human migrations and intermixture in Africa and elsewhere demonstrate the absurdity of racial categories that should ultimately be discarded. Yet even as he challenges the idea of "Negro" as a meaningful signifier, he's willing to deploy its logic to undermine white supremacist ideologies. Speaking of the whitening of ancient Egypt by European and American historiography, he writes: "We may give up entirely, if we wish, the whole attempt to delimit races, but we cannot, if we are sane, divide the world into whites, yellows, and blacks, and then call blacks white."[84]

Du Bois's challenge to Africa's erasure in dominant scholarly and diplomatic discourse is also stated through his self-conscious use of an array of secondary sources, even though, as he admits, the method may call his study's legitimacy into question. Useful to his project are Marx (despite his shortcomings vis-à-vis Africa) and Marxist social scientists; often-ignored European sources that were critical of colonialism and slavery; historical works written by African American and anticolonial activists and scholars; contemporary critics of U.S. society; and works by students of Africa and colonialism that had been deemed too controversial for publication. The reinscription of African peoples into world history is, then, a global intellectual project, dependent on far-ranging dialogue that exceeds established scholarly practice.[85]

Abdul-Karim Mustapha valuably describes how *The World and Africa* works through the responsibilities of the "Negro intellectual" toward Africa at midcentury. At a moment when some African American intellectuals operated as avatars of empire because U.S. hegemony was dependent upon a partial realization of racial democracy, Du Bois's work suggests an alternative task, which is "to produce a fissure in [the] framework" of geopolitics. Mustapha continues, "Du Bois suggests that the responsibility of the intellectual—the Negro intellectual, no less—is to impose a contradiction on the system itself at the level of narration, politics, and history." Du Bois thus presents in *The World and Africa* a kind of Pan-Africanist globality, which "asserts itself as an edification of [an alternative] world sense rather than as a reproduction of world sense as the idealized geopolitical gaze [promoting the interests of empire]."[86]

Writing Africa into world history is also foundational to the project of writing a rights-bearing African political subject into the moral complexity of the present. Du Bois opens the final chapter, "Andromeda," with a brief telling of the Greek myth, in which the daughter of the Ethiopian king and queen, Cepheus and Cassiopeia, doomed to be sacrificed to appease Poseidon, is rescued by Perseus, who marries her. Mustapha argues that Du Bois presents "Andromeda's exposure" as both "the first sign of violence of the world-system and the rise of European imperialism" and "the figure whose power, emanating from its exposure, the Negro intellectual ought to recapture in the movement of his own constitution as a global figure."[87] But this story also establishes the future global vision to which the intellectual should adhere. Although Du Bois admits that its meaning for the present is not entirely clear, "we must remember that this folk tale was part of the culture complex of the Mediterranean area where there was no color bar and no name for race; and where, at least in theory, the world was a fight between civilization and barbarism. Perhaps then in some way this legend may guide us in the present and the future." Global cooperation ideally defines the future, and that goal is dependent on the "future of black folk." Neither elimination, segregation, or cultural or physical assimilation are desirable for Africa. Instead, we must ask the questions: "Does the world need Africa? What has Africa to offer Europe, Asia, and America? Does Africa need the world?"[88]

The answers to these questions in the past were fundamentally determined by slavery and colonialism, with the latter continuing in the present, albeit with a civilizing face, as capital pours into the continent and African labor continues to extract resources for the global community.[89] Better that the world acknowledge Africa's place in the world, historically and in the present, as a means of enabling a deeper understanding of political economy necessary to social transformation and a more far-reaching concept of democracy. The role of the United States in Africa's future is given particular prominence. Although Du Bois is deeply worried about the United States' imperialist aspirations defining that future, there is still hope for a more mutually beneficial arrangement. He poses a two-pronged question: "What is America, and what duty and opportunity has it toward Africa and the peoples of African descent who live within her borders?" The answer is that reciprocity with Africa is crucial for a more democratic future in the United States, with a growing commitment to public welfare, redistribution of resources, and a commitment to "world democracy": "By releasing black Andromeda, [we] by that act release ourselves." And there is also "salvation" in the knowledge systems and ethical sensibilities established in Africa and Asia—he mentions the teachings of Gandhi, the writings of the Ghanaian physician, poet, essayist, and eventual critic of Nkrumah, Raphael Armattoe, and the common ownership of land in some regions of Africa—and in the idea of a global civilization that includes the peoples of these continents.[90]

It is ultimately incumbent on the Pan-Africanist subject of the present, however, to reinscribe black humanity and remake the world morally, politically, and economically. As Du Bois surveys the "crisis" of Europe at war's end in chapter 1, he positions himself and the Pan-African Congress movement as witnesses to the calamity brought to Africa by Europe. Pan-Africanism, as an outgrowth of African American and Afro-Caribbean cultural and intellectual history, is critical for asserting an insurgent continental imaginary that potentially bears fruit in the present as it reinscribes Africans as human beings into the world community. And while the foregrounding of this history is, on one level, self-serving, reproductive of the privileged role he ascribed to himself and other diasporans when charting Africa's future, Du Bois explicitly addresses in the text the problems of the elitism of the movement and its lack of African representation.[91]

Moreover, in the chapter on Andromeda Du Bois discusses the Manchester conference as marking a significant "step toward a broader movement and a real effort of the peoples of Africa and the descendants of Africa the world over to start a great march toward democracy for black folk." He acknowledges that the project of Pan-Africanism gains momentum from national liberation and trade union activities in Africa, and that these movements are crucial for improving the positions of Africans politically and economically. Pan-Africanism is also important, Du Bois suggests, because it challenges the newly created United Nations and its member states to extend human rights and recognize the ways that colonial projects compromise those rights.[92]

Pan-Africanism, then, plays the Perseus role. Its collapsing of African difference for particular political purpose permits the inclusive and egalitarian universalism signified by the Andromeda myth's emergence in the "culture complex of the Mediterranean area where there was no color bar and no name for race." Despite the crude and cruel motives behind her shame and exposure, and her degradation and enchaining, "the fire and freedom of black Africa, with the uncurbed might of her consort Asia, are indispensable to the fertilizing of the universal soil of mankind, which Europe alone never would nor give this aching earth."[93]

This feminine representation of the continent illustrates that *The World and Africa* was consistent with earlier creative and analytical works that similarly deployed a gendered global imaginary. By figuring Africa as a maternal figure, as Alys Weinbaum has noted regarding other texts, Du Bois insisted on "black belonging in the world" at the national, international, and historical levels through reproductive metaphor. Moreover the symbolic intermarriage here and elsewhere signifies a kind of "international kinship that encompasses all the darker peoples of the world and constitutes a refutation of the U.S. nationalist maternalism that is at base racist."[94] Yet "mother Africa" often remained in need of rescue by masculine political response. We see this in the figuration of Africa as Andromeda, as well as in the earlier chapter "The Rape of Africa," which traces the history of the North Atlantic slave trade.[95] Casting rape in symbolic terms, of course, obviates the real sexual violence directed toward black women under regimes of slavery and colonization, while it energizes a redemptive political project gendered male. Du Bois indeed writes in masculinist terms against the presumably feminizing "myth" of the "docility of Negro slaves in America." He describes slave revolts as "the beginnings of the revolutionary struggle for the uplift of the laboring masses in the modern world."[96] And if Pan-Africanism is a moral project, carried out primarily by black male intellectuals, it rectifies the moral failings of European and white American men. As Du Bois describes the "blameless, cultured, beautiful young woman in a London suburb" as the paradox of colonialism, she is representative of the West's moral failings, at least in part because the men who engineered the economic and political project of colonialism have put her in this compromised position, "content to remain in ignorance of the source of her wealth and its cost in human toil and suffering."[97]

Du Bois's recent reimmersion in Pan-Africanism had already replicated the masculinist intellectualism that had long defined his career. During early planning for the 1945 Congress, Amy Jacques Garvey was compelled to urge Du Bois to take her ideas seriously despite her gender. Also telling is that Du Bois stopped answering her letters and later abandoned a seriously ill wife to attend the conference.[98] Moreover, Du Bois's remarks at the concluding session of the Pan-African Congress, framed as a response to the other "gentlemen" on the panel, ignored both the substance and female authorship of Amy Ashwood Garvey's panel remarks on the marginal position of black women in Jamaica's labor force and their exclusion from politics.[99]

Indeed, Michelle Stephens describes early-twentieth-century "black global imaginar[ies]" that "drew key elements of imperialism along in their wake, racialized and gendered elements of empire and nation that would shape their own visions of the black state in the twentieth century." Most notably, "the woman of color often becomes in black transnational discourse a figure for the more affective and hybrid dimensions of nation and diaspora, while male heroic figures function as types for an image of the consolidated, racially unified black nation."[100] And by linking slave revolts to the revolutionary subject of Pan-Africanism, Du Bois engages in a familiar, "pressing masculinist need to take on the responsibility of rewriting history" and thus, in an appropriation of feminized roles, "give birth to new black social formations and communities."[101]

Yet Stephens also locates in black anticolonial thought generated by men "alternative ways of imagining black freedom, alternatives that deviated from paradigms of empire" and their gendered legacies.[102] Although her argument applies specifically to male Caribbean intellectuals, it is in some ways analogous to feminist critiques of Du Bois that remain open to how his work reproduces gendered exclusions at the same time that one may locate within it "alternative" ways of thinking and being in the world. Moreover, it is precisely through feminist critiques of the national liberation question as a potentially limited strategy that we can open up further inquiry into the possibilities embedded in Du Bois's uncertain negotiation of the question of national liberation in the mid and late 1940s.

Some have viewed Du Bois's Pan-Africanist project as insufficiently at cross purposes, as it was constituted by commitments both to national liberation and to placing Africans within the universal category of global citizenship and civilization. Yet a feminist critical distance toward the assumed value of both orientations, because of their often-gendered exclusions, enables us to question the basis of critiques of Du Bois's midcentury Pan-Africanism, especially as they emphasize Du Bois's limited commitment to national liberation. It would be a mistake, of course, to argue that Du Bois was moving toward a gender critical perspective that Stephens identifies in some of the late writings of C. L. R. James. The point here is that we should be open to a potentially valuable perspective generated at the nexus of his twinned commitments to national liberation in the face of colonialism and to global citizenship in light of an exclusionary discourse on human rights. These commitments were, in turn, articulated with a politics that was open to African agency while still invested in a kind of symbolic possession of the continent. We can read into his contradictory positioning an acknowledgment that national liberation without adequate global inclusion is a dead end and that Africans' symbolic exclusion from the world community vis-à-vis the needs of capital must be resolved before autonomous political-economic development can be successful.

AFRICA AND THE COLD WAR WORLD

During the late 1940s and 1950s, Du Bois's writings on Africa responded to national liberation struggles on the continent and to Cold War politics. Eventually, the successes of the former would affirm one key component of his vision for a reconstituted relationship between Africa and the rest of the world, while his growing frustrations with U.S. foreign and domestic policies increasingly pushed him, especially after the mid-1950s, to theorize African liberation as a path forged through cooperation with the Soviet Union and China. Yet in the late 1940s and early 1950s his work was defined by a broader, socialistic, global vision of justice and cooperation, one that still imagined the United States as a key player in the reconstruction of democracy.

Du Bois pushed the NAACP to pay more attention to the continent in his last years with the organization. He wrote the memorandum in September 1948 that hastened his departure from the group in response to Walter White's requests for information that could assist him as a member of the U.S. delegation at the upcoming Paris UN meeting, where its Universal Declaration of Human Rights would be adopted. White and other board members had been actively working to expand the scope of this document so that it addressed economic as well as political rights and included, ideally through a strong covenant, some mechanism for enforcement.[103] Ironically, they were working at cross-purposes with Eleanor Roosevelt, an NAACP member and United States' delegate to the Human Rights Commission. As Carol Anderson notes, in keeping with Truman's and the State Department's goals, Roosevelt promoted the United States' moral authority while simultaneously making sure that the proposed declaration and covenant would be difficult if not impossible to enforce and that "neither individuals nor nongovernmental organizations would have any authority to petition the UN for redress of human rights violations."[104]

White had initially suggested that Du Bois represent the NAACP at the meeting because of his grasp of the complexity of human rights issues, but the organization's board, worried about Du Bois's inflexibility and commitment to socialism, insisted that White take on the role.[105] Du Bois confirmed the board's fears. He initially refused to help because he believed that a declaration on human rights was meaningless without mechanisms for enforcement. When he finally responded to White's request, he lamented the failure of the *Appeal* and attacked White for ignoring the NAACP's commitment to nonpartisanship in his speeches in 1948 attacking Progressive and Republican candidates. More to the point, he castigated the organization for shirking its duty "to take a stand concerning Africa, Asia, the islands of the Pacific and the Caribbean, not to mention the colonial problems of all colored and oppressed peoples" at a moment when the United States was becoming more "international" in its actions. As the United States worked to end colonialism with deliberate speed, while augmenting its investments in the colonies, Du Bois argued that the organization had the duty to point out the hypocrisy of U.S. policy and support anticolonialism. For White to join the U.S. delegation at this moment was unacceptable, given its lack of support for the *Appeal* and its "sid[ing] with the imperial powers" on the UN Trusteeship Council; it would link the organization to the "reactionary, warmongering colonial imperialism of the present administration."[106]

Du Bois's take on Africa during this period was increasingly influenced by the CAA, which beginning in 1946 ratcheted up its critique of U.S. state and corporate investments in the colonial enterprise and attempted to intervene in African affairs through the United Nations. For example, the organization joined forces with the African National Congress (ANC) in attempting to thwart South Africa's continuing efforts to annex South-West Africa, lobbying instead to have it placed into the trusteeship program under the UN Charter. Rather than submitting a petition, they engaged in a publicity campaign, launched protests, and lobbied UN delegates. The United States tried to mediate, as it saw the bad publicity as a threat not only to South Africa's standing but also to its own stewardship of strategically important mandated territories in the Pacific islands. The United States helped thwart South Africa's plans but also resolutions that would have put South-West Africa under an international trusteeship. In the end, South Africa maintained control of the region as a mandated territory.[107]

Du Bois joined the CAA in 1947, initially as head of a special committee investigating internal conflicts generated by the administrative improprieties of its founder, Max Yergan. He was offered the unsalaried position of vice chairman when the NAACP dismissed him the following fall and was given office space and secretarial support. That same year, the U.S. attorney general put the group on a list of subversive organizations, in the wake of a lengthy investigation by the FBI for its potentially treasonous relationships with foreign entities. Things became more precarious for the CAA in 1948, as Yergan took a sharp and public turn to the right in the face of Cold War persecution. He attempted to get the group to renounce the left and fire Alphaeus Hunton. Eventually, Yergan was expelled from the group, which led some liberals to resign from or distance themselves from it. It also made the organization even more suspect in the eyes of the state. The CAA endured substantial scrutiny and persecution during the 1950s. Robeson had his passport revoked in 1950, and some of its members, including Hunton, were jailed. The CAA finally disbanded in 1955 as a result of conflicts among its members and legal fees associated with its struggle to avoid prosecution for not registering as a communist-front organization under the 1938 Foreign Agents Registration Act. Du Bois's associations with the CAA, combined with the government case against him for his work with the Peace Information Center (discussed in chapter 4), led to the loss of his passport beginning in 1952. Yet he worked with the organization until the end.[108]

Much of Du Bois's journalism during this period focused on Africa. He devoted all forty-nine of his columns in Adam Clayton Powell Jr.'s and Ben Davis's *People's Voice*, running from March 1947 to March 1948, to African issues. These pieces, written about a fifth of the time under the title "Pan-Africa," discussed precolonial and colonial African histories, examined the machinations of contemporary colonial administrations and South Africa's regional imperial ambitions, explored the inadequacy of trusteeship relations, and documented the struggles of labor and political groups.[109] However, as independence remained an unrealized goal and Western capital investment in the colonies increased, his tone became more urgent. As he noted in the CAA's own journal, *New Africa*, in 1949, a U.S. Army pronouncement that Africa "seems destined to play an even greater part in the world's economic and political affairs" indicated that "there is impending an increase of colonial imperialism" revolving around agriculture and mineral extraction, with the potential "use of force to put Africa to work for the benefit of the white peoples of the world."[110] "Before this rebirth of colonialism," he wrote in another article for *New Africa*, "the United Nations stand dumb and helpless, mumbling formulas on human rights and denying the wretched even the right to complain."[111] Ultimately, the bigger problem was the potential for future, generalized violence across the globe that would stem from increased U.S. and European investment in Africa. Building from his long-standing concerns with war's and peace's exclusions and dovetailing with his immersion in the international peace movement discussed in the following chapter, he emphasized the liberation of Africa from colonialism as necessary to world peace.[112]

These newspaper columns give an inkling of Du Bois's continuing interest in the political potential of a revived Pan-Africanism as a means of organizing various freedom struggles across the continent and a desire that the UN live up to its potential and play some role in liberating it.[113] He wrote to Padmore in March 1948, suggesting that the UN General Assembly meeting in Paris that September might be the time and place for a "real Pan-African Congress" at which delegates would hail primarily from Africa and which would again put forth the demand that the body represent African peoples at the UN meeting.[114] Two years later he thought Pan-Africanists might still leverage political pressure on the United Nations, which he perceived as retreating from its already limited commitments to the interests of colonized and decolonizing peoples.[115]

But in an unpublished article from 1948 titled "The African Roots of

Peace" he took things even further.[116] Building again from the premises that World War II illuminated the importance of Africa to the world and that the continent was becoming imperialism's last stand, Du Bois sought, in the face of conflicting and distorted information, to survey the political, economic, social, administrative, and educational challenges facing different African regions. This survey, by definition, involved an assessment of different regimes of power across the continent, as well as a consideration of the broader issue of its incomplete and unequal integration into the global networks.

Du Bois concluded by referencing his essay of 1915, "The African Roots of the War," from which the title of the piece was drawn. What distinguished the later piece from the "similar survey" that preceded it was the context. The issue in 1948 was not simply the possibility of achieving global peace and the empowerment of labor but the choice between "peace or the end of civilization in its present form." The "white world," he argued, "is facing suicide. Not, to be sure, complete physical annihilation, but a cultural collapse and a moral breakdown which many centuries will be required to restore, if restoration will ever be possible." And Africa and its diaspora face being "worked for other races profit; and spiritually suppressed for the uplift of the rest of the world." The solution lay in dismantling the colonial system, with Europeans and Americans engaging in "cooperation with the emerging intelligentsia, in Africa itself, and in the Negroids of all America; with the help of renascent Asia; and particularly with the direct aid of the socialist labor movement in all the world." Du Bois pointed to different instances of black/white solidarity ("Negroes are pouring into the trade unions of America") and, anticipating Bandung, to Afro-Asian cooperation (Gandhi's support for native South Africans, Vijaya Pandit's support for African independence at the UN founding conference, and so on) before placing ultimate duty on Africans. "These facts put on the Africans themselves, the onus of forcing the final overthrow of colonialism by continued and increased determination to be modern men. Their movement is spearheaded by their kin in America. They cannot fail. Their triumph is Peace, because colonialism and labor exploitation are the ultimate causes of war."

In an attempt to put such a vision into practice, Du Bois in January 1949 proposed to Mordecai Johnson, president of Howard University, that the school host a conference on Africa organized by the CAA to address specifically the place of Africa in the future of the world. "If Africa is going to be developed as the last stronghold of colonial imperialism," he told Johnson, "that will drag the world in one direction. On the other hand, if it is going to develop toward independence and self-sustaining cultures, as part of a new democratic world, that is another thing." Recognizing competing visions of what Africa's place in the world might entail, he suggested the conference should include representatives of colonial powers; independent African countries; African colonies; the Phelps-Stokes Fund, which, as a philanthropic funding agency with ties to Africa since the nineteenth century, represented both a tradition of missionary work and emergent area studies paradigms; "Big-Business as represented by [former secretary of state Edward] Stettinius [who through his Liberia Company had a substantial financial stake in the country] and other investors"; "the United Nations and the various organizations for world government"; and, in keeping with his sense that definitions of human rights should include an attention to economic as well as political rights, the Soviet Union. Although Johnson supported Du Bois's idea, the conference never took place.[117]

Du Bois's comments and actions here represent a kind of apex of his thinking about the integration of Africa in the world by a kind of mutual consent among Africans and those who benefit from and/or are potentially harmed by its exclusion from the world community. Although Cold War lines were already drawn, Du Bois still saw possibilities in U.S.–Soviet dialogue regarding world affairs and in the United States changing the nature of its relationships with the colonial world. Although, as he put it in one column, the United States was "leading this new colonial imperialism," it still represented "the highest proof of the possibilities of human kind."[118]

However, over the course of the 1950s, as independence movements came to fruition, and as European and American policies and discourse developed to accommodate and limit these movements, Africa less and less represented for Du Bois the possibility of democratic, global integration and exchange that would redeem the United States and build democracy at a moment of global crisis. In part because of the influence of the anticommunist Padmore, Du Bois would through Bandung champion a nonaligned position for emerging African nations and a Pan-Africanism that would reject a bipolar world and "bring the African nationalists and the progressive people of the whole world into union and understanding." Although he worried about the influence of "British and especially American capital," communism for Africa was an option but one of last resort, to be engaged if a more appealing, independent democratic socialism could not be achieved.[119] But he was frustrated by his own political alienation (and persecution) and increasingly dismayed over American and African American complicity in a limited conceptualization of Africa in the world. As the CAA was dissolving in 1955, he argued that African Americans were increasingly unaware of African affairs and doing little to lend assistance. He saw this as a return, on some level, to a nineteenth-century mind-set, before the Pan-African Congress movement had raised people's consciousnesses about the continent. Worse yet, as the civil rights movement picked up steam, African Americans had traded progress at home for acquiescence to American and European oppression of other peoples: "It is fair to admit that most American Negroes, even those of intelligence and courage, do not yet fully realize that they are being bribed to trade equal status in the United States for the slavery of the majority of men."[120]

Indeed, Du Bois wrote at a moment of a changing discourse about Africa in U.S. and African American circles as strategic interest in the region grew. Such conversations sought to bring Africa into the world, albeit under conditions different from those Du Bois imagined. U.S. policy toward Africa for most of the decade also sought a global equilibrium, a common ground between people in the colonies and metropoles, but one that was skewed significantly toward the interests of Western powers. Anticolonial movements were to be supported but on the United States' terms. They should not proceed too quickly, they should not go socialist, and they should not impede the extraction of raw materials from the continent. This state project was abetted by an area studies paradigm, often funded by Rockefeller and Carnegie money, that was rooted not in a historical materialist understanding of Africa's place in the world but in more conservative, positivist approaches and, more specifically, as Brenda Gayle Plummer notes, by development theories that stressed a deliberate pace of change, the benevolence of markets, and the universalism and implicit authority of "Western culture." The most visible American proponent of African inclusion of the world in the mid-1950s was the interracial American Committee on Africa, established in 1953, which eschewed a Marxian critique of imperialism and specifically distanced itself from the CAA. It instead drew upon Gandhian and Christian principles. It supported anticolonial movements but only insofar as these were not communist and would be inclined to participate in a hegemonic global order led by the United States.[121]

Accompanying such views was a revamping of paternalist and primitivist perceptions of Africa, at the very moment when its nations were beginning to achieve independence. As Von Eschen argues, the period witnessed a "rewriting of race," where legacies of imperialism were erased and through which the United States became not a perpetrator of racism but the wellspring of antiracism.[122] Du Bois was particularly troubled by a growing sense among African Americans that they and Africans were less and less of the same world. Although there was an increased interest in anticolonialism and burgeoning internationalist black nationalism after Bandung, Ghanaian independence, and the decolonizations that followed, the trend among many African American leaders and journalists was to focus on the dream at home, to give short shrift to the state of African affairs, and at times to reproduce stereotypes about the continent's putative backwardness or savagery.[123]

Over the remaining years of his life, Du Bois looked to Africa less as a partner with and corrective to, and more as an alternative to, political and social life in the United States. While he remained respectful of Padmore's (who would die in 1959) and Nkrumah's efforts to steer a nonaligned course in Ghana, Du Bois's perspective was diverging from theirs. In 1958, for example, in an address read by Shirley Graham Du Bois to the All-African People's Conference in Accra, Du Bois argued that the path to African development lay more firmly in cooperation with the Soviet Union and China as well as with left nationalist movements in Asia and the Middle East.[124]

THE WORLD TODAY

Du Bois ended his days in Ghana, trying to maintain his belief in African socialism during the authoritarian moves, corruption, and economic troubles that eventually led to Nkrumah's ouster. He moved there in 1961 at the invitation of Nkrumah to work anew on his *Encyclopedia Africana*. The project was reenergized first under the auspices of the Soviet Africa Institute, which was created by Moscow in 1959 in response to a Du Bois proposal, and then with the support of the Ghana Academy of Learning.[125] Shortly before leaving for the African nation, Du Bois joined the Communist Party of the United States (CPUSA), telling its chairman Gus

Hall in his letter of application that his decision "was long and slow in coming." He told of his willingness over the years to consider various paths toward socialism among nations but described how that view had faded during the Cold War. He was now convinced that capitalism was "doomed to self-destruction" and that "in the end communism will triumph."[126] Two days before receiving Nkrumah's invitation he again noted in his growing dissatisfaction with African American political cultures and his sense that blacks in the United States were being left behind by those in Africa in imagining a liberatory future. He criticized African Americans for their complicity in an economic system that was dependent upon the "domination of African cheap labor and free raw materials," for their participation in and acquiescence to red baiting in the United States, and for, in certain cases, participating in U.S. State Department public relations trips to Africa. Du Bois concluded by asking: "Would it not be wise for American Negroes themselves to read a few books and do a little thinking for themselves? It is not that I would persuade Negroes to become communists, capitalists or holy rollers; but whatever belief they reach, let it for God's sake be a matter of reason and not of ignorance, fear, and selling their souls to the devil."[127]

Such events suggest one conclusion to the story of Du Bois's vision for world and Africa, which might emphasize an eventual lack of faith in the possibility of crafting a just global order for black folk in conjunction with the U.S. project. One might also end the story with the disillusion that many African American expatriates experienced in Ghana during its early years of independence, given their disappointment in Nkrumah or the suspicion they fell under among Ghanaians as potential tools of the U.S. government.[128] Yet as an alternative to either denouement, I wish to contemplate the place of Africa in the world today in relation to Du Bois's somewhat earlier formulation of this conundrum.

The question of Africa's relationship to the world today is complicated and vexing, for Africans and for others. To begin to comprehend this relationship, one must understand the resonances of its colonial past in its postcolonial present. Africa's exclusionary social and political networks; dysfunctional governments; citizens with few or no political rights; arbitrary expressions of power and, especially, violence; and twenty-first-century manifestations of biopower that consign millions to death from malnutrition, AIDS, and other preventable ills are products of the legacies of colonial sovereignties and of the ways they have been articulated through postcolonial sovereignties and with neoimperial sovereignties. One must also be attuned to the ways emergent (neoliberal, underground economic, informational, technomilitarisic) and residual (colonial, neo-colonial) global processes articulate with one another to produce Africa's unequal and piecemeal integration into the international economy. This creates in the African social geography, in James Ferguson's words, "a patchwork of discontinuous and hierarchically ranked spaces, whose edges are carefully delimited, guarded, and enforced."[129]

And we must think about race. As the gap between rich and poor countries widens, and Africa emerges as the embodiment of the "age and space of *raw life*," as a "place and a time of *half-death* — or, if one prefers, *half-life*,"[130] an older mode of racial and sometimes racist thinking about the relationship of Africa to the world returns. David Theo Goldberg describes two fundamental senses of historical time informing concep-tualizations of race. The earlier conception, "racial naturalism," assumed that racial others were "fixed in time," whereas a more recent "racial historicism" "elevates Europeans and their (postcolonial) progeny over primitive or undeveloped Others as a victory of History, or historical progress, even as it leaves open the possibility of those racial Others to historical development." Although racial naturalism has persisted in vari-ous guises, after World War II "racial historicism could claim victory in the name of racelessness, sewing the assumptions of (now historicized) racial advancement silently into the seams of post-war and postcolonial reconstruction."[131]

In other words, although there were racial and sometimes racist as-sumptions undergirding the logic of liberalism in general and liberal developmentalism in particular, there remained a sense that the poorer nations of the global south could progress. Today this ameliorated turn in racial thinking is being reversed in ways that serve the projects of neoliberalism and empire. "As people lose faith in developmental time," Ferguson states, "the global status hierarchy comes to be understood in new and disturbing ways." One prominent way is an "understanding of global statuses as de-temporalized. Rather than the poorest countries being understood as *behind* 'the West' playing catch-up, developing, or emerging — they are increasingly understood as naturally, perhaps even racially, *beneath* it."[132]

When contemplating Africa's relationship with the world, Ferguson stresses the need to reconsider the collective critique of developmentalism's focus on modernization and integration. He acknowledges the Eurocentrism and imperial self-service of developmental discourse and programs in the past and present. Indeed, as Sylvia Wynter argues, "The goal of *development* together with its related subgoal of 'economic growth' functions to lay down the prescriptive behavioral pathways instituting our present world system."[133] Yet Ferguson stresses that modernization remains a relevant and often necessary category for Africans who continue to seek better health care, employment, and education. Such an orientation, he argues, "do[es] at least acknowledge (and promise to remedy) the grievances of political-economic inequality and low global status in relation to other places."[134]

Meanwhile, Achille Mbembe argues that African philosophy, forged in a critique of slavery and colonialism, has yet to come to terms with the "never-ending *process of brutalization*" in contemporary Africa that may have its beginnings in European barbarisms but which is articulated with and through various modes of power in the post-colony. His project is, in part, "to force Africa to face up to itself in the world."[135] Although a commitment to black humanity was foundational to anticolonial struggle, "both the asserted denial and the *reaffirmation* of that humanity now look like the two sterile sides of the same coin. What distinguishes our age from previous ages, the breach over which there is apparently no going back, the absolute split of our times that breaks up the spirit and splits it into many, is again contingent, dispersed, and powerless existence . . . [that] reveals itself in the guise of arbitrariness and the absolute power to give death any time, anywhere, by any means, and for any reason."[136] This political failure has existential consequences, even threatening to destroy the idea of a better future that is so central to struggles for justice: "The promise has been replaced by the lack of expectation. Enclosed in an impossibility and confined on the other side of the world, the natives no longer expect anything from the future."[137]

Into these dilemmas we can bring Du Bois and his midcentury reflections about and activism around the place of Africa in the world. As argued in chapter 1, one of the lessons of Du Bois's racial analysis is to remain attuned to shifts in the ontology of race while simultaneously looking out for the return of older racial logics. Writing about Africa in the 1940s and 1950s, Du Bois understood the roots of its exclusionary inclusion in world affairs through a history of racial imperialism, and he worried about how Africans would fare in future economic relationships and in light of limited application of human rights. The inadequate mechanisms in the UN for protecting the rights of African peoples were intertwined with the more general inability of the world community to put aside self-serving political and economic agendas and act toward Africans as if they were fully within the category of the human. But Du Bois also understood the implications of the continued marginalization of Africa for the racial future of the rest of the world. As he argued in his *Foreign Affairs* piece in 1943, "Unless this question of racial status is frankly and intelligently faced it will become a problem not simply of Africa but of the world. More than the welfare of the blacks is involved."[138] Du Bois's work, then, suggests that rethinking the place of Africa in the world is a necessary step for attending to the problem of race in its future.

Du Bois's work also suggests that this engagement can productively emerge at the nexus of historical imagination and ethics, which resonates today in particular ways when academic writing and popular culture texts reengage African history, and especially in the United States, the British colonial experience in Africa. As Harilaos Stecopoulos argues, such texts, even when putatively liberal and critical of the racism and economic exploitation of colonialism in the past, can provide cover for U.S. imperial power in the present by looking nostalgically to what is represented as the benevolent side of the colonial enterprise. And this power derives from simultaneous investments and disinvestments in a racial logic: "The fact that these narratives concern the experience of another white people allows the U.S. public to indulge in feelings of innocence where Africa is concerned—after all, we never held African colonies—and attempt to learn from the British record at the same time. For once, raced history comes with no guilt attached!"[139] "A critical relationship to history," Stecopoulos concludes, "remains our best defense against the temptations of a nostalgia that leaves America at peace with imperialism itself."[140]

Surely, explicating colonial and neocolonial abuses and their resonance in neoliberal restructuring on the continent does something in this regard, but does that fulfill the historian's task given Africa's unequal integration into the global community and the depth of belief about its failings? Might not the historian, rather than generating guilt, shame, or outrage about contemporary Africa and its future, seek instead to decenter Western knowledge production structuring the continent and perhaps, by extension, even promote a sense of collective responsibility for its future? As Wynter proposes, the analytic response to crisis in Africa and its place in the world, requires nothing less than "a move, beyond our present epistemological order. . . . Any such strategy will, therefore, call for the displacement of the economic goal/telos of 'development' and 'material progress'/'growth' and the counter-positing, from the neo-lay or liminal perspectives of 'we-the-underdeveloped,' of the jobless poor, and of the peoples of Africa and African descent of the hegemony of social goals based on reciprocity." Wynter's work suggests it might be possible, then, from a position outside, to help create a kind of shared commitment "to move toward a new human-species interest and ecosystemic sense of right, and therefore, toward a new order of *culture-scientific truth*."[141]

Du Bois, who was not without his own prejudices toward Africa and Africans, was through his activism and writing invested in negotiating a middle ground between support for autonomous national liberation movements and a global vision that would transform Africa's relationship with the world from one of labor exploitation and extraction to one of mutual political and economic uplift. His orientation was of course socialistic, and his vision would eventually depend on the guidance of the Soviet Union and China. But for several years he thought Africa could learn much from a broader sweep of the world's community and vice versa. Although one can find fault through eventual outcomes with simultaneous investments in a masculinized, nation-based program of anticolonial activism *and* a reformist state socialism, there seems value in the core goal of a rapprochement between Africans and others that would transform existing political-economic relationships, expand the terrain of human rights discourse, raise ethical standards globally, and, ultimately, eliminate one key cause and effect of the global color line. Even though he embraced the "framework of rationality" and "master discipline of economics" that Wynter identifies at the heart of the crisis-producing epistemological regime, Du Bois wanted nothing less than to reconfigure modernity in more humane terms through a reconsideration of Africa's place in the world.

Operating at a moment of political crisis in Europe and America, Du Bois wrote the history of the world and Africa in a way that catalogued a long history of European, and particularly British colonial, abuses and predicted a potential imperialist future led by the United States. But he surmised that an alternative way forward involved reconceptualizing the world's responsibilities toward Africa. It is important that rather than merely seeing this as a project for elites, he considered people of African descent in the United States and their current and future relationships with Africa. Centering reconciliation as an African American "problem" enabled him to theorize how race was a mode that could simultaneously disadvantage and privilege minorities in the global North. Du Bois was aware that African Americans, as they made domestic-based demands of inclusion, could be implicated in the racially imperial projects of their government, while at the same time he understood that the continued exploitation of Africa presented a perpetual threat to the economic stability and status of African Americans, other racial minorities, and working people more generally.[142]

Du Bois's orientation suggests that we consider how an emergent racial naturalism vis-à-vis Africa, concomitant with the West's willingness to let Africa suffer, may articulate with and perhaps even enliven other racial exclusions. Many have commented on the development of a "global apartheid," which has been described not only as a system of exclusion but as "a productive system of *hierarchical inclusion* that perpetuates the wealth of the few through the labor and poverty of the many." It is a system defined by growing disparities in wealth, health and safety; increased spatial segregation; growing rates of incarceration; and a proliferation of surveillance and policing that abets this growing prison population and keeps the rest of the population in check.[143] As we contemplate how such exploitative social logics make their way from Africa (or the global South more generally) to the global North, we should consider the extent to which the ways the West lets Africa suffer and then blames it for its suffering enables such transit by emboldening a resurgent hostility to people of color and augmenting an exhaustion with them and their "problems" in the putatively postracial present.

This is complicated terrain, no doubt. Apathy about Africa is countered by the increase of concern for the continent discussed at the beginning of the chapter. Despite the problems with such concern, it also shows a willingness to embrace humanity across the divisions manufactured by an emergent racial naturalism. But rather than ameliorating the hostility directed to racial subjects in the United States and elsewhere in the overdeveloped world, such identifications with Africa may simultaneously reflect and enable an unwillingness to attend to thorny issues at home pertaining to growing racial and class divisions in the context of neoliberal economic changes, global war, immigration and globalization, and so on. As Mbembe reminds us, Africa, as "that something invented," has long "play[ed] a key role, both in the world the West constitutes for itself and in the West's apologetic concerns and exclusionary and brutal practices towards others."[144]

At the heart of this complex matter—enabling a global racism but potentially challenging it as well—is the interface of exclusion and possibility that has long marked Africa's place in the world but which took a critical turn at midcentury. At that moment, Du Bois posed a moral challenge to the West in general, to African Americans in particular, and to Africans as well for taking responsibility for the manifestations of the colonial exclusions and for the social and moral limitations in Western societies that derived from these past and present exclusions. The linked futures of Africans and African Americans provided the litmus test for the future of democracy across the globe. Although Du Bois did not in this regard escape the trap of imposing non-African views on Africa, he did, in dialogue with Africans and anticolonialist activists from different lands, shift his perspective and attempt, in various ways, to work beyond the economy of guilt and blamelessness that characterized the moral scene pertaining to Africa.

Reading Du Bois's placement of Africa in the history of the world today, we are moved toward a collective sense of responsibility for Africa's past, present, and future, which is a key component to the existence of racism in the past, present, and future. This sense of responsibility is dependent on a deep understanding of political economy and of the consequences of racist ideologies both in the past and in the present. Du Bois suggests the need for an epistemological and moral intervention into what Ferguson calls the "demoralizing aspects" of neoliberal policy, which privilege individual economic freedoms and property rights and call upon Africans to atone for their irresponsible behaviors of the post-independence past. Like "African traditions of moral discourse on questions of economic process," Du Bois offers a potential resource for the future.[145] Reading him in the present helps give rise to an alternative orientation that must be fundamentally informed by our own individual and collective—whether African or non-African—implications in and responsibilities for Africa's position in the world. In other words, only with Andromeda's collectively charted release can race as a global phenomenon even begin to be dismantled.

In "20th Century: The Century of the Color Line," a pamphlet published in 1950 by the *Pittsburgh Courier*, Du Bois reflected upon the century's first five decades. Referencing his turn-of-the-century statement "The problem of the Twentieth Century is the problem of the color-line," he troubled his and other early civil rights activists' prognostications that the future would bring "peace, progress, and the breaking of the color line." Fifty years later, he reminded his readers, the world experienced "war, hate, the revolt of the colored peoples and the fear of more war."[1]

Writing at a time when the NAACP and other groups were mounting successful challenges in the courts to the legal edifice supporting white supremacy in the United States, and shortly before grassroots activists in the south would enter the national scene as they put their bodies on the line in pursuit of social justice, Du Bois offered a reflection on a long civil rights movement dedicated, in part, to integrating black people into the American nation, both structurally and symbolically. He catalogued valuable, albeit limited, efforts to secure equality in education, voting and other rights, better wages, fair housing and an end to spatial segregation, the development of a freer press, and "social equality." Not surprisingly, he emphasized his own role in these efforts.

Yet even as he longed for more successes within the domestic sphere of racial justice, he problematized black inclusion in the United States. At a moment when "the whole trend of the thought of our age is toward social welfare; the prevention of poverty by more equitable distribution of wealth, and business for general welfare rather than private profit," African Americans were not only overly concerned with accruing individual wealth but were complicit in a nationalistic, imperialist political project as well. "The effort of Negroes to become Americans of equal status with other Americans is leading them to a state of mind by which they not only accept what is good in America, but what is bad and threatening so long as the Negro can share equally."[2] African Americans should know the United States is not a "successful democracy and that until it is, it is going to drag down the world." They should develop from their subordinate position *and* their relative privilege as racialized citizens a more sustained and worldly political critique. Rearticulating his take on African Americans' responsibilities for the reconstruction of democracy, Du Bois cautioned his black readers: "We may find it easy now to get publicity, reward, and attention by going along with the reactionary propaganda and war hysteria which is convulsing this nation, but in the long run America will not thank its black children if they help it go the wrong way, or retard its progress."[3]

Du Bois called on African Americans to reject a patriotism defined via a simplistic nationalism or a will to consume. Instead, they should forge a more complex cosmopolitan web of loyalties: to socialism; to economic and social justice more generally; to often-ignored democratic principles that were still central to any just political future in the United States and in a world shaped by American hegemony; and to a transnational intellectual community who deemed peace and economic justice as inseparably linked and who he hoped would transform the world, "not by revolution, not by war and violence, but by reason and knowledge."[4]

Du Bois wrote this pamphlet at a moment of heightened Cold War conflict, when he was heavily involved with the CAA's anticolonial efforts in Africa and with the communist-led, Soviet-affiliated international peace movement seeking to ban the atomic bomb. He was also pursuing reconciliation with the Soviet Union through the National Council of American-Soviet Friendship. He wrote in 1949 and 1950 and tried to publish a book, tentatively titled "America and Russia," that described his travels to the Soviet Union and urged rapprochement with the communist nation. In 1950 he ran for U.S. Senate on the American Labor Party (ALP) ticket. Such activities eventually led to his indictment for failing to register as a foreign agent under the Foreign Agents Registration Act of 1938, a subsequent trial and acquittal, the loss of his passport in 1952, and the political alienation that would define his intellectual production for his remaining years.

I complete this consideration of Du Bois's midcentury thought by foregrounding the question of the rights and responsibilities of U.S. citizenship, and that of minority subjects in particular. As noted at various moments in this book, Du Bois's transnational and international perspectives on imperialism and war, their impacts on black and brown peoples across the globe, were intertwined with his concern for the reconstruction of democracy in the United States. Yet certain texts produced at this moment put compelling emphasis on the question of loyalty to a U.S. political project in which there was still potential but whose progressive elements were under attack by Cold War conservatism and liberalism alike. The shift in perspective in this chapter — from the global concerns evident in Du Bois's ruminations on Africa to his conception of critical citizenship in the United States — is inspired by his work and also by the ways that black intellectuals and activists have more recently, during the early years of the twenty-first-century global war on terrorism, raised their own concerns about where U.S. political culture is headed and about black complicity in and exclusion from it.

The chapter takes its title from Julianne Malveaux and Regina Green's twenty-first-century description of "the paradox of loyalty" as "the perfect distillation of the mixed feelings that many African Americans feel about our country. African Americans are the perfect Americans; caught between hope and despair, believing in the American dream despite evidence to the contrary because our disbelief would make us nihilistic and disengaged. African Americans who vote, engage, and criticize America are, in our opinion, the ultimate Americans, offering their criticism as a form of service."[5] As various black responses to September 11 and its aftermath suggest, such criticism should be simultaneously aware that racial inequalities in the United States are part and parcel of economic, political, and militaristic processes that reproduce racial inequalities on a global scale. Moreover, this commentary brings home the fact that loyalty to and location within the nation — defined through modes of gender, sexuality, and class, as well as race — continues to implicate African Americans in the project of empire, thus placing an added urgency on this form of service.

So, I examine Du Bois's attempts to define himself as a kind of "ultimate American" during a period of increased alienation. As analyzed by Du Bois and embodied by him as a fallen African American intellectual at this moment, African Americans' paradoxes of loyalty at midcentury were informed by a history of social exclusion and incomplete inclusion in the national project. They were also influenced in the moment by a Cold War scenario in which geopolitical aspirations required the state to include black people and their activism into the body politic, even as it continued to exclude them by refusing to intervene more actively in southern apartheid, in part because of the radical social vision such action would legitimate.

I argue that Du Bois's highly charged response to the political crisis circa 1950 anticipates the challenges facing those we can define as "suspect citizens" today. As M. Jacqui Alexander defines it, the "suspect citizen" is a racialized category, encompassing those who might possess citizenship through naturalization or birthright but whose "'loyalty' is perennially suspect and, therefore, ultimately threatening."[6] Yet my use of "suspect citizen" is also attentive to the ways that black people, through a process that Devon Carbado calls "racial naturalization," have been symbolically incorporated into the nation, regardless of formal status as citizens, through processes that are simultaneously inclusive and exclusive.[7]

I explore how Du Bois's contemplation of his own "racial naturalization" positions African Americans as suspect citizens while attempting to imbue the category with critical potential. I focus on Du Bois's participation in the peace movement between 1949 and 1951 and on his account, in his memoir *In Battle for Peace* (1952), of his personal and political ordeal that followed. Therein lies an interrogation of citizenship and loyalty as racially inflected Cold War political categories, as well as a description of his own, often competing, loyalties at a moment when he was experiencing a profound sense of alienation and pushing the limits of what was politically possible and permissible.

Twenty-first-century African American voices addressing post–September 11 political cultures, as well as others who examine the changing interface of race, gender, sexuality, class, and citizenship today, energize my treatment of Du Bois's negotiation of racialized loyalty at a midcentury moment of heightened global conflict, an emergent security state, and imposed political quiescence. Building on this literature also enables a more intersectional and comparative engagement with issues regarding race, war, and imperialism, developed in previous chapters by foregrounding a racialized, sexualized, gendered economy of neoimperialism at home and elsewhere.

At the beginning of 1948 Du Bois accepted an invitation to join the National Council of Arts, Sciences and Professions.[8] Later that year, he began helping it plan its Cultural and Scientific Conference for World Peace, held at New York's Waldorf-Astoria hotel in March 1949. The chair of the organization was the Harvard astronomer Harlow Shapley, whose call for the conference emphasized the dangers to intellectual freedom and cultural expression in the United States during the Cold War, the social problems accompanying increased military spending, and the need to "re-establish American-Soviet understanding and cooperation, which alone can make peace possible."[9] Du Bois was honored at and spoke at the panel on writing and publishing, which included, among others, Shirley Graham, the author Norman Mailer, the American studies doyen F. O. Matthiessen, the screenwriter Howard Fast, and the Soviet writer Peter Pavlenko.[10] Du Bois also gave a lengthy introduction to Shapley's appearance at the conference's closing session at Madison Square Garden.

The Waldorf conference occurred at a moment of growing opposition to atomic weaponry among pacifists, scientists, proponents of world government, religious folk, and others in the United States. It was also a period of growing anti-Soviet sentiment in the United States across the political spectrum but one in which there was still significant support for reconciliation with the Soviet Union given the heightened saber rattling between the two superpowers.[11] Stalin's blockade of Berlin beginning in June 1948 was countered by an airlift of food and supplies by the United States, France, and England. In July Truman sent to England sixty B-29's, capable of delivering atomic bombs to Eastern Europe. As the Soviet Union tightened its control of most of Eastern Europe, negotiations between the United States and Europe led to the North Atlantic Treaty, eventually signed in April 1949, which created an alliance for fighting Soviet military aggression against any of the signatories.

The Waldorf conference generated controversy even before it began because of its support by the Communist Party USA (CPUSA) and its connection to the communist-led, Soviet-affiliated international peace movement that drew together scientists and activists within and outside of communist parties. Although the Soviet Union did not always view the midcentury peace movement's goals as perfectly in sync with its own, its officials did see it as useful, sought to shape its contours, and provided funding for organizations such as the Partisans of Peace and its successor, the World Peace Council. The Soviet Union had much to gain geopolitically by portraying itself as committed to peace and the United States as an imperialist aggressor. Members of Communist parties within and outside the Soviet Union saw support for the popular cause of peace as potentially bringing more support for their political vision. Stalin himself viewed the peace movement in the late 1940s as an important check on Western anti-Soviet aggression and resolve. He saw some of it goals — banning nuclear weapons and opposing NATO and German rearmament — as more in his interests than those of the United States, which held a clear military advantage. Even after the Soviets' own atomic weapons program was made public a few weeks after its successful test on August 29, 1949, Stalin continued to view the peace movement's efforts to ban the bomb as useful given his doubts about his nation's ability to keep up with U.S. weapons production. The U.S. response to the news about the Soviet weapon test was, after all, to initiate plans to expand its own weapons program, including the development of the hydrogen bomb.[12]

The pro-Soviet orientation of this wing of the peace movement was not lost on other peace activists, and Cold War repression made affinity with it all the more difficult. In the United States, almost all nonaligned peace and world government groups eventually refused to participate in communist-affiliated peace activities, and many individuals who did participate were criticized from the left and from the right. In this context, tensions ran high as preparations were being made for the Waldorf conference. The U.S. State Department admitted a handful of "official" delegates from the Soviet Union and Eastern Europe but denied visas to most "individual" delegates from Latin America and Western Europe, seeking, it seemed to some observers, to overemphasize Eastern bloc influence on the proceedings. The FBI spied on conference organizers, and National Council officials found their offices searched after the event. The daily press was generally dismissive of the conference, and one local paper called on New York's citizens to picket outside the sessions. This call was taken up by, among others, the American Legion and Catholic groups. Still, thousands of ordinary citizens and many progressive figures from science, the arts, and politics attended and found the experience valuable, regardless of their affinity for the Soviet Union. Others — including some, like Pablo Picasso, who had been denied visas to attend — sent messages of support from overseas.[13]

Ironically, the principles of intellectual freedom and freedom of expression that the conference organizers used to galvanize support for the event and which were highlighted in many Waldorf presentations were central to criticisms of it. Cold War liberals and members of the anti-Stalinist left used the meeting to point out the shortages of these principles in the Soviet Union and in a peace movement they viewed as driven by Soviet interests. The CIA assisted the efforts of the recently formed anti-Soviet group Americans for Intellectual Freedom, led by the philosopher Sidney Hook, to disrupt the conference. Members of the organization — including the educator George Counts, *Partisan Review* affiliates Dwight MacDonald and Mary McCarthy, and the poet Robert Lowell — raised pointed questions to speakers and audience members at the panel on writing and publishing about intellectual and creative freedom in the USSR. Conference organizers did not help their cause by refusing some nonaligned pacifists, like A. J. Muste, a chance to speak. Norman Cousins was among the few nonaligned pacifists invited to address the conference. Although he initially refused, he changed his mind in order to challenge the conference agenda. Defending critics of the conference, he said they "are not speaking out against the idea of peace or the need of peace or the possibility of peace." Instead, "they are speaking out against a small political group in this country which has failed to live up to the rules of the game in a democracy." Given their allegiance to an outside government, he continued, American communists were "without standing and without honor in [their] own country." Peace would come, not from a communist-led movement but through the work of the United Nations.[14]

For his part, Du Bois used his stage at the panel on writing and publishing to define "intellectual freedom" as a human value that transcended political ideologies but was necessary to social change. After offering a meditation on the role of human creativity in furthering science but also in providing an alternative source of freedom when "physical law and even . . . biological and psychological compulsions" presented restraints, he concluded by identifying two fundamental barriers to human freedom: "the persistent relic of ancient barbarism — war" and "the world-old habit of refusing to think ourselves, or to listen to those who do think." "Against this ignorance and intolerance," he continued, "we protest forever. But we do not merely protest, we make renewed demand for freedom in that vast kingdom of the human spirit where freedom has ever had the right to dwell."[15]

In his introduction of Shapley at Madison Square Garden, Du Bois justified his intellectual commitments as part and parcel of his loyalty to higher principles of peace and justice. He praised the delegates to the conference for gathering in New York "in a time of hysteria, suspicion and hate." They were "not traitors nor conspirators; and far from plotting force and violence it is precisely force and violence that we bitterly oppose." He praised the Soviet Union and, while acknowledging that recent reports of its aggression might be true, he chose to be skeptical and to refuse condemnation of the communist power because of the ways the press in the United States had distorted facts in the present, as evidenced by coverage of the Waldorf conference, and in the past, given the ways the press "has lied" about "American Negroes for 300 years." This comment pointed to the issue that ultimately superseded for him the question of whether reconciliation with the Soviet Union was permissible. For "there arises before this conference the plight and cause of the vast majority of mankind who are not white." Commitments to peace and intellectual freedom must be attuned to the persistent problem of racism, and in turn, these commitments were necessary components of global antiracism. Contrary to Cousins's faith in the organization, Du Bois averred that the UN was failing in its pursuit of peace because it was not adequately addressing legacies of imperialism and racism. Du Bois noted that activism was on the increase in the colonized world and among racial minorities in independent nations. Yet this was not a politics of "revenge." "What we want," he continued, "is a decent world, where a man does not have to have a white skin in order to be a man, where poverty is not a means of wealth, where ignorance is not used to prove race superiority, where sickness and death are not part of our factory system. And all this depends first on world peace. Peace is not an end. It is the gateway to real civilization. With peace all things may be added. With war, we destroy even that which the toil and sacrifice of ages have builded [*sic*]."[16]

Du Bois had argued for a racially just commitment to peace and written favorably about the Soviet Union for decades, but he was stepping into a political and ideological maelstrom at a moment of geopolitical tension when such statements appeared to serve Soviet interests. Moreover, an African American activist troubling the Manichaean logic of the Cold War by promoting peace and reconciliation as part of an antiracist agenda raised other issues. Since the 1930s anticommunism had been deployed as a bogeyman to stifle African American claims for social justice. Thus Soviet-friendly comments by African Americans particularly enraged and vindicated segregationists and other conservatives. Yet by midcentury, at a moment when U.S. hegemony on the global stage necessitated a measure of liberal reform at home, other political figures tried to uncouple anticommunism from racism while simultaneously marginalizing the radical aspects of the civil rights movement. Civil rights could now be defined as being in the interests of "national security," yet "national security" remained a powerful check on radical political projects that pushed too hard for racial reform and a mechanism for scaling back the civil liberties of individuals involved in those projects.[17]

In addition to the political hostility Du Bois received at this moment, he has since been roundly condemned from both left and liberal perspectives for his seemingly naive or doctrinaire pro-Soviet affiliation and commentary during these years—a judgment often enhanced by what we know in hindsight about the depth of Stalin's crimes and the eventual failure of the Soviet project. It is indeed striking that the worry Du Bois expressed in *Color and Democracy* about how the Soviet project would be compromised should the nation emerge from the war as an imperial power was dissipating at the moment when it was clearly moving in this direction. It is also surprising, given Du Bois's iconoclasm, contrariness, and still vigorous intelligence, that he did not have more critical perspective on the Soviet Union's manipulation of the left at this moment and did not, like C. L. R. James, develop an analytical Marxism that was simultaneously anti-Stalinist and critical of Western racism and imperialism.[18]

Yet Gerald Horne emphasizes that, despite its faults, the Soviet Union offered to Du Bois the possibility of socialism in practice and, through its rhetoric, a useful critique of imperialism. Moreover, Du Bois's refusal to condemn Stalin was often motivated by his conviction that whatever the truth in anti-Soviet rhetoric, it must be read in light of the limitations of the racial politics of the United States. Not only were anti-red sentiments still intertwined with antiblack racism despite government efforts to disassociate the two; the treatment of African Americans at home demonstrated that the United States' commitment to freedom—despite its rhetorical juxtaposition to the totalitarianism of the USSR—was seriously lacking in its own right.[19] Building from Horne's analysis, Kate Baldwin argues that while it is important to maintain a critical perspective on Du Bois's Soviet affinities, "a space must be carved out wherein the commitment of Du Bois to the Soviet Union can be acknowledged without condemning his vision."[20]

These perspectives help us understand that, contrary to the claim that Du Bois's affinity for Stalin and later Mao was merely the telos of his authoritarian streak, we can consider instead how his long-standing ruminations on race, war, peace, and imperialism were given new sustenance by similar critiques voiced by the Soviet Union and communist parties more generally. Increasingly invested in the necessity of some kind of socialist response to problems of racism, poverty, and disease engendered by unequal capitalist economic relationships, Du Bois refused the negatively productive political role to which the Soviet Union was consigned during the Cold War. He instead insisted that, despite its problems, the Soviet Union should serve as a source, at a symbolic level at least, for conceptualizing fairer economic relationships and a more just social order.

Du Bois also pointed out the function of anti-Soviet propaganda in shaping political life in the United States. In an address delivered in February 1950 Du Bois discussed how anti-Soviet rhetoric championing democracy and freedom served the interests of capital and circumscribed democracy and might even lead to totalitarianism in the United States and elsewhere: "I mention Russia not to defend her or justify her every act but only to insist that the use of that Bogey to halt socialism and the welfare state in this land, to hold up a national health program, a decent system of public schools; the control of industry in the interest of a welfare state instead of for the amassing of colossal fortunes to buy our newspapers, magazines and books; instead of such tactics coupled with the insane notion of world conquest, we should return to normalcy and common-sense."[21]

Moreover, as his comments at the Waldorf plenary that put the struggle for peace in a racial context indicate, his work with the pro-Soviet peace movement, whatever its limitations, provided a mechanism for generating a critical perspective on the global racial order and its interface with the rights and responsibilities of U.S. citizenship and attendant questions of loyalty. As I will emphasize over the rest of this chapter, this perspective is still valuable today. Du Bois, in his public support for the peace movement, put the question of color and democracy back on the table, insisting that a black reconstruction of democracy as a project that was simultaneously rooted in a home-grown radicalism and a cosmopolitan vision was still in order. He articulated this perspective through the ways he commented on, inhabited, and refused the racial category of suspect citizen.

Still, we must move carefully into this analysis, keeping in mind the cautionary tales, rather than dismissals and deflections, that some have brought to Du Bois's final decades. William Cain has argued that a fundamental problem with Du Bois's late work still relevant today was that he was so invested in criticizing the United States that he refused to acknowledge the brutality and failures of Soviet policies.[22] This observation points to not only the basic analytical problem of political dogmatism but also the affective and political challenge of synthesizing patriotism and cosmopolitanism; of balancing a critique of one's own society and external affinities with a recognition of the problems that exist outside of it; and, more specifically, of coming to terms with how cosmopolitan impulses (left, liberal, and otherwise) often do underwrite imperial and sometimes even genocidal projects.[23] One lesson of Du Bois's failures in this regard, especially in the middle 1950s, is that any reasonable antiracism in the present must keep in mind multiple forms of abjection. We must be attuned not only to those produced by the United States but also those created by other racial states; by various sovereign entities (NGOs, religious movements, corporations); by the complicity in racism of global elites and middle classes, regardless of race; and by populist movements (often including or led by people of color) that are energized by nativism, ethnic or tribal affiliations, anti-Semitism, and so on. However, I hope to show that we can take these lessons to heart while simultaneously learning from what Du Bois's inability or willingness to recognize certain forms of power at a distance enabled him to focus on close up.

DEFINING LOYALTY

In April 1949, the month after the Waldorf conference, Du Bois cochaired the World Congress of the Partisans of Peace meeting in Paris. This meeting drew more than two thousand delegates from over seventy countries. Here Paul Robeson made his much vilified statement that effectively brought to a close his career in the United States. He suggested that African Americans would not go to war "on behalf of those who have oppressed us for generations [the United States] against a country [the Soviet Union] which in one generation has raised our people to the full dignity of mankind." Although Du Bois would not feel the heat until later, he too lambasted the United States in Paris. Du Bois framed the current global conflict not in terms of a choice between freedom and totalitarianism as it was commonly put in the United States but as a choice between socialism — "spreading all over the world and even in the United States" — and the racial project of colonialism: "Leading this new Colonial Imperialism comes my own native land, built by my fathers' toil and blood, the United States. The United States is a great nation: rich by grace of God and prosperous by the hard work of its humblest citizens. . . . Drunk with power we are leading the world to hell in a new colonialism with the same old human slavery which once ruined us; and to a Third World War which will ruin the world."[24]

That summer, Du Bois testified in front of the House Committee on Foreign Affairs against Truman's proposed Mutual Defense Assistance Act, which authorized funding for NATO and for assorted governments battling leftist movements. His protest again resonated with the assumption that the United States' utter failure at racial democracy at home severely limited its ability to act in the interest of the world's majority in its international affairs.

> How have we equipped ourselves to rule the world? To teach democracy we chose a Secretary of State [James Byrnes] trained in the democracy of South Carolina. When we wanted to unravel the worst economic snarl in the modern world, we chose a general trained in military tactics at West Point [probably George Marshall, architect of the Marshall Plan, who was actually educated at Virginia Military Institute]; when we want to study race relations in our borders we summon a baseball player [a reference to Jackie Robinson's HUAC testimony refuting Robeson's questioning of black loyalty]. . . . We who hate niggers and darkies propose to control a world full of colored people. Will they have no say in the matter?[25]

Du Bois returned to Europe that August, in part to attend, as the sole American representative, the all-Soviet Peace conference in Moscow. His address there revisited arguments made in *Black Reconstruction* about race, labor, and the creation of U.S. society. He echoed comments, made in Paris, that the history of racial discrimination that had compromised

American democracy could be redressed and an alternative, more demo-cratic future realized, through a commitment to socialism, reconciliation with the Soviet Union, and a more extensive dedication to peace.[26]

In the summer of 1950 Du Bois was drafted to run for U.S. Senate on the New York American Labor Party (ALP) ticket, with a campaign theme of "Peace and Civil Rights." Although he knew he had no chance of winning, he saw it as an opportunity to generate support for ALP leader Vito Marcantonio's ultimately unsuccessful bid to keep his congressional seat. Moreover, given narrowing "opportunit[ies] to write for publica-tion," he viewed this as potentially his "last and only chance to tell the truth as I saw it."[27] Created in 1936, the American Labor Party was a Popular Front formation that had been heavily influenced by the Com-munist Party after 1941. However, Marcantonio's 1950 campaign drew progressives disenchanted with the CP's adherence to Soviet doctrine and weakened status. The ALP also had a particular appeal to African Ameri-cans and Latinos because of its support for political representation from these communities, attention to civil rights, and anti-imperialist stances.

In his statement announcing his Senate campaign, Du Bois made ref-erence to the McCarran bill being considered by Congress as the "Fugi-tive Slave Law of 1950." What ultimately became the Internal Security Act (1950) required the registration of communist organizations; poten-tially prevented from becoming citizens or stripped the citizenship of per-sons deemed to be engaged in "un-American" activities; provided greater means for denying entry to or deporting from the United States for-eigners deemed a threat; and allowed for the detention for those deemed dangerous, disloyal, or subversive in times of war. The Fugitive Slave Law of 1850 legislated that southern slave owners had the right to re-trieve their escaped "property," even if said person was physically in a "free" state. As Du Bois noted, it was "a bill that made kidnapping of any Negro possible without trial, that made a man prove his freedom instead of forcing masters to prove property; and tried to make anti-slavery opinion a crime."[28] The decision was also, following Devon Car-bado, a critical mechanism not simply for affirming African Americans' lack of rights as citizens but also their incorporation into the nation in an exclusionary manner.[29] By drawing parallels between the way "Slave Power ruled the nation" via racist legislation in 1850 and the way "Wall Street rules it today" — at a moment when the state, supported by corpo-rate power, stifled dissent and produced loyalty through the Internal Security Act and other measures — Du Bois implicitly defined Cold War politics as a racial project that subverted black rights claims via the litmus test of loyalty while simultaneously using a potential black disloyalty to foment a sense of political crisis, thereby justifying other trajectories of political repression or inaction.[30]

Yet Du Bois also remained attentive to the dangers of black inclusion. As civil rights reforms were starting to challenge the edifice of white supremacy, both the limitations and successes of such reforms could further the Cold War racial project, at home and abroad. In an address at Yale University in January 1951, Du Bois discussed three recent U.S. Supreme Court decisions chipping away at segregation in higher education and interstate transportation. Not only had such cases done little to alter the de jure and de facto exclusions structuring black life but there was also a potential danger to social justice and dark bodies at home and abroad when small steps toward progress were defined as success: "When thus by accident or good will, by cost or fear, the color-line yields a fraction, and a real fraction here and there, and now and then, in such cases we have evolved an extraordinary procedure. We go into a national snake dance, we sound the tom-toms and yell vociferously and call the attention of the world to the fact that the United States is now at last safe for democracy, and the color line is disappearing so rapidly that it is good as gone." On the domestic front, "this basic habit of ours of refusing to face the facts with regard to our Negro population, of refusing to honestly right these wrongs and of continually excusing our mistakes by declaring to the world that we have already done that which we hope sometime to do" gave power to a morally relativistic calculus that served the needs of capital and facilitated the growth and seamless coordination of militarism, consumerism, and political acquiescence. More broadly, refusal and excuse remained "a prime cause why this land is heading toward a world war of races between the white world and Asia and Africa, with reckless willingness to risk civilization, rather than yield the right to exploit the darker world for the profit of American millionaires."[31] The specific challenge for African Americans, then, given early victories in the legal struggle for civil rights and black participation in the warfare state, was to reconcile the struggle for minority rights with the responsibilities stemming from their positions as suspect citizens in a society that was perpetually preparing for imperial wars — that is, one should work for peace.

The year 1950 also saw Du Bois helping a committee of activists to establish and then agreeing to chair a new organization, the Peace Information Center (PIC). The group came together early that year out of the desire to ramp up the peace movement in the United States. Some of the group's members were specifically inspired by the Paris Partisans of Peace meeting. Understanding that forming a U.S. branch of the Partisans of Peace would be illegal under what Du Bois termed "new legislation" (probably the 1950 Internal Security Act), the organizers "adopted a plan which seemed to us all unusually apt and legal, and that was, as we decided at a later meeting in a private home, to form a Peace information Center, the object of which should be simply to tell the people of the United States what other nations were doing and thinking about war."[32]

The PIC issued a series of "peacegrams" informing U.S. citizens of various pleas for peace from across the world and produced its own pamphlets advocating the cause. The group's most visible activity was the reprinting and circulation of the Stockholm Appeal beginning in July 1950. The Appeal was issued by the Partisans of Peace that March, in response to Truman's suggestion that the United States would develop a hydrogen bomb. Its dissemination was given urgency by the recently begun war in Korea. The petition called for the banning of atomic weapons under strict international control, defined such weaponry as "an arm of terror," argued that the first government to use these weapons in the future "will be committing a crime against humanity and should be treated as a war criminal," and called upon "all people of good will throughout the world to sign this appeal." According to Du Bois, over a half billion people worldwide signed the petition, with the PIC collecting 2.5 million signatures of support in the United States. The PIC made special efforts to target religious and labor groups, prominent artists and intellectuals, and the African American community. However, many of these targeted individuals and groups, while often sympathetic to the ideals of the Appeal, refused to sign or withdrew support because of the Soviet connection via the Partisans of Peace.[33]

The PIC's activities engendered a swift and negative reaction from the U.S. government. With the Korean War only two weeks old, Secretary of State Dean Acheson issued a statement on July 12, 1950, arguing that the Appeal was merely "a propaganda trick in the spurious 'peace offensive' of the Soviet Union." He implied that potential charges of war crimes would not deter the United States from using nuclear weapons and charged that "the real crime against humanity" was the Soviets' support of North Korean "aggression in defiance of the United Nations."[34] A day later HUAC issued its own report condemning the "Communist 'Peace Petition' Campaign."[35] The day after that Du Bois issued a lengthy press release, published in the *New York Times* three days later, excoriating Acheson and HUAC for being trapped in a bipolar logic and a militaristic mindset that could at any moment condemn millions to injury or death in another world war. He also defined the peace movement as an effort whose interests were synonymous with those of the majority of Americans and, indeed, with humanity writ large.[36] Less than a month later the Justice Department informed the PIC officers that it was "engaged in activities within the United States which require its registration with the Department under the terms of the Foreign Agents Registration Act [FARA] of 1938, as amended."[37] And so began an arduous fifteen-month period that saw Du Bois indicted and stand trial for his activities with the PIC.

Du Bois's initial response to the demand for registration—sent from Paris, where he had traveled after attending a Partisans of Peace meeting in Prague—was to refuse to do so on the grounds that the government did not "indicate on whose behalf we are supposed to be acting." He described the PIC as "an entirely American organization devoted to the cause of world peace."[38] After a few months of fruitless attempts to meet with Justice Department officials and otherwise negotiate a way out of registration on these grounds, the PIC officers publicly shut down the organization in October, although winding down its business kept the group in operations until the end of the year. But on February 2, 1951, the group was informed that dissolution did not preclude it from registration, and a week later the PIC officers were indicted for "failure to register as agent of a foreign principal." The indictment accused the PIC of acting as publicity agent for, reporting information to, and serving "at the request of, the Committee of the World Congress of the Defenders [Partisans] of Peace and its successor the World Peace Council."[39] On February 16, Du Bois and his colleagues were arraigned in Washington, D.C., and freed on bail.

The trial did not begin until November, and Du Bois spent a good part of the year trying to elicit support for his cause and defense funds from potential allies at home and abroad. One bright spot through this ordeal was his marriage to Shirley Graham, pushed up to February 14 so that she might have visitation rights if Du Bois was jailed after his arraignment and so she could not be compelled by the prosecution to testify at the trial.[40] Du Bois was also buoyed by statements of support from prominent artists, intellectuals, and political figures, particularly from overseas, and a healthy dose of encouragement from African American workers. Yet he would be profoundly disappointed that members of the African American middle class, even erstwhile friends and allies, failed to come to his defense. The NAACP tried to cut off his pension after his indictment, and his eighty-third birthday celebration, scheduled for February 23 at the Essex House in New York, was abruptly cancelled by its management. Former friends and allies withdrew acceptances and declined invitations so as not to be publicly affiliated with the controversial figure. Although the event went forward at Small's Paradise in Harlem, with stalwart friends like E. Franklin Frazier and Paul Robeson praising him and greetings sent to the event by luminaries like Langston Hughes, Mary Bethune, and Leonard Bernstein, the symbolic abandonment by others in his time of need left a bitter taste and fueled his critique of elite African Americans.[41]

Ultimately, Du Bois and his co-defendants went free. First, the judge in the case ruled that the jury could not consider the circumstantial case that the PIC was, through the Partisans of Peace, an agent of the Soviet Union. He then dismissed the case after the defense attorney and former congressman Vito Marcantonio successfully argued a motion for acquittal on the grounds that the state had failed even to establish that the relationship between the PIC and Partisans of Peace was one of "agency and principal."[42] David Levering Lewis has also suggested that the trial was a political mistake on the part of the government, with Du Bois in particular cutting a sympathetic figure as a defendant, especially among African Americans. Two of Du Bois's co-defendants believed that the judge's ruling was at least in part influenced by the Truman administration's recognition that a conviction would reflect badly on it, as would Albert Einstein's planned testimony as a character witness for Du Bois and the defendants being given the opportunity to articulate on the record the principles guiding their activities.[43]

In Du Bois's case, such testimony would have almost certainly included both scathing condemnation of U.S. foreign and domestic policies and, in the context of having his loyalty challenged, seeking to prove it via an alternative definition. Du Bois did, however, have a chance to air such sentiments publicly in his memoir *In Battle for Peace* (1952), which was published by *Masses and Mainstream*, a journal associated with the CPUSA and co-edited by his friend and associate Herbert Aptheker.[44]

In Battle for Peace is clearly a self-interested, extended performance of righteousness, produced at a moment when Du Bois's loyalty and judgment were called into question by both the Cold War state and erstwhile friends and allies. But Du Bois valuably redefines loyalty by suggesting that a more just social and economic order requires multiple commitments: to socialism, to communities of workers and intellectuals, to ideas, and to the democratic principles upon which, even if in retreat at the moment, the United States was putatively founded. Time and again, Du Bois talks about his actions as highly moral, motivated by humanitarian instincts, democratic values typically defined as American, and the ethical challenge that the Soviet Union poses to a people who are overly concerned with the accrual of capital and consumer goods.

The motivation of the state and its witnesses, on the other hand, reflects some of the worst aspects of U.S. society. The state's prosecution of the PIC officers represents yet another Cold War retreat from its commitment to civil liberties. Former PIC member John Rogge, who had become state's witness after breaking with the group over what he saw as its intransigent, pro-Soviet orientation, represents the perfidy of mid-century political culture given how he helped establish the organization and encouraged Du Bois's participation, before testifying for the government. Rogge also, via what Du Bois characterizes as his hasty and opportunistic education in the law, represents "the nation's rush to get rich off the world's calamity."[45] Ultimately, as Keith Byerman notes, "the problem is not Du Bois's politics; rather the nation itself has become un-American."[46]

While recognizing the problems of a jingoistic loyalty to the nation, Du Bois maintains a belief in the nation's institutions so long as they can be transformed: "I know what America has done for the poor, oppressed and hopeless of many other peoples, and what indeed it has done to contradict and atone for its sins against Negroes. I still believe that some day this nation will become a democracy without a color-line. I work and shall work for an America whose aim is not solely to make a few people rich, but rather to stop War, and abolish Poverty, Disease and Ignorance for all men." Yet he believes he is still permitted affinity with the USSR: "While, then, I am and expect to be a loyal citizen of the United States, I also respect and admire the Union of Soviet Socialist Republics." And though he may have erred in his praise of the Soviet Union, as in other venues, here he importantly avers that political and intellectual freedom builds from a cosmopolitan perspective generated out of affinity for and critical distance from U.S. democracy and Soviet socialism, as domestic and global projects: "As, then, a citizen of the world as well as of the United States of America, I claim a right to know and think and tell the truth as I see it. I believe in Socialism as well as Democracy. I believe in Communism wherever and whenever men are wise and good enough to achieve it; but I do not believe all nations will achieve it in the same way or at the same time."[47]

Dovetailing with Du Bois's commentary about his loyalty to the nation and its principles is that pertaining to his previously held commitments to racial analysis and African American politics. Du Bois concludes the penultimate chapter, focusing on his acquittal, lamenting the failure of most "business and professional Negroes" to support him in his time of need. This is symptomatic, he argues, of the ways black leadership and a black intelligentsia, across the diaspora, are "following in the footsteps of western acquisitive society." He has been compelled to rethink his own vision for a black reconstruction of democracy developed in the 1930s and early 1940s. Du Bois states that this vision was predicated on the assumption that an "ancient African communism, supported and developed by memory of slavery and experience of caste" would serve to maintain group unity and preclude the "development of economic classes and inner class struggle." Yet with the "loosening of outer racial discriminatory pressures," the result was not "a new cultural unity, capable of absorbing socialism, tolerance and democracy, and helping to lead America into a new heaven and new earth. But rather, partial emancipation is freeing some of them to ape the worst of American and Anglo-Saxon chauvinism, luxury, showing-off, and 'social climbing.'" Support during this ordeal came not from unified African American action but from his few remaining allies among the black intelligentsia joining forces with an interracial and international community of workers and activists. "Without the help of the trade unionists, white and black, without the Progressives and radicals, without Socialists and Communists and lovers of peace all over the world, my voice would now be stilled forever." Recent experience, Du Bois writes, "is tending to free me from that racial provincialism which I always recognized but which I was sure would eventually land me in an upper realm of cultural unity, led by 'My People.' "[48] Later, when describing a journey from his struggles against racial prejudice before World War I through his formulation of a "thesis of socialism for the American Negro in my *Dusk of Dawn*," Du Bois argues that World War II "sent all my formulations a-whirl. Not from the inner problems of a single social group, no matter how pressing, could the world be guided. I began to enter into a World conception of human uplift and one centering about the work and income of the working class."[49]

It is tempting, as some have done, to view Du Bois's account of his move to "a World conception of human uplift" as marking a shift from a focus on race to a focus on class as his fundamental analytical category for understanding society. Yet taking him at his word, so to speak, does not do justice to the complexity of his theorizing of the interface of race and political economy throughout the 1940s and 1950s and of the ways he implicates black subjects in the future of democracy. Even though she is among those who identify this shift from race to class via this passage, Kate Baldwin valuably shows how Du Bois's engagement with the Soviet Union in *In Battle for Peace* and contemporaneous texts extends and revises arguments made in *Dusk of Dawn*, where he drew upon Marxism to analyze racism's role in capitalist development while revising Marxism in the process; deepened his understanding of race as a transnational phenomenon intimately connected to imperialism; and theorized "the paradox of race as both an impossibility and a fact," which negatively determined black social existence and potentially "incorporated [Negroes] into the system of Americanization that he came to equate with whiteness." In the context of the Cold War, it became increasingly clear to Du Bois that African American incorporation into the national body politic could not only enable U.S. imperial ambitions but also deflect analysis of the economic basis of racism at home.[50]

Baldwin's comments suggest that we can read *In Battle for Peace* as another consideration of the ethical responsibilities Du Bois imparted to suspect citizens like himself for the reconstruction of democracy in the United States and elsewhere. Du Bois pays attention to the ways citizenship exclusions based on loyalty build upon those enacted racially in past eras and serve racial projects in the present. At a moment when the state needed civil rights reforms and when even relatively moderate forms of civil rights activism could be met with reprisal from the government because of the assumed disloyalty of their agents, Du Bois theorizes an appropriate African American response to the simultaneous exclusion of black subjects from the imagined nation and their incorporation into the Cold War project.[51] He moves toward an embrace of a disidentificatory Americanism, forged from a simultaneously alienated and complicit position.[52] Inhabiting this identity requires for black subjects a consideration of the extent to which resistance to white supremacy through incorporation into nationalist state and consumerist projects might ultimately enable it as a global project. And it necessitates, for both survival and an ultimate concern for justice in a world structured by U.S. hegemony, "criticism as a form of service." We can thus read through *In Battle for Peace* the development of an African American political practice that balances competing loyalties while critically examining the power and privileges of citizenship and the reproduction of its exclusions.

Du Bois registers shock and disillusionment with his prosecution and with the ways many erstwhile allies turn their backs on him. As an African American he knows very well the unfair practices of the legal system, but now he finds himself doubly suspect as both racial subject and political dissenter: a situation he describes as a "gruesome experience."[53] He comes to terms with the concurrent marginality and privilege of African Americans defined further by racism's production of blackness in simultaneously differentiating and essentializing ways. This is evident in his musings about African Americans' paradoxical status as citizens. He is aware of the ways that class generally determines the ways the racial state is brought to bear on human bodies. He recognizes how some elite African Americans are "becom[ing] American in their acceptance of exploitation as defensible, and in their imitation of American 'conspicuous expenditure.'" He also comments on the ways other African Americans draw upon recently accessed power to put pressure on the political system; he suggests that he himself benefited during his trial from appeals to the Truman administration by "the highest placed Negro Democrats." Yet, his trial also brings home the fact that his freedom depends significantly on his access to resources and publicity, while others, particularly poor black others, continue to be unfairly imprisoned by the criminal justice system: "There is desperate need of nation-wide organizations to oppose this national racket of railroading to jails and chain-gangs the poor, friendless and black."[54] But even with this class differentiation, black people as an aggregate are a bloc against which American citizenship is defined. While praising the efforts of the International Committee in Defense of Dr. W. E. B. Du Bois, he notes, "What the foreign signers of this appeal did not realize was that in the United States a Negro is not regarded as an American; as a Negro works for Negroes, he has certain nuisance value, which is often recognized as natural; but his contribution to the nation, much less to humanity at large, is practically never considered."[55] Still, African Americans have important roles to play. Du Bois notes the visible and symbolic importance of African American political struggle in inspiring activism across the globe. The challenge for Du Bois, then, is to articulate not just a commitment to solidarity across national boundaries but an intellectual and ethical standpoint rooted in his position as a suspect citizen and the responsibilities that follow.

Du Bois expresses his loyalty to freedom of thought and commitment to the truth that stems both from the responsibilities of citizenship in the United States but which is also grounded in a commitment to global citizenship that transcends and may have to reject restrictive aspects of national citizenship imposed on or available to him. He talks repeatedly in the volume about the solace he finds in being in dialogue with and garnering support from intellectuals across the ideological spectrum in different parts of the world. Socialism, the right to work toward it, and the potential in international solidarity provide part of the inspiration. Yet even as he commits to Marxism, his intellectual affinity resists programmatic restrictions from the party as well. As noted earlier, as "a citizen of the world as well as of the United States of America, [he claimed] a right to know and think and tell the truth as [he saw] it. [He] believe[d] in Socialism as well as Democracy."[56] Socialism, then, and to some extent the political project of the USSR, are the vehicles by which Du Bois can partially detach from domestic political imperatives and answer to a higher cosmopolitan calling.

In another instance, Du Bois relates the Justice Department's offer to have him plea *nolo contendere* in exchange for the charges to his FARA case being dropped. He claims the government was worried that his prosecution might indicate a democratic society flirting too closely with totalitarianism.[57] And we can add that a conviction of this venerable civil rights leader would work contrary to Cold War racial reforms. Du Bois, though, refuses this Cold War hegemonic move, this attempt to keep alive a global racial project predicated on racial reform at home. His refusal of this deal, his continued, expressed affinity for the United States and Soviet Union alike in his memoir, constitutes an embrace of the identity of the suspect citizen and imbues it with critical potential — even if such an embrace is politically disastrous in the short term.

THE SUSPECT CITIZEN AND THE POSSIBILITIES OF LOYALTY

Twenty-first-century and specifically post-9/11 writings on the paradoxes of loyalty among African Americans and other racialized subjects have addressed both the difficulties of and necessity of identifying critically, or disidentifying, with the neoimperial state. In these final sections, I put Du Bois's commentary on the responsibilities of the suspect citizen into dialogue with this recent work and from there suggest ways that his comments on black loyalty might guide us in the future.

M. Jacqui Alexander identifies a present-day gendered, sexualized, and racialized regime of U.S. neoimperialism, in which citizenship is increasingly produced through discourses and practices of domestic and global militarism, ardent nationalism, free markets, and expectations of loyalty to these principles.[58] Alexander is particularly interested in the production and function of the "new citizen patriot." This juridically produced "hypermasculine" and "heteromasculine" figure serves the interests of the state through his active loyalty and his willingness to withhold criticism of the state. Additionally, he helps to define limits of nation and citizenship by allowing himself to serve symbolically as the "originary citizen" who settled the imagined homeland: "This (white) originary citizen is in sharp contradistinction to the (dark) naturalized citizen, the dark immigrant or even the dark citizen born of the dark immigrant whose (latent) 'loyalty' is perennially suspect and, therefore, ultimately threatening."[59] This symbolic, heteromasculine patriot, Alexander continues, is defined against a demasculinized and often sexual perverse "dark enemy," whom the state must position as feminine and aberrant enough to be defeated but still dangerous enough to justify war, more restrictive immigration policies, increased surveillance, and potential restrictions to civil rights and liberties.[60] She suggests obliquely that people of color can serve as citizen patriots, but they operate more trenchantly in her analysis as the domestic casualties of a neoimperial agenda and the threat that justifies it: "The racialized citizen patriot, the noncitizen nonpatriot, the disloyal suspect immigrant, and the suspect citizen are all made to occupy this underworld as the urban internal enemy — the violence against whom underwrites the forms of massacre directed against the external enemy."[61]

Du Bois's analysis in *In Battle for Peace*, of course, does little by itself to weave the categories of sexuality and gender into examinations of the interface of citizenship, race, and social class. His critique of Cold War political culture, for example, does not include commentary on ascendant, antifeminist, domestic ideologies. On the contrary, this book that valuably articulates a powerful critique of national identity and capitalism and imagines transnational identities and affiliations not only subordinates gender as a category of analysis but also, as in other Du Boisean texts, reproduces a masculinist political and intellectual project. Shirley Graham's short "comments" at the end of several of the book's chapters serve a supporting role in the narrative structurally while enshrining Du Bois's masculine intellectualism. For example, at the end of chapter 1, Graham notes the early influence of the archetypical race man, a "symbol of our hopes and aspirations."[62] The book's construction of Du Bois in heroically masculinist terms is also apparent in his own disparaging comments about John Rogge's and Henry Wallace's refusal of the self-sacrifice he saw himself as embodying for remaining true to his leftist commitments.[63] And we see it in another of Du Bois's deployments of a rape metaphor to describe geopolitics, with communist and de-colonized Asia now taking the place of Africa: "I was witnessing the blood-stained collapse of Atlantic culture finding burial on the ancient ruins of the Mediterranean efforts to civilize mankind. I saw this caricature and contradiction of mighty ideals, in frantic, dying struggle, trying with lewd incest again to rape the All-Mother Asia from northern heartland to southern sea, from Russia to India."[64] Still, we can again engage in a "politics of juxtaposition" by putting *In Battle for Peace* in dialogue with twenty-first-century works more critical of gender and sexual formations.

Keeping in mind Du Bois's attention to the responsibilities of the black suspect citizen in the context of Cold War complicity and marginalization can lead us to think about similar imbrications and political potentialities vis-à-vis the neoimperialist security state during the war on terror. It can also prompt us to extend Du Bois's thinking in a more comparative and intersectional direction. On one level, Du Bois's analysis, responsive to the unfolding of the Cold War racial project, compels us to make central to our own analyses of the present the historical antecedents of the processes by which foreign and domestic wars on terrorism contribute to the abjection of poor people, people of color, and sexual minorities in the United States and elsewhere during the twenty-first century. He compels us to pay attention to genealogies of outright exclusions, genealogies of inclusions that have been incomplete, and genealogies of incomplete inclusions predicated on someone else's exclusions.

Indeed, Melani McAlister has demonstrated how, from the early Cold War to the present, U.S. foreign interventions and concomitant acts of domination and violence toward racial others have been justified by the production of racial innocence at home via both real and artificial commitments to racial inclusion. In the late 1940s and 1950s, the support the United States voiced for anticolonialism abroad and civil rights domestically undergirded the doctrine of "benevolent supremacy," holding that an altruistic American hegemony in a postwar world would be of great benefit for the global community.[65] During the Gulf War, "military multiculturalism"—that is, the demonstrable racial diversity of the military and representations of it as such—"provided the mandate for . . . power" and helped cultivate the sense that its inclusiveness defined "America as different from, and superior to, the putatively less liberal identities of other nations, particularly those in the Middle East."[66] During the post-9/11 era, when incidents like the torture and killing of prisoners at Abu Ghraib or mass civilian casualties across Iraq sparked charges of racism, the "inclusive" nature of the military became a ready-made defense. And the surveillance of Arabs, Muslims, and Middle Easterners was justified in the Patriot Act and elsewhere by a rhetoric of pluralism that foregrounded the multicultural foundations of the United States.[67]

These narratives of inclusion were exclusionary in both theory and practice. Military multiculturalism, as McAlister notes, was a deeply gendered and sexualized discourse, dependent, despite the presence of women warriors, on the objectification of women and their consignment to normative roles (the worrying mother, the faithful wife, and so on) as well as on a policy ("don't ask, don't tell") that excluded gay men and lesbians.[68] Leti Volpp argues that September 11 "facilitated the consolidation of a new identity category of people who appear to be 'Middle Eastern, Arab, or Muslim.'" This process of racialization largely revolved around members of this socially constructed group being "identified as terrorists and disidentified as citizens" through current conceptions of nation, identity, and citizenship; through the revivification of "old Orientalist tropes"; and through "the fact and legitimacy of racial profiling."[69] Yet this mode of racialization was also propelled by contradictory claims of inclusiveness on the part of the state, through, among other things, the Patriot Act's condemnation of hate crimes and emphasis on protecting the civil rights and liberties of members of these and other groups.[70]

Indeed, one of the more striking racial phenomena in the immediate post–9/11 period has been the way emergent racial formations have been constructed relationally and ambivalently via the perceived loyalties of different groups. Although racial profiling and various forms of exclusion and suspicion based on assumed citizenship status continue to wreak havoc on other communities of color, and while such inclusive multicultural configurations are fragile, September 11 and its aftermath precipitated the creation of, in Volpp's words, a "national identity that was both strongly patriotic and multiracial," where certain groups — "whites, African Americans, East Asian Americans, and Latinas and Latinos" — were, in a geopolitical sense at least, "safe and not required to prove their allegiance."[71] Evelyn Alsultany has argued, building on Agamben and his theorization of "the state of exception," that the current war on terrorism has, in fact, been founded in part on an ambivalence towards racism, which is deemed simultaneously "unjustifiable and necessary." In this context, inclusive moves toward other people of color based on their assumed loyalty affirm the state's racial innocence. Such moves, in turn, justify the state's racialization of Arabs and Muslims — an act that may be illegitimate in theory but is condoned because of the temporary necessity of protecting its more loyal citizenry from terrorists.[72]

Du Bois's analysis also compels us to consider the ways nonwhite subjects may be implicated in the ideology of what Alexander calls "the secure citizen" — both through acts of loyalty in the present and through a history of participation in struggles for more inclusive definitions of citizenship. As various commentators have noted, members of various racialized groups, having been asked to prove their loyalty, have done so with an enthusiasm rooted in necessity. Jasbir Puar and Amit Rai discuss the production of "docile patriots" in the post-9/11 period, a category inhabited not just by the originary citizens identified by Alexander but as well by some of those deemed suspect. They note in particular the actions of mainstream Sikh American groups who, in the post-9/11 period, amid and following a rash of hate crimes directed against members of their community, sought to demonstrate their loyalty by positioning themselves as "model minority citizens," educating people about their religion, and making it clear that they should not be confused with the Muslim enemy.[73] Other members of marginalized groups saw September 11, the war on terrorism, and the resulting, if temporary, transformations in patterns of racialization as opportunities to improve their social status by supporting the racial profiling of Arabs, Muslims, and Middle Easterners.[74] Such moves, of course, produced an array of normative behaviors and expectations of these behaviors. Among other things, the post-9/11 period witnessed the veneration of familiar figures traditionally deployed to produce nationalism along axes of gender and sexuality: the reproductive family; the patriotic wife and mother; and the masculine citizen soldier who serves also as rescuer and defender. And we have seen how acts geared toward proving loyalty reproduce exclusionary racial norms and stifle solidarities within and among marginalized groups.[75]

In the face of such normative identifications, Du Bois's midcentury work, if we update it in more comparative and intersectional ways, suggests the possibilities emanating from African American meditations on suspect citizenship. We can explore this as a productive political and intellectual space that refuses such normativity and insists instead on a critical distance from both the United States and its others. It offers "criticism as a form of service" to one's own nation while insisting on the right to establish loyalties to a wider array of populations and ethical and political principles.

Clearly, black people have been decentered from racial politics and discourses in the United States by globalization, shifting patterns of immigration, emergent political claims rooted in identity, the war on terrorism, and what Thomas Holt has described as their significant "exclusion . . . from productive relations" in the post-Fordist economy. Yet Holt, like others, is still attuned to the continuing ways that blackness and black people anchor race's ontology in our "postracial" and post–black/white binary moment.[76] The philosopher Lewis Gordon argues that one consequence of a history of explicit antiblack racism and its contemporary occult forms is a "racism [that] is a white-black phenomenon with enough semiotic flexibility to mask itself as living 'beyond' such a dichotomy. . . . if we take any other 'racial formation,' we will find that its members' identity is a function of its distance or nearness to the two extremes, which means, in the end, that if the extremes are eliminated, new extremes will emerge. Every 'in between' is a whiteness or blackness waiting to emerge."[77] And Carbado reminds us that the inclusive exclusion of black people in the United States works dialectically with the naturalization of nonblack immigrants. Blacks and nonblacks, he argues, have long been "American-ized" via the antiblack racism of the latter.[78]

In other words, although some African Americans have a certain privi-lege of status when compared to some recent immigrants and residents of the United States, in terms of standards of living, access to consumer goods, the ability to exercise political rights and the like, blackness and African Americanness still anchor racism's ontology and remain catego-ries of abjection in the eyes of billions of people on this planet, including many of those "noncitizen nonpatriots," "disloyal suspect immigrants," and others placed outside the category of formal citizenship that African Americans generally possess. The novelist and essayist John Edgar Wide-man brings this together quite nicely in a meditation on September 11 and its aftermath:

> Like all my fellow countrymen and women, even the ones who won't admit it, the ones who choose to think of themselves as not implicated, who maintain what James Baldwin called a "willed innocence," even the ones just off boats from Russia, Dominica, Thailand, Ireland, I am an heir to centuries of legal apartheid and must negotiate daily, with just about every step I take, the foul muck of unfulfilled promises, the apparent and not so apparent effects of racism that continue to plague America (and, do I need to add, plague the rest of the Alliance as well). It's a complicated muck, muck that doesn't seem to dirty Colin Powell or Oprah or Michael Jordan or the black engineer in your firm who received a bigger raise than all her white colleagues, muck so thick it obscures the presence of millions of underclass African Americans living below the poverty line, hides from public concern legions of young people of color wasting away in prison.[79]

Wideman calls attention to the simultaneous marginalization and privi-lege of African Americans in the twenty-first century and the ways that all inhabitants, including new immigrants, within the nation's borders are implicated in a racism that, regardless of its multidimensionality, multiple applications, and global reach, continues to derive meaning from both histories of black exclusion and the abjection of blackness.

Moving Du Bois's thinking about the power of the suspect citizen forward in light of present-day formulations of African American posi-tionality suggests that we consider what collective critical potential for addressing "the problem of the future world" may be found in revisiting and revising in intersectional and global directions the symbolic power of black activism and particularly the cosmopolitan array of loyalties that has in part defined what Robin D. G. Kelley has described as the "black radical imagination" in the United States.[80]

On one level, Du Bois's antiracism and ruminations on black loyalty at midcentury point to the particular responsibilities of the simultaneously privileged and marginalized black population of the United States. His work suggests that for African Americans, there is need for critical reflection on the parochial definitions of freedom and the struggles for it, as well as on black complicity in the U.S. imperial project. In *What Next*, his meditation on the political responsibilities of African Americans in the post–September 11 era, the novelist and essayist Walter Mosley compares his reaction to witnessing the destruction of the World Trade Center to his father's politicization through participation in World War II. His father's experience of German troops treating him as an American by virtue of targeting him with their guns helped him realize his citizenship and enabled him, upon returning to the United States, to go "out in the world and [struggle] to make this realization a fact." Mosley, on the other hand, "saw in that column of smoke" emanating from the remains of the World Trade Center that "we — Black men and women in every stratum of American society — live in and are part of an eco-system of terror. We, descendants of human suffering, are living in a fine mansion at the edge of a precipice. And the ground is caving in under the weight of our wealth and privilege."[81] His concern is that the "heirs" of the civil rights movement, with its inclusionary demand honed during World War II and the Cold War, have become complicit in a neoimperial project that creates human suffering and stifles democracy in the United States and elsewhere.[82]

The challenge for black people in the United States, Mosley argues, at least those with some modicum of social power and privilege, is to build from their "singular perspective on the qualities of revenge, security, and peace" and reorient African American struggle in anticapitalist, antimilitarist, and simultaneously global and local directions as a means of reconstructing democracy.[83] Although Mosley does not engage in a feminist analysis of the ways that race articulates with gender and sexuality within the terrain of imperialism, militarism, citizenship, and loyalty, he provides a platform for further work building from this "singular perspective" that could be energized by engagements with the work of Alexander and others. This work would be more accountable to the limitations of black freedom struggles in the past and attentive to a multiplicity of intersections of power and the struggles against them in the present.[84]

Du Bois's analysis also suggests the importance of the ideas and actions of the broader collective of human beings in the United States connected to its black population by the complex ideological matrix of Negrophobia/Negrophilia. While this population may not be at the vanguard of large-scale future justice movements in a globalized world, it will play an important role, one way or another. As Arundhati Roy reminds us, even at a moment of declining U.S. power, "The fact is that the only institution in the world today that is more powerful than the American government is American civil society. American citizens have a huge responsibility riding on their shoulders." "The rest of us," she adds, "are subjects of slave nations. We are by no means powerless, but you have the power of proximity."[85] And even as Du Bois lamented black complicity in and abjection by the Cold War project, he implied in *In Battle for Peace* that African American struggle, because of the paradoxical position of its agents, still provided important inspiration for others in the United States and across the globe.

Moving forward is no easy task. I revise these concluding remarks a year after the first African American president's inauguration. The bracing array of invocations and refusals of race that have surrounded Barack Obama (and have sometimes been uttered by him) during his campaign and after his election will surely keep scholars busy for many years to come. Observations that his candidacy and then victory showed that we are now "post-racial," that the lingering problems of racism and outdated modes of black politics have been eradicated, illustrate some Americans' naïve investments in the ideology of colorblindness in the face of evidence to the contrary. Especially when one considers claims during the run-up to the election that Obama was a "dangerous," crypto-Muslim, the equally hysterical calls by "birthers" after the election for Obama to prove his U.S. citizenship and thus his legitimacy as president, and the public desire of some of our white citizenry to get their "country back" during the recent debates over his health care proposals. Such commentary demonstrates the persistence of old racisms (that blackness and non-subordinate Americanness are still, for some, incommensurate) and their articulation with emergent ones. Indeed, if anything, such phenomena are indicative of the ways that "post-race" has become a mechanism for masking, and sometimes justifying, a resurgent racism.

The depth of hate and vitriol directed to Obama over his proposed reforms to the nation's health care system has been particularly revealing. Obviously, there are many sources for the antigovernment sentiment that has emerged in the wake of Obama's proposals, which can be criticized convincingly from various places across the political spectrum. However, it remains fascinating that critiques of this moderate liberal president often revolve around the charge that he is a socialist and, less frequently, that he is a totalitarian dictator who can be compared to Hitler and Stalin. Not only does this discourse speak to some fundamental misunderstandings of history, political ideology, and about how the U.S. government operates; it also speaks of a deep-seated, populist, conservative animosity to progressive politics that has been skillfully framed in racial terms by elites since the Reagan administration. As Du Bois's critique of Cold War politics, among other sources, tells us, the fact that this animosity has been and continues to be so easily mobilized makes Du Bois's vision for a reconstruction of democracy via the transformation of the state so difficult to realize. Such a vision must work, not simply against articulated and unarticulated versions of racism but also against an antistatist populism, predicted on a racial logic. It is a logic that holds without irony that government intervention on behalf of the racially privileged — although such benefits are often not shared significantly across class lines — is racially neutral and nonintrusive, while state projects promoting racial democracy are not only intrusive but undemocratic. The difficulty of the task of challenging this logic was made clear recently during the health care debates when commentators who suggested that racism may have informed the populist rage against Obama were identified as racist themselves.

We also cannot forget that recent history has witnessed the continued racial blind spots of progressives. For some, the question of black liberation has been displaced or perhaps is no longer relevant in a racial terrain defined by a growing collection of diverse voices demanding redress. Transnational anti-imperialist critiques sometimes lose sight of the connections between current regimes of global racism and an older antiblack racism, as well as the possibilities that might emerge from linking long-standing claims for black redress and emergent antiracisms.[86] Among the unfortunate outcomes of the 2001 World Conference Against Racism in

Durban, South Africa, was that the momentum for redress and reparation movements for black subjects was displaced among some progressives in the wake of the Durban Declaration identifying slavery and the slave trade as "crimes against humanity." First, there were controversies over language about Israel and Zionism (which led to Israel and the United States walking out of the proceedings), and then there were concerns over emergent racisms intertwined with the war on terrorism.[87] We must also contend with the moral excess that people impose on black politics. In the fallout over the passage of Proposition 8 in California, outlawing gay marriage, we saw an important critique of homophobia in the black community and religious institutions that are symbolic of the parochialism of some black freedom struggles, historically and in the present. Yet, in the hard-hitting blame for the proposition's passage on black Californians who make up a relatively small percentage of that state's electorate, we also saw reflected the long-standing political practice by nonblacks of putting excessive responsibility on black people for both creating and rectifying society's failings. This often devolves into chastisement of the black masses for failing to live up to their assumed progressive duties.

Yet we must not lose sight of the political possibilities still sedimented in the unfinished, cosmopolitan black and left political projects of the twentieth century for reconstructing democracy across the globe. Although some may wish to avoid the duties, power, or the responsibilities of U.S. citizenship, and as much as we may want to look elsewhere for inspiration and blame, the reconstruction of democracy as a global racial project, as Du Bois suggested, depends at least in part on the actions of black folk and others in the United States who find themselves drawn into or who actively participate in the paradoxes of loyalty theorized by an earlier generation of black activists. To do nothing, to live a normative citizenship rather than act upon these paradoxes, means to be part of a bloc forged out of heterogeneity, where a fragmented population, positioned in impossibly complicated ways, with an almost infinite array of affiliations, can operate globally as one, when articulated with and through the exercise of national economic and political power.

We have seen in recent elections in the United States how diverse working-class and middle-class communities, deeply distanced from one another by geography, race, and the competition for resources, have found common ground over "god, gays, and guns" and similar themes, helping to consolidate the power of the right and further enabling a neoliberal racial order defined by, among other things, the prison industrial complex, a failing health care system, a lack of affordable housing, chronic joblessness, inhumane immigration and other policies at home, as well as a host of injustices outside the United States that bring much greater suffering, especially, to racialized human beings.

Yet, returning to Obama and his presidency, we can also see a glimmer of hope in his election, perhaps even an inkling of a reconstruction of democracy. We see this not in his administration's continuation of neoliberal logics when handling the financial crisis or in selections of political centrists and, in some cases, foreign policy hawks for cabinet positions and administrative posts that suggest further reproduction of the colonial past. Nor is it evident in his administration's decision to forgo a potential leadership role in the global conversation about racism by boycotting the 2009 Durban Review Conference, designed as a follow-up to the 2001 World Conference on Racism. We also do not see it in Obama using his acceptance speech for the Nobel Peace Prize to justify (without naming) U.S. imperial ambitions and, with some regret, to articulate a stay-the-course strategy in Afghanistan. But alongside the growing hysteria on the right there has been a palpable sense that Obama's ascendancy has been symbolic of other possibilities: those evident in the tears that flowed on election night; on the face of my student the next day, explaining how she, her siblings, and her cousins decided for the first time to exercise their right to vote in their twenty-something lives; and when the many recognized, whatever the limitations of Obama's politics or future legacy, how his victory was, on some level, a product of a history of black struggle for democracy and provided an occasion for reflection on the exclusions and possibilities of this democracy that have been identified by black activists and intellectuals since the eighteenth century. This event also inspired people outside the United States to reconsider what is possible in a world structured by race, to think carefully about the limitations of those possibilities and the work that still needs to be done, and to shift their perspectives on what is possible in the United States and, by extension, through its actions in the world. This, perhaps, is one reason some members of the Nobel Prize committee chose Obama for the award. The challenge, of course, is to know what to do with this glimmer of hope, to avoid complacency and naiveté and harness such sentiments in a political practice that does them justice.

And while the historically specific state socialist project through which Du Bois hoped his reconstruction of democracy would happen founders on the ruins of the Soviet Union and on Russia's and China's free market and imperialist adventures in the present, the project of transforming the state to better promote economic and racial justice remains a necessity, as evidenced by the economic crisis unfolding as I write this. Gilbert Achcar argues that "the collapse of 'really existing socialism,' together with the thorough discrediting of the very idea of socialism" have enabled the emergence of twenty-first-century barbarisms, of the global North and of the global South. Even if societies cannot and should not be transformed in ways imagined in the past, "it is necessary for a credible progressive alternative to neoliberal capitalism to emerge again. . . . [and channel] social discontent toward transformative action in the pursuit of democracy and justice."[88] Such a vision informed Du Bois's midcentury radical commitment at its best, which was simultaneously cosmopolitan and American, expansively species oriented and racially attuned in the face of a different political crisis and its attendant, narrowing opportunities.

I hope, in the end, that I have shown that we can be inspired by Du Bois's midcentury example, even with his shortcomings, to find the solutions to the seemingly intractable problems facing us in the present. The future of "civilization," as he might have put it, may very well depend on it.

NOTES TO INTRODUCTION

1. See, for example, Du Bois, "On Stalin," *National Guardian*, March 16, 1953, in Aptheker, *Newspaper Columns*, 910–11. This and other pro-Stalin pieces are discussed in Cain, "From Liberalism to Communism."

2. Du Bois, *Autobiography*, 19, 57–58.

3. Most dismissive were Broderick, *W. E. B. Du Bois*, and Harold Isaacs's assessment of Du Bois in *The New World of Negro Americans*. For valuable summaries of the early historiography on Du Bois, from which this analysis is drawn, see Marable's "Bibliographic Essay," in *W.E.B. Du Bois*, 267–73; Marable, "Reconstructing the Radical Du Bois"; Horne, *Black and Red*, xi, 3–4.

4. See Marable, "Bibliographical Essay," for more details.

5. See my bibliography for references to part of the extensive collection of volumes of Du Bois's writings edited or reprinted by Aptheker.

6. Robinson, *Black Marxism*, 266–348.

7. Lewis, *W. E. B. Du Bois: The Fight for Equality*, 570.

8. Rampersad insists that Du Bois engaged the postwar world "with a still vigorous intelligence," but as he identifies Du Bois's retreat into "the certitudes of Marxist-Leninist teaching" and teleological move toward Communist Party membership, he obfuscates the quality, nuance, and historical specificity of individual texts, especially from the 1940s and early 1950s. Rampersad, *The Art and Imagination of W. E. B. Du Bois*, 170, 245–49, 262–64. Lewis devotes roughly 80 percent of *W. E. B. Du Bois: The Fight for Equality* to the years 1919 to 1940, 20 percent to the years 1940 to 1963. Moreover, his analysis of Du Bois's writings from his final two decades tends to be overshadowed by accounts of Du Bois's divergence from the mainstream. Du Bois thus comes across as a somewhat tragic figure, steadfastly holding on to radical beliefs while the world around him moved to the right. Lewis, *W. E. B. Du Bois: The Fight for Equality*, 516–17, 524–26.

9. Marable engages in a bit of self-critique in his reassessment of his book two decades later. "In retrospect, *Du Bois: Black Radical Democrat* was also much too narrowly preoccupied with presenting a response to the still-influential scholarship of both Cold War liberals and anti-Communist Negro integrationists that denigrated Du Bois." Marable, "Reconstructing the Radical Du Bois," 11.

10. Appiah suggests in "The Uncompleted Argument" that by holding on to the concept of race as an analytic or vehicle for social activism we engage in erroneous thinking and potentially reproduce systems of racist exclusion. Appiah revised his assessment several years later, arguing that one could build upon Du Bois "to reconstruct a sociohistorical view that has more merit than I have previously conceded." See Appiah and Gutmann, *Color Conscious*, 74–83.

11. See, for example, Wald, *Constituting Americans*, 207–12; Outlaw, "'Conserve' Races?" and Gooding-Williams, "Outlaw, Appiah, and Du Bois's 'The Conservation of Races.'" Outlaw and Gooding-Williams appear in Bell, Grosholz, and Stewart's *W. E. B. Du Bois on Race and Culture*. Others in this volume also offer substantial engagements with Appiah's essay.

12. See, for example, Holt, "The Political Uses of Alienation"; Lott, "Du Bois on the Invention of Race," in *The Invention of Race*; Mostern, *Autobiography and Black Identity Politics*; Olson, "W. E. B. Du Bois and the Race Concept"; Shuford, "Four Du Boisian Contributions to Critical Race Theory."

13. Olson and Shuford, for example, address the construction of both whiteness and blackness in Du Boisean texts, although they differ significantly in their assessments of the value of the "abolition" of whiteness. Although not centered specifically on Du Bois, prominent texts in "whiteness studies" influenced by Du Bois include Roediger, *The Wages of Whiteness*; Harris, "Whiteness as Property"; Ignatiev and Garvey, *Race Traitor*.

14. The list of sources addressing one or more of these issues is extensive. The following represents a sampling of influential work not otherwise discussed in this literature review: Gilroy, *The Black Atlantic*; Kaplan, *The Anarchy of Empire*; Prashad, *Everybody Was Kung Fu Fighting*; Sundquist, *To Wake the Nations*; Weinbaum, "Reproducing Racial Globality."

15. See, for example, Balfour, "Unreconstructed Democracy"; Shuford, "Four Du Boisian Contributions to Critical Race Theory."

16. For example, Du Bois's research projects like the *Philadelphia Negro* and meditations on method such as "The Study of Negro Problems" and the unpublished essay "Sociology Hesitant" continue to serve as mechanisms by which scholars engage thorny questions about social scientific objectivity and the ways institutionalized racism and racial discourse structure putatively color-blind academic research. See, for example, Katz and Sugrue, *W. E. B. DuBois, Race, and the City*; Edwards, "W. E. B. Du Bois Between Worlds"; Williams, "The Early Social

Science of W. E. B. Du Bois"; and the special issue of *boundary 2* (27:3), edited by Ronald Judy.

17. See, for example, Davis, *Women, Race, and Class*; Giddings, *When and Where I Enter*; B. Aptheker, "On 'The Damnation of Women': W.E.B. Du Bois and a Theory for Woman's Emancipation," in *Woman's Legacy*.

18. For useful surveys and bibliographies of these critiques, see Marable, "Reconstructing the Radical Du Bois"; Washington, "Introductory Essay"; Weinbaum, "Reproducing Racial Globality."

19. Carby, *Race Men*; Ferguson, "W. E. B. Du Bois"; James, *Transcending the Talented Tenth*.

20. Hancock, "W. E. B. Du Bois."

21. Gillman and Weinbaum, *Next to the Color Line*, 3, 8; emphasis in the original.

22. Although neither is particularly invested in applying Du Bois's work in the present, Shamoon Zamir's *Dark Voices* focuses primarily on his earliest years, while Raymond Wolters's *Du Bois and His Rivals* does not significantly address texts after 1940. Robert Gooding-Williams's more recent treatment of Du Boisean thought in *In the Shadow of Du Bois* does apply his insights to the post-Jim Crow period, but the analysis centers primarily on *The Souls of Black Folk*. Adolph Reed Jr.'s *W. E. B. Du Bois and American Political Thought*, discussed later, provides a deep historical contextualization of Du Bois's earlier works and significant engagement with post-1940 texts. Yet, even while offering a critique of scholars' focus on the early years, Reed tends to discuss later works as extensions of an intellectual project established decades earlier rather than historicize them in the moment in which they were produced. Reiland Rabaka's *W. E. B. Du Bois and the Problems of the Twenty-First Century* and his *Du Bois's Dialectics* are significant for their engagements with a broad range of post-1940 texts, but Rabaka rejects periodization and deep historical contextualization, seeking instead to make sense of, as he puts it in the first volume, "a single, protracted, critical, and conjunctive thought process" (189). Although most of the thirteen essays and the afterword in Bell, Grosholz, and Stewart's *W. E. B. Du Bois on Race and Culture* use *Dusk of Dawn* or the posthumously published *Autobiography of W. E. B. Du Bois* as sources for historical information or biographical data, only one provides substantial analysis of post-1940 writings. Two of three pieces discussing Du Bois's Pan-Africanism cite his *The World and Africa* (1947), but the authors use it primarily for background and perspective on Du Bois's vision without analyzing it substantively in its context. In "The Study of African American Problems," a special issue on Du Bois in the *Annals of the American Academy of Political and Social Science*, only three of eighteen essays cite Du Bois's works published after 1940, and only four of eighteen cite anything published as late as *Dusk of Dawn*. Brent Edwards's analysis of Du Bois's depiction of romance in his

Mansart trilogy is the only piece in the Gillman and Weinbaum volume that centers on post-1940 writings. See "Late Romance," in Gillman and Weinbaum, *Next to the Color Line*, 124–49.

23. The attention to *The Souls of Black Folk* is no doubt in part a result of the popularity of that text in its moment and a late-twentieth-century canonization of Du Bois that celebrated, if not his radicalism, then his militancy when compared to the political quiescence of Booker T. Washington, whom he took to task in that text. Moreover, given disciplinary interests and comfort zones, it simply makes sense for sociologists to be most interested in *The Philadelphia Negro* and turn-of-the-century essays on emergent social science practice; for literary scholars to read *The Quest of the Silver Fleece* or *Dark Princess* before *Color and Democracy*; and for philosophers and political theorists to be more invested in the general contours of his thinking than with historicizing it. And given the foundational role that Appiah's work has played in shaping the field of Du Bois studies, his focus on "The Conservation of Races" and *Dusk of Dawn* has played no small role in determining the texts around which debates about Du Bois and his race concept often revolve.

24. Commenting on a series of centennial celebrations of Du Bois's best-known book, *The Souls of Black Folk* (1903), Marable argues that the feting of *Souls* not only privileged the early part of Du Bois's career but also revealed a liberal rewriting of Du Bois, as someone working "toward the realization of a color-blind, racially integrated American society." Marable, "Reconstructing the Radical Du Bois," 2. Reed similarly suggests that the interest in Du Bois's notion of double-consciousness, discussed famously in *The Souls of Black Folk*, is "part of a strain that depoliticizes and dehistoricizes accounts of the Afro-American experience." Reed, *W. E. B. Du Bois and American Political Thought*, 177.

25. Baldwin, *Beyond the Color Line and the Iron Curtain*, 156.

26. Thanks to Bettina Aptheker for helping me better understand this point. For details on these relationships, see Horne, *Black and Red*, especially 289–311.

27. See, for example, Cain, "From Liberalism to Communism." Here the value of Du Bois's late thought is primarily to caution members of the left from engaging in naive, shortsighted intellectual and political behavior.

28. Marable, "Reconstructing the Radical Du Bois," 19, 22.

29. Gates, "The Black Letters on the Sign." It must be noted that even as he encourages others to explore Du Bois's later work, he insists on the "centrality" of *The Souls of Black Folk*.

30. Winant, *The World Is a Ghetto*, 135; emphasis in the original.

31. Barkan, *The Retreat of Scientific Racism*; Degler, *In Search of Human Nature*; Holloway, *Confronting the Veil*; Tucker, *The Science and Politics of Racial Research*. As Carey McWilliams characterized the situation in 1951: "Encouraged by new scientific findings, the spokesmen for equality became increasingly insistent that

the old barriers should be removed, and at the same time the defense of these barriers began to assume a ludicrous quality, shrill, falsetto, croaking. The more support these new scientific findings provided for the American creed of equality, the more interest they aroused — with the result that the myths formerly used to rationalize prejudiced attitudes have lost their power to coerce people's thinking about race relations." McWilliams, *Brothers under the Skin*, 13.

32. Indeed, as the basis of racial rule was challenged by science and insurgencies across the globe at midcentury, Winant notes, it created "an unstable equilibrium between the old and new racial orders. Since that time, two openly contradictory world-historical racial *projects* have coexisted: deeply rooted and dearly held attachments to white supremacy on the one hand, and fierce implacable and partially institutionalized legal and social commitments to racial justice, universalism, pluralism, and democracy on the other." Dual commitments to maintaining and ending racial inequities have been enshrined through a hegemonic give-and-take in various juridical, political, educational, economic, and social institutions. Although many of its elements are no longer visible, the old racial system "live[s] on informally, vampire-like, as the organizing principle of the worldwide social structure it was crucial in creating." Winant, *The World Is a Ghetto*, 6, 289.

33. Ibid., 137; emphasis in the original.

34. Gilroy, *Postcolonial Melancholia*, 14. M. Jacqui Alexander is also instructive on this point, as she describes a U.S. neo-imperialism whose "contradictions form the basis for an understanding of the U.S. state that is not automatically, self-referentially democratic, although democracy characterizes its self-representational impulse." See Alexander, *Pedagogies of Crossing*, 234.

35. Anderson, *Eyes off the Prize*; Borstelmann, *The Cold War and the Color Line*; Dudziak, *Cold War Civil Rights*; Plummer, *Rising Wind*; Prashad, *Everybody Was Kung Fu Fighting*; Singh, *Black Is a Country*; and Von Eschen, *Race against Empire*.

36. Holt, *The Problem of Race in the Twenty First Century*, 4–5; emphasis in the original.

37. Ibid., 24.

38. Omi and Winant, *Racial Formation in the United States*, 55.

39. "Unlike in the early twentieth century," Holt argues, "race no longer follows a color line. The racialized other may well be white and hail from the Caucuses." Holt, *The Problem of Race in the Twenty First Century*, 100.

40. Hall, "Gramsci's Relevance for the Study of Race and Ethnicity," 413.

41. Reed, *W. E. B. Du Bois and American Political Thought*, 4–6, 179. Reed also identifies the analytical limitations of "'if-x-were-alive-now' laments [which] have a prelapsarian quality that posits a golden age of heroic antecedents purer, clearer, and smarter than ourselves."

42. Ibid., 181–84; emphasis in the original.

43. Scott, *Conscripts of Modernity*, 1, 3. Rather than merely transposing the insights of an earlier generation of anticolonial writers to a postcolonial context or, conversely, illuminating the flaws in their analyses, he suggests that a more productive engagement with such work can be achieved when one is attuned to "the *difference* between the questions that animated former presents and those that animate our own."

44. Ibid., 210. Scott writes, "It seems to me, therefore, that a tragic sensibility is a particularly apt and timely one because, not driven by the confident hubris of teleologies that extract the future seamlessly from the past, and more attuned at the same time to the intricacies, ambiguities, and paradoxes of the relation between actions and their consequences, and intentions and the chance contingencies that sometimes undo them, it recasts our historical temporalities in significant ways."

45. Kelley, *Freedom Dreams*.

46. Baldwin, *Beyond the Color Line and the Iron Curtain*, 155.

47. See Agamben, *Homo Sacer*.

NOTES TO CHAPTER 1

1. "A Pageant in Seven Decades," a shorter piece written for his seventieth birthday in 1938, provided the "skeleton of the manuscript." Lewis, *W. E. B. Du Bois: The Fight for Equality*, 472.

2. Du Bois, *Dusk of Dawn*, 651.

3. Ibid., 551.

4. Appiah, "The Uncompleted Argument," 34.

5. See, for example, Holt, "The Political Uses of Alienation"; Mostern, *Autobiography and Black Identity Politics;* Olson, "W. E. B. Du Bois and the Race Concept"; Shuford, "Four Du Boisian Contributions to Critical Race Theory."

6. Du Bois, *Dusk of Dawn*, 555–58.

7. Du Bois, "The Colonial Groups in the Postwar World," in Aptheker, *Against Racism*, 231.

8. Gilroy, *The Black Atlantic*, 113–17, 125.

9. Rampersad, *The Art and Imagination of W. E. B. Du Bois*, 242.

10. Du Bois, *Dusk of Dawn*, 556.

11. Ibid., 577.

12. Of course, the reader can still locate in *Dusk of Dawn* a sometimes essentialist investment in racial kinship rooted in his nineteenth-century dabbling in Herderian folk nationalism, Hegelian historicism, Afrocentrism, and occult mysticism. For assessments of the continuing influence of nineteenth-century paradigms on Du Bois's twentieth-century writings, see, for example, Gillman, *Blood Talk*; Reed, *W. E. B. Du Bois and American Political Thought*; Moses,

"Culture, Civilization and the Decline of the West"; Guterl, *The Color of Race in America*.

13. Du Bois, *Dusk of Dawn*, 602–3.

14. Ibid., 622–24.

15. Mullen, *Afro-Orientalism*, 15–19.

16. Du Bois, "The Negro Mind Reaches Out," in Locke, *The New Negro*, 386. This piece was reprinted with revisions from *Foreign Affairs* 3, no. 3 (April 1925). He adds that one must "view the European and white American labor problem from this side perspective, remembering always that empire is the heavy hand of capital abroad."

17. As he wrote to Mary White Ovington in 1938, "Communism is the hope of us all but not the dogmatic Marxian program with war and murder in the forefront. Economic communism by the path of peace is possible." Du Bois to Mary White Ovington, March 21, 1938, in Aptheker, *The Correspondence of W. E. B. Du Bois*, vol. 2, 163. See also Lewis, *W. E. B. Du Bois: The Fight for Equality*, 310–11; Marable, *W. E. B. Du Bois*, 157–58; Du Bois, *Dusk of Dawn*, 771–72; Du Bois, *Autobiography*, 264.

18. Du Bois, *Dusk of Dawn*, 773–74. For further discussion, see Lewis, *W. E. B. Du Bois: The Fight for Equality*, 306–10. Lewis states, "Racism, then, was not for Du Bois the epiphenomenon described by Marx, a fixation existing in the penumbra above and around the reality of class antagonisms. Racism had to be understood as an integral component of the dynamic of class, possessing a life of its own, and equal in the power of its agency to class." Du Bois's early *Crisis* editorials developing this position include "Toward a New Racial Philosophy" (January 1933), "Karl Marx and the Negro" (March 1933), and "Marxism and the Negro Problem" (May 1933).

19. For perhaps the earliest articulation of this plan, see the September 1933 *Crisis* editorial "On Being Ashamed of Oneself: An Essay on Race Pride."

20. Du Bois, "A Pragmatic Program for a Dark Minority," *The Papers of W. E. B. Du Bois*, reel 83, frames 158–66. Handwritten notes on this document suggest it was written in 1935, "for New Deal book."

21. Holloway, *Confronting the Veil*, 4–16, 150–54; Lewis, *W. E. B. Du Bois: The Fight for Equality*, 318–24. Du Bois voiced frustration in *Dusk of Dawn* about his Armenia critics' naive "economic determinism." See 773–74.

22. Du Bois, *Dusk of Dawn*, 765–66.

23. Lewis, *W. E. B. Du Bois: The Fight for Equality*, 301, 314–17, 324–48; Du Bois, *Autobiography*, 293–303. The Atlanta University deal had been in the works over a year, and Du Bois had been working there as a visiting professor since January 1933. Another push factor was that the *Crisis*'s Depression-era financial difficulties had made his job increasingly difficult; he even donated portions of his own salary from time to time to keep the magazine afloat.

24. Du Bois, *Black Reconstruction*, 13.

25. Ibid., 700. The direct association of these wages with the category "whiteness" is, of course, made by David Roediger in *The Wages of Whiteness*.

26. Du Bois, *Black Reconstruction*, 630.

27. Du Bois, *Dusk of Dawn*, 679, 716.

28. Eric Sundquist, *To Wake the Nations*, 564.

29. Kate Baldwin, *Beyond the Color Line and the Iron Curtain*, 183.

30. Du Bois, *Dusk of Dawn*, 625.

31. Ibid., 629–39.

32. Ibid., 639–40.

33. Ibid., 651.

34. Ibid., 654.

35. Ibid., 639.

36. This recent work is indebted to Cedric Robinson's analysis of *Black Reconstruction* as both a historiographic intervention and a "political work" that refashions Marxist theory and historiography and compels them to be more attuned to race. See Robinson, *Black Marxism*, 266–348.

37. Holt, "The Political Uses of Alienation," especially 309–10, 319–20. As Holt puts it, "From Marx he learned that there was a deeper structural basis for racial oppression; that it was not enough to fight for integration into a house that was inherently flawed. From Freud he learned to appreciate the irrationality of prejudice and its deep-seatedness."

38. Olson, *The Abolition of White Democracy*, 1–30.

39. Olson, "W. E. B. Du Bois and the Race Concept," especially 119–24. Olson suggests that the "purpose of Du Bois's theory of race is to undermine the undemocratic power of the white world" both through a "refut[ation of] all attempts to validate a biological *race-in-itself*" and the "facilitat[ion of] the construction of a *race-for-itself*, a collective united by a common experience of racial subordination and resistance to it." He argues that Du Bois's "mature" thinking about race as a social construction marks the "third phase" of this thinking about the concept, following his early understanding of race as a "scientific" and "world historical" category and a second phase of his thinking about race in terms of culture and geography.

40. Singh, *Black Is a Country*, 60–68, 86–87.

41. Ibid., 87–88; Brown et al., *Whitewashing Race*, 26–30; Lewis, *W. E. B. Du Bois: The Fight for Equality*, 326–28. On Du Bois's improving assessment of Roosevelt, see Rampersad, *The Art and Imagination of W. E. B. Du Bois*, 223; Marable, *W. E. B. Du Bois*, 154.

42. Singh, *Black Is a Country*, 63, 89, 94–96.

43. Gillman, *Blood Talk*, 176–78. Susan Gillman has highlighted Du Bois's "strategic self-citation" in *Dusk of Dawn*, through which he reworks key tropes and passages

from his sociological work — particularly regarding "science," "history," "truth" and the "Negro problem" — as he redefines the "race problem" from the singular to the plural. What becomes explicit in *Dusk of Dawn*, she argues, is what is latent in earlier sociological work: because the problems facing African Americans stem from multiple and contradictory racial factors, uncovering these "requires an analogous set of investigative methodologies that bridge the separate spheres of science and politics, objectivity and partisanship, the lyrical and the scientific. In short, it is occult history — attuned equally to all the contradictory forces, the rational and irrational, the visible and the veiled — that allows Du Bois access to what he calls in *Dusk of Dawn* the 'twilight zone' of race prejudice."

44. Du Bois, *Black Reconstruction*, 726. Burgess's *Reconstruction and the Constitution, 1866–1876* falls under the heading "Standard — Anti-Negro" in Du Bois's bibliography. Authors listed in this category "believe the Negro to be sub-human and congenitally unfitted for citizenship and the suffrage." See page 731. Also prominent in this category is the work of the historian William Dunning and his followers.

45. Du Bois, *Black Reconstruction*, 725.

46. Du Bois's critique in this regard is directed to Charles and Mary Beard's *The Rise of American Civilization* (1933), which can be read "with a comfortable feeling that nothing right or wrong is involved." See pages 715–16.

47. Du Bois, *Black Reconstruction*, note "To the Reader," presumably page 1.

48. Du Bois, "The Study of Negro Problems," in Green and Driver, *W. E. B. Du Bois on Sociology and the Black Community*, 81. Writing several years later about the Atlanta Conferences, Du Bois notes, "We have assumed that the Negro is a constituent member of the great human family, that he is capable of advancement and development, that mulattoes are not necessarily degenerates and that it is perfectly possible for the Negro people to become a great and civilized group." Du Bois, "The Atlanta Conferences," in Green and Driver, *W. E. B. Du Bois on Sociology and the Black Community*, 53–60; 57. Originally published in *Voice of the Negro* 1 (March 1904): 85–89.

49. Du Bois, *The Philadelphia Negro*, 387. Du Bois states here that the denial of black "humanity" "is, in America, the vastest of the Negro problems."

50. Du Bois, "The Study of Negro Problems," 76–77.

51. "The Study of Negro Problems," 71–72, 76–77, 81.

52. Du Bois, "The Atlanta Conferences," 54.

53. Du Bois, "The Study of Negro Problems," 80.

54. As Robert Williams argues, "Du Bois's activities implied that social scientifically informed activism (practice) was a mediating element between reality and conceptions of that reality. Researchers and the knowledge they generated were thereby part of the production of the truthfulness of our concepts of reality. Instead of being a disinterested party, the researchers of racial injustice would

scientifically seek knowledge of particular circumstances in space and time and then provide the analyses needed to fight White supremacism and to struggle against those conditions and structures oppressing African Americans." Williams, "The Early Social Science of W. E. B. Du Bois," 387. It must be pointed out that there is some debate on the intellectual genealogy of this move. Williams, for example, locates it in Du Bois's engagement with William James's pragmatist philosophy (see page 386). Barrington S. Edwards, on the other hand, downplays the influence of pragmatism and instead emphasizes the influence of German historical economists such as von Treitschke, Wagner, and Schmoller. See Edwards, "W. E. B. Du Bois Between Worlds."

55. In Ronald Judy's words, the essay is an investigation into how the "formation of an objective field of analysis, and the application of knowledge to the facts of that field in the form of action, does not derive from purely logical or methodological sources but can be understood only in the context of material social processes. For Du Bois, not only are facts products of complex social and historical processes, but science as a particular activity is a moment in the social process of production and is not self-sufficient. . . . Du Bois's critique of abstracting theoretical praxis from the interested motivations of social life practices aimed to demystify institutionalized racism and was grounded in his recognizing discourse — especially scientific discourse — as fundamentally political." Judy, "Introduction," 28–29.

56. Adolph Reed situates Du Bois in this context. See Reed, *W. E. B. Du Bois and American Political Thought*, 17–20, 45–47.

57. Lewis, *W. E. B. Du Bois: The Fight for Equality*, 422–26; Marable, *W. E. B. Du Bois*, 148–49.

58. Bunche, *A World View of Race*. For an excellent summary and analysis of this text, see Holloway, *Confronting the Veil*, 163–69.

59. Holloway, *Confronting the Veil*, 112; Lewis, *W. E. B. Du Bois: The Fight for Equality*, 361–65, 371–76; Marable, *W. E. B. Du Bois*, 146–47. Among the issues that incensed Left critics were pessimism about the possibilities of interracial solidarity, his use of the term "proletarian dictatorship" to describe black Reconstruction governance, and his failure to mark major social transformations between the antebellum and Reconstruction periods. Among his African American left critics were Ralph Bunche, Abram Harris, and Loren Miller, who focused specifically on the romantic racialism and talented-tenth assumptions they claimed distorted Du Bois's Marxist analysis.

60. Du Bois was criticized for relying too heavily on secondary sources and government documents. Ironically, as David Levering Lewis points out, the racial politics of southern archives during the 1930s was such that Du Bois would have great difficulty gaining full and, in some cases, even partial access to state and local records. See *W. E. B. Du Bois: The Fight for Equality*, 361.

61. Ibid., 426–33.

62. Holloway, *Confronting the Veil*, 16.

63. It was clear, as David Levering Lewis notes, that "the philanthropic-intellectual complex," while "troubled enough by the old 'scientific' racism and the New National Socialism to contemplate the possibility of a moderate reassessment of the race perennial," still operated through a mode of "genteel racism [that] recoiled from the prospect of learning more about Negroes from Negroes themselves." Lewis, *W. E. B. Du Bois: The Fight for Equality*, 433.

64. Du Bois, "Confidential Memorandum Regarding the Significance of the Proposed *Encyclopedia of the Negro*, in Aptheker, *Against Racism*, 160–64.

65. Lewis, *W. E. B. Du Bois: The Fight for Equality*, 434–37, 442–53, 566–68; Rampersad, *The Art and Imagination of W. E. B. Du Bois*, 227; Marable, *W. E. B. Du Bois*, 150; Editor's Note, Aptheker, *Correspondence*, vol. 3, 106.

66. Du Bois to Augustus Kelley, September 28, 1938, in Aptheker, *Correspondence*, vol. 2, 174.

67. Du Bois, "On the Scientific Objectivity of the Proposed *Encyclopedia of the Negro* and on Safeguards Against the Intrusion of Propaganda," 165.

68. "The Position of the Negro in the American Social Order: Where Do We Go From Here?," *Journal of Negro Education* 8 (July 1939): 551–70. Reprinted in Aptheker, *Writings in Periodicals*, vol. 3, 69–87. For a detailed discussion of how these social scientists, who were trying to transcend racial thinking, were in various ways constrained by race, see Holloway, *Confronting the Veil*. Du Bois was also recruited by *The American Scholar* to write the article "The Negro Scientist" (1939), which identified a number of black scientists overlooked by white academic institutions. Lewis, *W. E. B. Du Bois: The Fight for Equality*, 477. Several years later Du Bois likened recent questions about the objectivity of black social scientists to the more obvious racist exclusions emanating from the scientific community at the beginning of his career. See Du Bois, "My Evolving Program for Negro Freedom," 50.

69. Goldberg, *Racist Culture*, 3–7 (quote on page 6). Goldberg continues: "The more abstract modernity's universal identity, the more it has to be insisted upon, the more it needs to be *imposed*. The more ideologically hegemonic liberal values seem and the more open to difference liberal modernity declares itself, the more dismissive of difference it becomes and the more closed it seeks to make the circle of acceptability."

70. Ibid., 149.

71. Ibid., 7–8.

72. Du Bois, "Confidential Memorandum Regarding the Significance of the Proposed *Encyclopedia of the Negro*," 160.

73. Du Bois, *Black Reconstruction*, 183–86.

74. Ibid., 325.

75. Ibid., 377.

76. Du Bois, *Dusk of Dawn*, 654–55; my emphasis.

77. Ibid., 639.

78. Ibid., 654.

79. Ibid., 665–66.

80. Du Bois to F. P. Keppel, December 2, 1940, in Aptheker, *Correspondence*, vol. 2, 254–56. For additional statements by Du Bois about the Phylon Institute, see Du Bois, "Apology," in *Selections from Phylon*, 5–7; Du Bois to William Alfred Fountain Jr., Pres. Morris Brown College, July 15, 1941, in Aptheker, *Correspondence*, vol. 2, 290–91; Du Bois to Edwin R. Embree, November 3, 1942, in Aptheker, *Correspondence*, vol. 2, 349–52; Du Bois "The Twenty-Fifth Atlanta Conference," *Unity* 127 (November 1941): 145–46, reprinted in Aptheker, *Writings in Periodicals*, vol. 3, 139–42.

81. Aptheker, introduction to Aptheker, *Selections from Phylon*, 1–2; Du Bois to Rufus E. Clement, Pres. Atlanta U, March 1, 1940, in Aptheker, *Correspondence*, vol. 2, 224–26.

82. Du Bois to Ira De A. Reid, Atlanta University, April, 14, 1939, in Aptheker, *Correspondence*, vol. 2, 187–91: 188.

83. Du Bois, "Apology," in Aptheker, *Selections from Phylon*, 5–7.

84. Du Bois's "Autobiography" chapter on the Phylon Institute bears this title. See pages 308–25.

85. From a document Du Bois presented to a conference of presidents of "Negro land-grant colleges" in Chicago in 1941. Reprinted in Du Bois, *Autobiography*, 316; see also 312–17.

86. Du Bois, *Autobiography*, 310.

87. Du Bois, "Apology," 5. Joel Olson notes when discussing Du Bois's use of culture in *Phylon* and *Dusk of Dawn*, "even when he defines race as culture, the lines demarcating races are drawn by power." Olson, "W. E. B. Du Bois and the Race Concept," 124.

88. Du Bois, "Apology," in Aptheker, *Selections from Phylon*, 5.

89. See Jonathan Holloway's excellent summary of this debate and Franklin's career in *Confronting the Veil*, 123–56, especially 127–36.

90. Balibar, "Is There a 'Neo-Racism'?" in Balibar and Wallerstein, *Race, Nation, Class*, 21, 25.

91. Du Bois had been thinking about this feature at least since 1937, when he imagined that the new journal would include "a carefully selected and annotated chronicle of happenings touching races and interracial relations and forming a continuous, reliable, and comprehensive history of such developments." Du Bois, "Personal and Confidential Memo of the Conference," in Aptheker, *Against Racism*, 170.

92. Du Bois, "A Chronicle of Race Relations," *Phylon* 1, 2nd quarter 1940, in Aptheker, *Selections from Phylon*, 17–18.

93. See, for example, iterations of the Chronicle in the following volumes of *Phylon*: 1, 2nd quarter 1940, in Aptheker, *Selections from Phylon*, 17–35; 1, 3rd quarter 1940, in *Selections from Phylon*, 37–55; 1, 4th quarter 1940, in *Selections from Phylon*, 57–79; 2, 1st quarter 1941, in *Selections from Phylon*, 81–96; 3, 1st quarter 1942, in *Selections from Phylon*, 155–75.

94. Du Bois, "A Chronicle of Race Relations," *Phylon* 4, 4th quarter 1943, in Aptheker, *Selections from Phylon*, 263–66.

95. Du Bois, "Phylon: Science or Propaganda," *Phylon* 5, 1st quarter 1944, in Aptheker, *Selections from Phylon*, 395–99.

96. Ralph J. Bunche to Du Bois, March 8, 1940, reel 51, frame 359, *The Papers of W. E. B. Du Bois*; Du Bois to Ralph Bunche, March 12, 1940, reel 51, frame 360, *The Papers of W. E. B. Du Bois*.

97. Lewis, *W. E. B. Du Bois: The Fight for Equality*, 451–53. King, *Race, Culture, and the Intellectuals*, 39; Myrdal, *An American Dilemma*, xliii.

98. Myrdal was on the committee that helped draft the first of these UNESCO statements under the direction of the physical anthropologist M. F. Ashley Montagu, from whose own work he had drawn in *An American Dilemma*. The UNESCO group even went so far in their 1950 statement as to argue that there was a biological basis for "the ethic of universal brotherhood," although this was qualified in the 1951 statement after objections from physical anthropologists and geneticists who said there was no scientific basis for such a claim. Also participating in the drafting or revising of the first UNESCO statement were E. Franklin Frazier and Otto Klineberg, from whose work Myrdal had also drawn. For more details, see Baker, *From Savage to Negro*, 209; Degler, *In Search of Human Nature*, 204–205; UNESCO, *Race and Science*, 493–95.

99. As Penny Von Eschen notes, "In the retreat from explanations grounded in political economy. . . . Racism was portrayed as a 'disease,' and as a psychological or spiritual problem, or as a characteristic of backward peoples which could be eradicated by 'modernization' or, in more psychological language, 'maturity.'" Von Eschen, *Race against Empire*, 155. See also Singh, "Culture / Wars," 487; King, *Race, Culture, and the Intellectuals*, 22–23.

100. Singh, *Black Is a Country*, 38–39, 142–51; Baker, *From Savage to Negro*, 194.

101. A "modernization thesis" was, for example, central to the Commission to Study the Organization of Peace's report in 1944, *International Safeguard of Human Rights*. As Brenda Gayle Plummer notes, this report "differentiated Nazi racism, defined as state policy, from racism in the United States, defined as 'laggard customs.' Anticipating opposition to international interference in questions deemed domestic in many countries, the report provided an escape hatch for the

United States by means of a modernization thesis. American race problems, then, derived neither from a governmental nor a societal commitment to white supremacy. They were instead the products of uneven progress toward development." Plummer, *Rising Wind*, 115.

102. Singh, *Black Is a Country*, 135–36, 148–50.

103. Du Bois, *Dusk of Dawn*, 698, 700; emphasis in the original.

104. Ibid., 655.

105. Ibid., 666.

106. In a draft of the manuscript Du Bois titles this section "white dilemma." Manuscript fragment, reel 84, frame 1569, *The Papers of W. E. B. Du Bois*.

107. Du Bois, *Dusk of Dawn*, 674.

108. Ibid., 677–78.

109. Kate Baldwin makes a similar conclusion about this section. Speaking of the Van Dieman exchange and other passages, she notes, "Du Bois outlines the malleability of racial identity and the potential for Negroes to be incorporated into the system of Americanization that he came to equate with whiteness." See *Beyond the Color Line and the Iron Curtain*, 183.

110. Du Bois, *Dusk of Dawn*, 665.

111. Mustapha, "Constituting Negative Geopolitics," 175.

112. Du Bois, *Dusk of Dawn*, 678–80.

113. Brown et al., *Whitewashing Race*, 12–15. The authors note three primary tenets held by many whites in the United States. "First, they believe the civil rights revolution was successful, and they wholeheartedly accept the principles enshrined in civil rights laws. . . . Second, if vestiges of racial inequality persist, they believe that is because blacks [and certain others] have failed to take advantage of opportunities created by the civil rights revolution. . . . Finally, most white Americans think the United States is rapidly becoming a color-blind society, and they see little need or justification for affirmative action or other color-conscious policies." *Whitewashing Race*, 1–2.

114. Harvey, *A Brief History of Neoliberalism*, 2.

115. Goldberg, "Deva-Stating Disasters," 85. Elsewhere Goldberg describes this tendency in a more general frame as "born again racism," which "is racism without the categories to name it as such. It is racism shorn of the charge, a racism that cannot be named because nothing abounds with which to name it. It is a racism purged of historical roots, of its groundedness, a racism whose history is lost." Goldberg, "The End(s) of Race," 226.

116. Prashad, *Everybody Was Kung Fu Fighting*, 38; emphasis in the original.

117. Ibid., 46; emphasis in the original.

118. Lipsitz, *American Studies in a Moment of Danger*, 5–8.

119. Ahmed, "Liberal Multiculturalism is the Hegemony."

120. For example, Du Bois included information about the relatively higher repre-

sentation of African American women in the work force in a "Chronicle" survey of information from the preliminary 1940 Census but does not comment on it as he does on other facts. Du Bois, "A Chronicle of Race Relations," *Phylon* 2, 2nd quarter 1941, in Aptheker, *Selections from Phylon*, 101.

121. Byerman, *Seizing the Word*, 196.

122. Carby, *Race Men*, 9–41.

123. Hancock, "W. E. B. Du Bois."

NOTES TO CHAPTER 2

1. Hardt and Negri, *Multitude*, xi–xiii. This discussion, of course, follows their account of the changing contours of sovereign power in their much-debated volume *Empire*.

2. Ibid., 5–8; emphasis in the original.

3. Ibid., 18–20.

4. Mbembe, "Necropolitics," 14; emphasis in original. Paul Gilroy is also suggestive in this respect: "It is not just that rationally applied terror routinely became imperial administration but also that the critical figure of the person who could be killed with impunity or disposed without conscience moved out of the liminal position to which it had been allocated by the unruffled workings of the national state." See Gilroy, *Postcolonial Melancholy*, 49.

5. Gregory, *The Colonial Present*, 248–49.

6. Ibid., 140, 183. And even as, at the time of writing this chapter, the war in Iraq was a disaster for the United States, its allies, and most of all for Iraqis, the arguments for peace typically revolved around domestic costs (in blood and money) in the United States or the impossibility for victory. Anti-imperialist critiques were few and far between in mainstream political discourse.

7. See Lenin, *Imperialism*.

8. Du Bois, "The African Roots of the War," *Atlantic Monthly*, May 1915, 707–14. This essay was published as "The Hands of Ethiopia" in *Darkwater*. See Kaplan, *Anarchy of Empire*, 171–212, for a discussion of these texts and the issues they raise.

9. "Close Ranks," in Lewis, *W. E. B. Du Bois: A Reader*, 697. For an analysis of Du Bois's piece and his complicity in the project of U.S. empire at that moment, see Kaplan, *The Anarchy of Empire*, 181.

10. Writing in 1941, for example, at a moment when many were contemplating the United States' entry into World War II, Du Bois stated, "I have lived through one period of deliberate and prolonged propaganda for war and partially succumbed to it *until* I really believed that the first World War was a war to end war and that the interests of colored people in particular were bound up in the defeat of Germany. I have lived to know better and my opposition to war under any circumstances has been immeasurably increased." Du Bois to Andrew J.

Allison, February 3, 1941, in Aptheker, *The Correspondence of W.E.B. Du Bois*, vol. 2, 272–73.

11. Du Bois, "Social Planning for the Negro, Past and Present," *Journal of Negro Education* 5 (January 1936): 110–25. In Aptheker, *Writings in Periodicals*, vol. 3, 26–40.

12. For an example of this reading of Nazi economic organization as a model for other nations, see Du Bois, "Neuropa." For contextualization of his sympathetic commentary on Germany during the 1930s, see Lewis, *W. E. B. Du Bois: The Fight for Equality*, 388, 399–402, 420, 467–68.

13. Mullen, *Afro-Orientalism*, 3. For contemporaneous commentary on Japan's defeat of Russia, see Du Bois, "The Color Line Belts the World," *Collier's Weekly*, October 20, 1906, 20; reprinted in Aptheker, *Writings in Periodicals*, vol. 1, 330.

14. Du Bois, "Postscript," *Crisis* 40, no. 1 (January 1933), 20. Quoted in Mullen, *Afro-Orientalism*, 23.

15. Lewis, *W. E. B. Du Bois: The Fight for Equality*, 409–19, 461–62; Mullen, *Afro-Orientalism*, 26; Waldo McNutt to Du Bois, February 13, 1939, in Aptheker, *The Correspondence of W. E. B. Du Bois*, vol. 2, 184–85; Du Bois to McNutt, February 25, 1939, in Aptheker, *The Correspondence of W. E. B. Du Bois*, vol. 2, 185.

16. Plummer, *Rising Wind*, 37–56, 67–74; Von Eschen, *Race against Empire*, 11–17. It is worth noting here that Plummer's account of African American antiimperialism during these years emphasizes its immanence in black racial sentiment and downplays the influence of the left. Although I draw throughout this chapter from her excellent and detailed account of black foreign affairs, I see a greater influence of the left on the contours of African American antiimperialism as documented by Robin Kelley, Penny Von Eschen, Gerald Horne, and others.

17. Lewis, *W. E. B. Du Bois: The Fight for Equality*, 418–19.

18. Prashad, *Everybody Was Kung Fu Fighting*, 20, 33–34.

19. Torgovnick, *The War Complex*, xi.

20. Discussing a letter Ralph Ellison wrote to Richard Wright in 1940, Nikhil Singh argues that Ellison's views at this moment "suggest[ed] a wider repudiation among black thinkers of the ethical primacy of 'civilization' bankrupted by racial, colonial, and right-wing politics. . . . fascism, colonialism, and racism were interrelated phenomena, whose linkages undermined Anglo-American claims to special moral standing among nations." See Singh, *Black Is a Country*, 116.

21. Du Bois, "As the Crow Flies," *Amsterdam News*, February 24, 1940. In Aptheker, *Newspaper Columns*, 286–87.

22. Du Bois, "A Chronicle of Race Relations," *Phylon* 1, 3rd quarter 1940, in Aptheker, *Selections from Phylon*, 37. See also Du Bois, "Neuropa," 384–85.

23. Du Bois, "A Chronicle of Race Relations," *Phylon* 4, 3rd quarter 1943, in Aptheker, *Selections from Phylon*, 257–58.

24. Singh, *Black Is a Country*, 129–30.

25. Ibid., 109, 130–31.

26. This is, of course, a very brief summary of a complex historical process. See Singh, *Black Is a Country*; Von Eschen, *Race against Empire*; Plummer, *Rising Wind*; Boerstelman, *The Cold War and the Color Line*; Dudziak, *Cold War Civil Rights;* Anderson, *Eyes Off the Prize*, for more details.

27. Du Bois, "A Chronicle of Race Relations," *Phylon* 1, 2nd quarter 1940, in Aptheker, *Selections from Phylon*, 28–29. He made similar comments the following year. See "A Chronicle of Race Relations," *Phylon* 2, 4th quarter 1941, in Aptheker, *Selections from Phylon*, 135–39.

28. Du Bois, "As the Crow Flies," *Amsterdam News*, February 1, 1941, in Aptheker, *Newspaper Columns*, vol. 1, 356–57. Gesturing toward the United Nations, Du Bois also indicates that such goals would be pursued initially, given the current fact of war, by an "international police army" and eventually by a "World League of Peoples."

29. Borgwardt, *A New Deal for the World*, 3.

30. Singh, *Black Is a Country*, 104; Plummer, *Rising Wind*, 84–85; Von Eschen, *Race against Empire*, 25–28.

31. "A Declaration by Negro Voters," in Aptheker, *A Documentary History*, 468.

32. Von Eschen, *Race Against Empire*, 25–28; Plummer, *Rising Wind*, 79, 84–85, 110–115; Committee on Africa, the War, and Peace Aims, *The Atlantic Charter and Africa from an American Standpoint*; L. D. Reddick, "Africa: Test of the Atlantic Charter," *The Crisis* 50 (July 1943): 202–4, 217–18; Padmore, *Pan-Africanism or Communism*, 130.

33. Taylor, *The Veiled Garvey*, 151–60. In 1944 Garvey produced a memorandum toward this effort titled "Correlative of Africa, the West Indies, and the Americas," which appears to have been presented at the Council of African Affairs conference "Africa — New Perspectives" held in New York in April of that year.

34. Du Bois, "As the Crow Flies," *Amsterdam News*, August 30, 1941, in Aptheker, *Newspaper Columns*, vol. 1, 382–83.

35. Du Bois, "The Future of Europe in Africa" (April 1942), in Aptheker, *Against Racism*, 189.

36. Du Bois, "The Realities in Africa; European Profit or Negro Development?" *Foreign Affairs* 21 (July 1943), 721–32, in Aptheker, *Writings in Periodicals*, vol. 3, 170–78.

37. Plummer, *Rising Wind*, 76; Singh, *Black Is a Country*, 123.

38. Du Bois, "As the Crow Flies," *Amsterdam News*, February 14, 1942, in Aptheker, *Newspaper Columns*, vol. 1, 413–14.

39. Du Bois, "As the Crow Flies," *Amsterdam News*, March 14, 1942, in Aptheker, *Newspaper Columns*, vol. 1, 415–16.

40. Du Bois, "A Chronicle of Race Relations," *Phylon* 3, 3rd quarter 1942, in Aptheker, *Selections from Phylon*, 177–82.

41. Du Bois, "A Chronicle of Race Relations," *Phylon* 3, 2nd quarter 1942, in Aptheker, *Selections from Phylon*, 409–12. As Penny Von Eschen notes, other activists and journalists used the successful Japanese invasions of European territories in the Pacific in 1941 and 1942 to criticize colonialism. George Padmore noted that colonials' passivity to Japanese invasion showed knowledge that they'd be exploited no matter what. Chicago *Defender* columnist John Robert Badger stated, "Colonialism is incapable of defending a territory [or] population under its control." See *Race against Empire*, 23.

42. Du Bois, "The Future of Europe in Africa" (April 1942), in Aptheker, *Against Racism*, 185.

43. Du Bois, "The Future of Africa in America" (April 1942), in Aptheker, *Against Racism*, 183–84.

44. Du Bois, "The Future of Europe in Africa" (April 1942), in Aptheker, *Against Racism*, 185.

45. Du Bois, "A Chronicle of Race Relations," *Phylon* 4, 1st quarter 1943, in Aptheker, *Selections from Phylon*, 211–23.

46. Du Bois, "A Chronicle of Race Relations," *Phylon* 4, 3rd quarter 1943, in Aptheker, *Selections from Phylon*, 256.

47. Du Bois, "A Chronicle of Race Relations," *Phylon* 4, 1st quarter 1943, in Aptheker, *Selections from Phylon*, 212–13.

48. Du Bois, "A Chronicle of Race Relations," *Phylon* 3, 4th Quarter 1942, in Aptheker, *Selections from Phylon*, 201–2; Du Bois, "A Chronicle of Race Relations," *Phylon* 4, 2nd Quarter 1943, in Aptheker, *Selections from Phylon*, 239–41. Another example of Du Bois's more favorable view of the New Deal from the perspective of the 1940s is found in a *New Masses* piece from 1945, lamenting the passing of both Roosevelt and his social vision. See Du Bois, "What He Meant to the Negro," *New Masses* 55, no. 4 (April 24, 1945): 9, in Aptheker, *Writings in Periodicals, 1945–1961*, 1.

49. In a 1943 Chronicle entry Du Bois surveyed the challenges to empire articulated by both colonials who joined the war effort and those who were engaged in anticolonial agitation. See Du Bois, "A Chronicle of Race Relations," *Phylon* 4, 3rd quarter 1943, in Aptheker, *Selections from Phylon*, 245–51.

50. Du Bois, "The Future of Europe in Africa" (April 1942), in Aptheker, *Against Racism*, 191.

51. Du Bois, "The Cultural Missions of Atlanta University," *Phylon* 3, 2nd quarter 1942, in Aptheker, *Selections from Phylon*, 363.

52. Du Bois to editor, *Fortune* magazine, May 21, 1942, in Aptheker, *The Correspondence of W. E. B. Du Bois*, vol. 2, 325. According to Aptheker's editor's note on page 324, the June 1942 issue of the magazine had a feature, "The Negro and

the War," which may have inspired his own proposal. Either way, *Fortune* did not show any interest in Du Bois's piece. That same month he made similar points while arguing for the release of the imprisoned communist Earl Browder. Du Bois, "The Release of Earl Browder" (May 1942), in Aptheker, *Against Racism*, 198–202.

53. Du Bois, "Reconstruction, Seventy-Five Years After," *Phylon* 4, 3rd quarter 1943, in Aptheker, *Selections from Phylon*, 394.

54. Du Bois, "The Future of Africa in America" (April 1942), in Aptheker, *Against Racism*, 184.

55. Du Bois, "We fight for a Free World . . . This or Nothing!" Chicago *Defender*, September 26, 1942, in Aptheker, *Writings in Periodicals*, vol. 3, 143–45.

56. Anderson, *Eyes off the Prize*, 29–30.

57. Du Bois to Walter White, August 12, 1944. Quoted in Aptheker, introduction to Du Bois, *Color and Democracy*, 10.

58. Du Bois, "Prospects of a World without Race Conflict," *American Journal of Sociology* 49 (March 1944), in Aptheker, *Writings in Periodicals*, vol. 3, 184, 188–89. Du Bois's take on the prospects of "world without race conflict" is fairly pessimistic. See page 184 especially. Similarly, as Plummer notes, a 1944 *Negro Digest* poll showed that a majority of African Americans thought the war would enable, on some level, their struggles for democracy but would not end racial conflicts. See *Rising Wind*, 87–88.

59. Reprinted under the heading "Colonialism, Democracy, and Peace after the War," in Aptheker, *Against Racism*, 229–44. Aptheker notes that Du Bois gave four talks in Haiti at the invitation of the Haitian government and with the "encouragement" of the U.S. State Department. Two of these were published in *Cahiers d'Haiti*; the previously unpublished versions are reproduced in Aptheker's volume.

60. Aptheker, introduction to Du Bois, *Color and Democracy*, 10; Lewis, *W. E. B. Du Bois: The Fight for Equality*, 503–504; Du Bois, *Color and Democracy*, 3–16; Plummer, *Rising Wind*, 118–19; Horne, *Black and Red*, 34.

61. Quoted in Du Bois, *Color and Democracy*, 128. The source that Du Bois wrote this statement is Aptheker's introduction to Du Bois, *Color and Democracy*, 18. Also quoted in "FDR Urged to Fight Colonial Exploitation," Chicago *Defender*, September 23, 1944, 18. This article has September 12 as the date of transmission to the Roosevelt administration.

62. Quoted in Du Bois, *Color and Democracy*, 129–30.

63. Du Bois, "Imperialism, United Nations, Colonial People," *New Leader* 27 (December 30, 1944), in Aptheker, *Writing in Periodicals*, vol. 3, 225–26. Du Bois made similar comments in *Color and Democracy*, published the following year. See pages 3–16. See also Anderson, *Eyes off the Prize*, 36.

64. Du Bois, "Imperialism, United Nations, Colonial People," 228.

65. Du Bois to Roy Wilkins, March 2, 1945, in Aptheker, *Correspondence*, vol. 3, 4–5. He also mentions Bretton Woods briefly in *Color and Democracy*, 101. In March 1945 he responded to a document released by the high-profile Commission to Study the Organization of Peace, arguing that its vision for postwar recovery was too heavily invested in the project of imperialism and not rooted enough in the rights and autonomy of colonial peoples. Lewis, *W. E. B. Du Bois: The Fight for Equality*, 503–4.

66. Aptheker, "Introduction" to Du Bois, *Color and Democracy*, 5–6, 10–11.

67. Du Bois was using this stationery as early as March 1945, before the publication of the book. See Du Bois to George Padmore, March 22, 1945, in *Papers of W. E. B. Du Bois*, reel 57, frames 1028–29.

68. Du Bois, *Color and Democracy*, v.

69. Ibid., 53–54.

70. Ibid., 54.

71. Ibid., 56.

72. Ibid., 70.

73. Ibid., 56–57.

74. Ibid., 73.

75. Ibid., 77–83.

76. Ibid., 84.

77. Ibid., 74–76.

78. Ibid., 85.

79. Ibid., 85–91.

80. Ibid., 93–95.

81. Ibid., 5.

82. Ibid., 101.

83. Ibid., 103–107.

84. Ibid., 114–17.

85. Ibid., 98–99.

86. Ibid., 97.

87. Ibid., 139–41.

88. Quoted in Horne, *Black and Red*, 30.

89. "New York Anti-Colonialism Conference," in Aptheker, *Documentary History*, 558–60; Von Eschen, *Race against Empire*, 76–77.

90. Anderson, "From Hope to Disillusion," 534–35; Lewis, *W. E. B. Du Bois: The Fight for Equality*, 507; Plummer, *Rising Wind*, 126, 135–37. One of the points of contention among activists was the NAACP's relatively privileged status as a consultant organization to the U.S. delegation.

91. NAACP Board of Directors statement, March 12, 1945, and Du Bois, memorandum to U.S. delegation to the UN founding conference, in Aptheker, *Documentary History*, 557–58, 569–71. For general accounts of African American par-

ticipation in the UN founding conference, see Plummer, *Rising Wind*, 125–65; Von Eschen, *Race against Empire*, 78–83; Anderson, *Eyes off the Prize*, 39–57.

92. Borstelmann, *The Cold War and the Color Line*, 3–4.

93. Anderson, *Eyes off the Prize*, 43–51; Singh, *Black Is a Country*, 160; Plummer, *Rising Wind*, 126–32, 141–45. Language here is from Dulles's initial amendment as quoted in Anderson. For the final revised version, see the UN Charter, Article II, 7.

94. Du Bois, *An Appeal to the World*; Aptheker, editor's notes in Aptheker, *Correspondence*, vol. 3, 163, 166; Anderson, "From Hope to Disillusion, 544–54; Plummer, *Rising Wind*, 171–74, 178–79; Anderson, *Eyes off the Prize*, 58–93.

95. Anderson, *Eyes off the Prize*, 96–112; Plummer, *Rising Wind*, 178–83.

96. Borstelmann, *The Cold War and the Color Line*, 2.

97. Anderson, "From Hope to Disillusion," 557–63; Janken, "From Colonial Liberation to Cold War Liberalism," 1082–84; Lewis, *W. E. B. Du Bois: The Fight for Equality*, 505, 528–34; Plummer, *Rising Wind*, 178–83; King, *Race, Culture, and Intellectuals*, 22.

98. Horne, *Black and Red*, 24; Von Eschen, *Race against Empire*, 97–102; Plummer, *Rising Wind*, 169. As Plummer notes, the significance of Churchill making the "Iron Curtain" speech at a small college that did not admit black students was not lost on African American observers. White also in 1946 defended the Soviet Union during a UN debate over the schedule of its withdrawal from Iran.

99. Lewis, *W. E. B. Du Bois: The Fight for Equality*, 517–18, 526; Horne, *Black and Red*, 55–62; Plummer, *Rising Wind*, 185–87; Von Eschen, *Race against Empire*, 107.

100. Singh, *Black Is a Country*, 166–67, Von Eschen, *Race against Empire*, 3; Plummer, *Rising Wind*, 159.

101. Janken, "From Colonial Liberation to Cold War Liberalism," 1084–86; Horne, *Black and Red*, 64–65.

102. Lewis, *W. E. B. Du Bois: The Fight for Equality*, 522–27; Horne, *Black and Red*, 50–56.

103. Lewis, *W. E. B. Du Bois: The Fight for Equality*, 532–34, 538; Horne, *Black and Red*, 50–56, 90–102; Von Eschen, *Race against Empire*, 108, 120–21; Du Bois, memorandum to the Secretary and Board of Directors of the NAACP, September 7, 1948, in Aptheker, *Correspondence*, vol. 3, 243–45.

104. Wallerstein, *The Decline of American Power*, 46. Wallerstein's book as a whole provides a useful survey of various phenomena described in the remainder of this paragraph.

105. For a useful summary, see Harvey, *A Brief History of Neoliberalism*.

106. Nordstrom, *Shadows of War*, 92–94, 115, 124. Nordstrom notes as well that modern states find it necessary to keep such arrangements only partially visible through justificatory frameworks that rearticulate those which supported ex-

pressions of colonial sovereignty in the past. "Part of its [the modern state's] power rests on the optics of deception: focusing attention on the need for violence while drawing attention away from both the war-economy foundations of sovereign power and the price in human life this economy of power entails. This is the magician's trick: the production of invisible visibility." *Shadows of War*, 34.

107. David Levering Lewis suggests that Du Bois's intervention at the 1945 Bretton Woods briefing was prescient. His intervention was unwelcome, of course, for the "north-south problems of extreme economic disparity, of stillborn postcolonial nations doomed to uneven, artificial, contingent development, and to a simulacrum of prosperity at best — the spawn of Bretton Woods and its supranational money lenders, to be reckoned with a half-century later — were uncomfortable considerations to be hurried past by treasury officials and international bankers." See Lewis, *W. E. B. Du Bois: The Fight for Equality*, 504.

108. Quoted in Ferguson, *Global Shadows*, 170.

109. Torgovnick, *The War Complex*, 2, 4.

NOTES TO CHAPTER 3

1. Alex Williams, "Into Africa: For a Continent Célèbre, Blockbuster Interest," *New York Times*, August 13, 2006, sec. 9, 1, 8.

2. Mudimbe, *The Invention of Africa*, ix. Achille Mbembe similarly suggests that "narrative about Africa is always pretext for a comment about something else, some other place, some other people. More precisely, Africa is the meditation that enables the West to accede to its own subconscious and give a public account of its subjectivity." Mbembe, *On the Postcolony*, 3.

3. Mbembe, *On the Postcolony*, 1.

4. Ferguson, *Global Shadows*, 5–10.

5. Ibid., 16–17, 22. Considering Africans as global citizens, Ferguson continues, "puts the question of the unequal relation between Africa and the West back on the table in a radical way, after decolonization and national independence had channeled it, for a time, into the question of national development." See page 23.

6. Monteiro, "Being an African in the World," 220–23; Moses, "Culture, Civilization, and the Decline of the West," 245–49; Mullen, *Afro-Orientalism*, 4–6; Sundquist, *To Wake the Nations*, 546–69.

7. This essay was reprinted in *Darkwater*. The point referenced here is made on pages 34–36.

8. For histories of the CAA, see Anthony, *Max Yergan*, and Von Eschen, *Race against Empire*.

9. Du Bois, "As the Crow Flies," *Amsterdam News* (June 22, 1940), in Aptheker, *Newspaper Columns*, vol. 1, 307–8. Cited in Marable, "The Pan-Africanism of W. E. B. Du Bois," 209.

10. Plummer, *Rising Wind*, 109–10.

11. Du Bois to F. W. Keppel, Carnegie Corporation, May 30, 1939; Keppel to Du Bois, June 9, 1939, and August 29, 1939, *The Papers of W. E. B. Du Bois*, reel 49, frames 1144–45.

12. Du Bois to Edward Weeks, October 2, 1941; Du Bois to Weeks, November 20, 1941; Weeks to Du Bois, January 26, 1942, in Aptheker, *The Correspondence of W. E. B. Du Bois*, vol. 2, 302–6. Regarding the time and place of these talks, see Aptheker's editor's note in *Against Racism*, 173, 184, and Du Bois to Anson Phelps-Stokes, April 20, 1942, *The Papers of W. E. B. Du Bois*, reel 54, frame 84.

13. Du Bois, "The Future of Europe in Africa (April 1942)," in Aptheker, *Against Racism*, 185–87.

14. Du Bois did not note the influence of Herskovits's geographical and cultural groupings in this talk, but he did so earlier when dividing the continent into nine regions in *Black Folk Then and Now*. See page 5. He also divided Africa into nine regions in his short volume *Africa, Its Geography, People and Products* (1930).

15. Du Bois, "The Future of Europe in Africa (April 1942)," in Aptheker, *Against Racism*, 186.

16. Quoted in Mamdani, introduction to *The World and Africa*, xxvi. Mamdani notes that Du Bois, in *The World and Africa*, was responding to a racialized historical and geographical conception of Africa, but he does not connect his description of distinct African geographies, a discussion anticipated by this talk, to that intervention.

17. Du Bois, "The Realities in Africa; European Profit or Negro Development?" *Foreign Affairs* 21 (July 1943): 721–32, in Aptheker, *Writings in Periodicals*, vol. 3, 174; see also 170–78.

18. Anson Phelps Stokes to Du Bois, March 4, 1942; Stokes to Du Bois, March 16, 1942; Stokes to Executive Committee, April 1, 1942 (with minutes of February 7, 1942, Executive Committee meeting); Du Bois to Stokes, April 20, 1942; Stokes to General Committee, May 12, 1942 (with minutes of April 5, 1942, Executive Committee meeting). All in *The Papers of W. E. B. Du Bois*, reel 54, frames 69, 72, 79–83, 86–89. Portions of one of the memoranda are quoted in the volume. See *The Atlantic Charter and Africa*, 60.

19. The substance of Du Bois's April 28, 1942, letter is gleaned from Stokes to Du Bois, April 29, 1942, in Aptheker, *Correspondence*, vol. 2, 332–33. Unfortunately, the April 28 letter is not found in his papers. Stokes thought some of Du Bois's "extreme criticisms" were not appropriate for the report. He explained to Du Bois that the volume was, after all, a public document intended to influence international public opinion. But Stokes apparently did take some criticisms to heart and promised to revise the document.

20. Stokes to Du Bois, July 9, 1942, in Aptheker, *Correspondence*, vol. 2, 334–35. Stokes reported that he presented the report at a symposium on Africa, under the

auspices of the Foreign Missions Conference of North America, held June 19–25 at Otterbein College.

21. *The Atlantic Charter and Africa from an American Standpoint*, 6, 10.

22. Ibid., 1, 22. Plummer notes both the influence of this report and its accommodationist and paternalistic take. See *Rising Wind*, 110–13.

23. Appendix II, "Terms of the Mandate System," in *The Atlantic Charter and Africa*, 132–37.

24. *The Atlantic Charter and Africa*, 105.

25. Minutes of May 23, 1942, General Committee meeting. Enclosed in Stokes to Committee, May 27, 1942, *The Papers of W. E. B. Du Bois*, reel 54, frames 95–98.

26. Du Bois, "Books and Race," *Phylon* 3, 4th quarter, 1942, 435–37. Du Bois offered a briefer, more measured review of the volume in the *New York Herald Tribune*, January 10, 1943, 10. Stokes was happy with Du Bois's review in *Phylon*, even with its criticisms. See Stokes to Du Bois, November 9, 1942, in Aptheker, *Correspondence*, vol. 2, 336. He liked it more than other reviews in the black press. He mentioned one, by Eric Williams, that concluded: "It seems to me that in view of the widespread recognition that we live in tremendous times, when radical changes must be made in the condition of the colonial peoples, the report will seem to those most concerned, the African people, just another in a by now very lengthy list of mild palliatives for a desperate disease." See Eric Williams, "Africa and the Post-War World, *Journal of Negro Education* 11, no. 4 (October 1942): 534–36. The report was also reviewed by L. D. Reddick in *Opportunity* 20 (September 1942): 283–84.

27. Du Bois, "Books and Race," *Phylon* 3, 4th quarter, 1942, 435–37.

28. Du Bois, "The Future of Europe in Africa (April 1942)," in Aptheker, *Against Racism*, 195–98.

29. Some accounts of Du Bois's engagement with Africa in the 1940s have focused on the limitations of his thinking and intellectual positionality. Brenda Gayle Plummer, for example, characterizes Du Bois's relative marginalization from the revived Pan-African Congress movement as a product of his "dated" understanding of African politics that privileged African American stewardship and was not fully committed to national liberation (Plummer, *Rising Wind*, 155–56). Adolph Reed argues that while Du Bois eventually saw the need for African political autonomy and indigenous leadership, he retained a sense that there were "backward" and "advanced" peoples and a faith in a "civilizing mission." This mission, even when framed in socialist terms, was rooted in long-standing beliefs in rational planning and administration rooted in the West and, ultimately, in a universalist assumption embedded in them. "Du Bois saw Pan-Africanism," Reed concludes, "as an expression among blacks of the developmental logic of modern society" Reed, *W. E. B. Du Bois and American Political Thought*, 78–83.

30. Marable, "The Pan-Africanism of W. E. B. Du Bois," 199–202.

31. Von Eschen, *Race against Empire*, 9–10; Plummer, *Rising Wind*, 12, 15–19; Reed, *W. E. B. Du Bois and American Political Thought*, 79–80; Padmore, *Pan-Africanism or Communism*, 106–7.

32. Robinson, "Du Bois and Black Sovereignty." Quoted material from page 145.

33. Minutes of April 25 committee meeting, enclosure to Stokes to General Committee, May 12, 1942, *Papers of W. E. B. Du Bois*, reel 54, frames 87–89.

34. See *The Atlantic Charter and Africa from an American Standpoint*, 151–53. I could identify eleven committee members as African American: Claude Barnett, Ralph Bunche, Du Bois, George E. Haynes, Charles S. Johnson, Rayford Logan, Frederick Douglass Patterson, Channing Tobias, I. W. Underhill, Walter White, and Bishop Richard Robert Wright. The introduction to the volume identifies the "representative Africans in this country" who were invited to its meeting on February 21, 1942, at which a draft of the report was discussed: Walter F. Walker, Liberian Consul General in New York; Ako Adjei, a student from Gold Coast studying at Hampton Institute; Ross Lohr, a Sierra Leone student doing advanced graduate work at Teachers College; Francis Nkrumah of Gold Coast, teaching at Lincoln University and pursuing a Ph.D. in philosophy at the University of Pennsylvania; Ibanga Udo Akpabio of Nigeria, studying at Columbia. All were invited to prepare memoranda that would be discussed at the meeting. It was also noted that other students living at a distance from New York were invited to send memoranda for discussion. See page ix.

35. Du Bois, "The Future of Europe in Africa (April 1942)," in Aptheker, *Against Racism*, 187–88, 191.

36. Du Bois to Eric Cochrane, July 6, 1943, in Aptheker, *The Correspondence of W. E. B. Du Bois*, vol. 2, 366. Du Bois wrote this letter when asked to comment on the differences between his *Foreign Affairs* piece and another essay, more favorably disposed toward privatization in the African future, appearing in the same issue (July 1943). Per Aptheker's editor's note on page 365, the article Du Bois was asked to compare his article to was Karl Brandt's "Problems of Invasion and Occupation."

37. Amy Jacques Garvey to Du Bois, April 4, 1944, in Aptheker, *The Correspondence of W. E. B. Du Bois*, vol. 2, 375–77; Du Bois to Paul Robeson, April 7, 1944, ibid., 378; Du Bois to Harold Moody, April 7, 1944, ibid., 378; Du Bois to Amy Jacques Garvey, April 8, 1944, ibid., 378–79; Lewis, *W. E. B. Du Bois: The Fight for Equality*, 499–500; Taylor, *The Veiled Garvey*, 165; Von Eschen, *Race against Empire*, 45–46.

38. Taylor, *The Veiled Garvey*, 166–67, Amy Jacque Garvey to Du Bois, April 24, 1944, in Aptheker, *The Correspondence of W. E. B. Du Bois*, vol. 2, 379–83; Amy Jacques Garvey to Du Bois, April 16, 1944, ibid., 383. Garvey herself had some difficulty escaping the ideological trappings of an earlier version of Pan-

Africanism. She was more oriented toward cultural uplift than anticolonial agitation. She also deployed what Von Eschen describes as the "gender-laden language of nineteenth- and early twentieth-century Pan-Africanism," referring to
Africa as the motherland and praising Du Bois's struggles for the "manhood" of
African peoples. See Von Eschen, *Race against Empire*, 46; Amy Jacques Garvey
to Du Bois, April 4, 1944, in Aptheker, *The Correspondence of W. E. B. Du Bois*,
vol. 2, 375–77; Amy Jacques Garvey to Du Bois, April 5, 1944, ibid., 377.

39. Von Eschen, *Race against Empire*, 11–12, 45; Adi, "Pan-Africanism in Britain,"
11–13. Like Du Bois, some IASB members had written about the place of Africa
in world affairs as well as the concomitant role of imperialism in perpetuating
war. See, for example, Padmore, *Africa and World Peace*.

40. Lewis, *W. E. B. Du Bois: The Fight for Equality*, 501; Von Eschen, *Race against
Empire*, 49–50; Adi, "Pan-Africanism in Britain," 14–16; Henry Lee Moon to
Du Bois, April, 9, 1945, in Aptheker, *The Correspondence of W. E. B. Du Bois*, vol.
3, 57–59; Padmore, "Call for Pan-African Party in Paris Drafted by British Colonial Leaders," Chicago *Defender*, national edition, March 17, 1945, 19; Padmore,
"Pan-African Congress Plans Paris Meeting," *Pittsburgh Courier*, national edition, March 3, 1945, 1; Padmore, *Pan-Africanism or Communism*, 133.

41. This document was eventually published by Moody's League of Coloured Peoples as "Manifesto on Africa in the Post-War World." The language of some of its
points differs slightly from that of those put forth by Padmore in the *Defender*
piece. Signatories of the manifesto were Moody, Padmore, K. A. Chunchie, J. S.
Annan, H. N. Critchlow, Samson Morris, R. W. Beoku-Betts, T. A. Bankole,
K. A. Korsah, J. A. Garba-Jahumpa, and C. B. Clarke. See *The Papers of W. E. B.
Du Bois*, reel 57, frames 534–36. Although Moody joined various labor activists
in support of this manifesto, he remained suspicious about labor's role in the
upcoming congress. See Moody to Du Bois, April 28, 1945, *The Papers of W. E. B.
Du Bois*, reel 57, frames 527–28.

42. Padmore, "Call for Pan-African Party." For a brief discussion of the manifesto,
see Adi, "Pan-Africanism in Britain," 16–17.

43. Du Bois to Padmore, March 22, 1945, in Aptheker, *The Correspondence of W. E. B.
Du Bois*, vol. 2, 56–57; Padmore to Du Bois, April 12, 1945, ibid., 64. Du Bois to
Padmore, July 9, 1945, ibid., 67–68.

44. Lewis, *W. E. B. Du Bois: The Fight for Equality*, 499–500; Alphaeus Hunton to
Du Bois, January 23, 1945, *The Paper of W. E. B. Du Bois*, reel 57, frame 387.
Moon became director of public relations for the NAACP in 1948.

45. Du Bois to Padmore, April 11, 1945, in Aptheker, *The Correspondence of W. E. B.
Du Bois*, vol. 3, 60–61; Du Bois to Harold Moody, April 11, 1945, ibid., 61–62,
Von Eschen, *Race against Empire*, 50–52.

46. Lewis, *W. E. B. Du Bois: The Fight for Equality*, 502, 512–13; Von Eschen, *Race
against Empire*, 52–53; Plummer, *Rising Wind*, 154–60.

47. Resolution reprinted in Du Bois, "Pan-Africanism: A Mission in My Life," *United Asia* (Bombay), March 1955, 23–28; reprinted in Aptheker, *Writings in Periodicals*, vol. 4, 233; see also 227–33.

48. Du Bois's comments come at the end of the final session of the Congress, on October 19, 1945. Du Bois is listed as "rapporteur" of this session. Reproduced in Padmore, *Colonial and Coloured Unity*; reprinted in Adi and Sherwood, *The 1945 Manchester Pan-African Congress Revisited*, 100–101.

49. Adi, "Pan-Africanism in Britain," 19–21.

50. Plummer, *Rising Wind*, 117–18; Von Eschen, *Race against Empire*, 70–74.

51. Du Bois, memorandum to U.S. delegation to the UN founding conference, in Aptheker, *Documentary History*, 569–71; Anderson, *Eyes off the Prize*, 50–51; Plummer, *Rising Wind*, 153–54; Charter of the United Nations, http://www .un.org/aboutun/charter/.

52. Walter White to Du Bois, March 23, 1946, in Aptheker, *The Correspondence of W. E. B. Du Bois*, vol. 3, 160; Du Bois to White, March 26, 1946, ibid., 160–61; Du Bois, draft of press release, March 28, 1946, ibid., 161–62.

53. See Von Eschen, *Race against Empire*, 85, on India's representation of South African Indians.

54. White to Du Bois, March 28, 1946, in Aptheker, *The Correspondence of W. E. B. Du Bois*, vol. 3, 161; Du Bois, draft of press release, March 28, 1946, ibid., 161–62.

55. Du Bois to Walter White, March 28, 1946, in Aptheker, *The Correspondence of W. E. B. Du Bois*, vol. 3, 161; Du Bois to White, November 14, 1946, ibid., 166–67.

56. Du Bois to George Padmore, April 1, 1946, in Aptheker, *The Correspondence of W. E. B. Du Bois*, vol. 3, 138–39; Padmore to Du Bois, April 16, 1946, ibid., 139; Padmore to Du Bois, May 21, 1946, ibid., 139–41; Du Bois to Padmore, July 12, 1946, ibid., 141–44; Padmore to Du Bois, August 9, 1946, ibid., 144–49.

57. Du Bois to Padmore, July 12, 1946, in Aptheker, *The Correspondence of W. E. B. Du Bois*, vol. 3, 141–44; Du Bois to Oswald Villard, July 24, 1946, ibid., 149–51. A list of some of the organizations to which Du Bois sent this letter can be found on page 151.

58. Du Bois to Oswald Villard, July 24, 1946, in Aptheker, *The Correspondence of W. E. B. Du Bois*, vol. 3, 150.

59. The petition and the list of organizations that endorsed it are reprinted in Aptheker, *The Correspondence of W. E. B. Du Bois*, vol. 3, 154–56. See Nkrumah to Du Bois, November 4, 1946, in Aptheker, *The Correspondence of W. E. B. Du Bois*, vol. 3, 156–57, for the endorsement of the West African National Secretariat.

60. Du Bois to Trygve Lie, September 4, 1946, in Aptheker, *The Correspondence of W. E. B. Du Bois*, vol. 3, 153. Per Aptheker's note, there is some question as

to whether Lie ever responded or whether the two men met to discuss the matter. Another note by Aptheker indicates the petition was sent on September 11. See *The Correspondence of W. E. B. Du Bois*, vol. 3, 153. See a third editor's note (166) on Du Bois bringing together representatives from twenty organizations to meet at the Schomburg Library on October 4, 1946, to discuss the substance of the petition. This meeting was reported in the *New York Times*, October 6, 1946, 34.

61. Du Bois to George Padmore, January 28, 1946, in Aptheker, *The Correspondence of W. E. B. Du Bois*, vol. 3, 137; Du Bois to Padmore, July 12, 1946, ibid., 141–44; Du Bois to Walter White (memorandum), November 14, 1946, ibid., 166–67; Lewis, *W. E. B. Du Bois and the Fight for Equality*, 521; Aptheker, editor's notes, in *The Correspondence of W. E. B. Du Bois*, vol. 3, 152–53, 166.

62. Du Bois to George Padmore, December 30, 1946, in Aptheker, *The Correspondence of W. E. B. Du Bois*, vol. 3, 159.

63. Du Bois, letter to editor, *New York Times*, November 6, 1946 (as drafted), November 28, 1946 (as published). Reprinted in Aptheker, *Writings in Periodicals*, vol. 4, 21–23. The reprinted version in this volume includes both the published sections and those edited out of Du Bois's original, with the omitted sections in italics.

64. Du Bois to editor *New York Times*, November 1, 1946, *The Papers of W. E. B. Du Bois* reel 59, frames 120–23. This is an even longer version than the "as drafted" version reproduced in Aptheker's edited volume. After sending this longer letter, Du Bois was asked to edit it down to half its length. See *New York Times* to Du Bois, November 5, 1946, *The Papers of W. E. B. Du Bois*, reel 59, frame 124.

65. Du Bois, Letter to editor, *New York Times*, in Aptheker, *Writings in Periodicals*, vol. 4, 23.

66. Du Bois, "Memorandum to the Secretary [Walter White] on Africa," December 2, 1946, in Aptheker, *The Correspondence of W. E. B. Du Bois*, vol. 3, 168.

67. Ibid. Interestingly, Du Bois pointed out that without the NAACP's work on this, the job of collecting information on Africa would be left to African studies at the University of Pennsylvania. This seems to indicate that he had a problem with emergent area studies paradigms.

68. Du Bois to Viking Press, January 17, 1945, in Aptheker, *The Correspondence of W. E. B. Du Bois*, vol. 3, 29. Aptheker's editor's note makes the connection to *Color and Democracy*.

69. Du Bois approached Henry Luce, requesting a meeting to discuss placing something along these lines in one of his publications. See Du Bois to Henry Luce, December 17, 1945, in Aptheker, *The Correspondence of W. E. B. Du Bois*, vol. 3, 94–95. Per Aptheker's editor's note on page 94, it's unclear whether Luce

granted the meeting, but it is clear that nothing like this appeared or was mentioned in Luce's publications.

70. Du Bois to George Padmore, July 12, 1946, in Aptheker, *The Correspondence of W. E. B. Du Bois*, vol. 3, 142; Viking Press, Inc. "to the book review editor" (generic letter), Februrary 5, 1947, in *The Papers of W. E. B. Du Bois*, reel 61, frame 9.

71. Du Bois, *The World and Africa*, viii, xii.

72. Ibid., 80.

73. Ibid., 2.

74. Ibid., 23.

75. Ibid., 250–55.

76. Ibid., 17–19.

77. Ibid., 41–42.

78. Ibid., 74.

79. Ibid., 254–55.

80. Ibid., 80.

81. Mandani, introduction to Du Bois, *The World and Africa*, xxvii.

82. Du Bois, *The World and Africa*, 163.

83. Ibid., 91–97.

84. Ibid., 119.

85. Ibid., viii–xii.

86. Mustapha, "Constituting Negative Geopolitics," 173–76, 187, 190.

87. Ibid., 184–85.

88. Du Bois, *The World and Africa*, 227.

89. Ibid., 227–31.

90. Ibid., 250, 256, 259–60. He quotes Raphael Armattoe, *The Golden Age of West African Civilization*: "I believe it is specifically the mission of African civilization to restore ethical principles to world civilization. Unless this attempt is made all civilization must come to an end. The African by virtue of his detachment, his direct vision, and his innate kindness, is qualified to bring humanitarianism to the technical and materialistic concepts of the Western World."

91. Du Bois, *The World and Africa*, 7–12.

92. Ibid., 244.

93. Ibid., 260. It should be noted that elsewhere on this page Du Bois is seemingly at odds with the rest of his anti-imperialist, pro-peace agenda by noting sympathetically black contributions to the war effort, including the role of black scientists in the development of the atomic bomb.

94. Weinbaum, "Reproducing Racial Globality," 16, 31. See also Mullen, *Afro-Orientalism*.

95. Du Bois also figures Africa as the victim of rape in *Darkwater*, 42.

96. Du Bois, *The World and Africa*, 60–62.

97. Ibid., 41–42.

98. Taylor, *The Veiled Garvey*, 168–69; Lewis, *W. E. B. Du Bois: The Fight for Equality*, 513.

99. Reproduced in Adi and Sherwood, *The 1945 Manchester Pan-African Congress Revisited*, 98–101.

100. Stephens, *Black Empire*, 15–16.

101. Ibid., 209.

102. Ibid., 20.

103. Anderson, *Eyes off the Prize*, 136–38.

104. Ibid., 131–33. Roosevelt also saw it necessary to leave out the racial discrimination clause in order to get approval from southern senators.

105. Ibid., 139.

106. Du Bois to Secretary and Board of Directors, NAACP, memo on UN and NAACP, September 7, 1948, in Aptheker, *The Correspondence of W. E. B. Du Bois*, vol. 3, 243–45. In good Du Boisean fashion, he charged that much of the problem with NAACP policy stemmed from his being kept out of the loop in its discussions of foreign policy. Carol Anderson suggests that Du Bois ultimately should have supported the Human Rights Declaration and Covenant, as they actually provided a potential mechanism for redress that could have been developed further. See *Eyes off the Prize*, 151–52.

107. Von Eshen, *Race against Empire*, 84–95. Von Eschen also discusses how the CAA supported India's efforts to secure the right to represent South African Indians at the UN and to initiate charges with the General Assembly that South Africa's treatment of this population violated the human rights clause of the UN Charter. India's petition resulted in a nonbinding resolution asking that they and South Africa come to an agreement about the matter and report back to the assembly. The United States sought to mediate the conflict and ultimately was among the nations voting against the resolution, a position likely related to its strategic interest in South Africa's uranium deposits.

108. Ibid., 115–16, 122–24, 141–43; Horne, *Black and Red*, 115, 119, 185–91; Lewis, *W. E. B. Du Bois: The Fight for Equality*, 539–40; Anthony, *Max Yergan*, 228–34; Aptheker, editor's notes, *The Correspondence of W. E. B. Du Bois*, vol. 3, 255, 347–48; Du Bois form letter, June 18, 1953, in Aptheker, *The Correspondence of W.E.B. Du Bois*, vol. 3, 348–49.

109. These columns ran almost every week from March 15, 1947, through March 6, 1948. The title "Pan-Africa" was given to columns published from July 26, 1947 through October 4, 1947. The *People's Voice* columns are reproduced in Aptheker, *Newspaper Columns*, vol. 2, 771–854.

110. Du Bois, "Africa Today," *New Africa* (February 1949), in Aptheker, *Writings in Periodicals*, vol. 4, 103–4.

111. Du Bois, "To Save the World, Save Africa!" *New Africa* (May 1949), in Aptheker, *Writings in Periodicals*, vol. 4, 117–18.

112. Du Bois, "The Winds of Time," Chicago *Defender* (January 11, 1947), in Aptheker, *Newspaper Columns*, vol. 2, 704–5; Du Bois, "The Winds of Time," Chicago *Defender* (November 15, 1947), ibid., 741.

113. See specifically the column "Pan-Africanism Growing Slowly," *People's Voice* (October 25, 1947), in Aptheker, *Newspaper Columns*, vol. 2, 822.

114. Du Bois to George Padmore, March 1, 1948, in Aptheker, *The Correspondence of W. E. B. Du Bois*, vol. 3, 198.

115. Du Bois to James Coleman, February 18, 1950, in Aptheker, *The Correspondence of W. E. B. Du Bois*, vol. 3, 276–77; Du Bois to George Padmore, March 17, 1950, ibid., 280–81; Du Bois to Padmore, July 10, 1951, ibid., 316–17.

116. "The African Roots of Peace," *The Papers of W. E. B. Du Bois*, reel 83, frames 407–18. Du Bois sought to place this piece in *Atlantic Monthly*, but the magazine rejected it on the grounds that it could not be edited down to an appropriate length without compromising the argument. See Du Bois to editor, *Atlantic Monthly*, June 8, 1948; Edward Weeks to Du Bois, June 18, 1948; Weeks to Du Bois, July 14, 1948; Du Bois to Weeks, July 26, 1948; Du Bois to Weeks, September 27, 1948; Weeks to Du Bois, September 20, 1948, *The Papers of W. E. B. Du Bois*, reel 61, frames 408–11.

117. Du Bois to Mordecai Johnson, January 26, 1949, in Aptheker, *The Correspondence of W. E. B. Du Bois*, vol. 3, 255–56; Mordecai Johnson to Du Bois, February 3, 1949, ibid., 256.

118. Du Bois, "To Save the World, Save Africa!" *New Africa* (May 1949), in Aptheker, *Writings in Periodicals*, vol. 4, 117–18.

119. Du Bois to Robert C. Bennett, February 16, 1954, in Aptheker, *The Correspondence of W. E. B. Du Bois*, vol. 3, 355; Du Bois to George Padmore, December 10, 1954, ibid., 374–75; Du Bois, "The Giant Stirs," in Du Bois, *The World and Africa*, especially 279–80. "The Giant Stirs" is comprised of ten articles from the *National Guardian*, published between February 14 and April 10, 1955. These are reprinted in Du Bois, *The World and Africa*, 265–91. Kevin Gaines notes the influence of Padmore and the friendly debates he and Du Bois had about the relationship of Pan-Africanism and communism through the 1950s. See *American Africans in Ghana*, 148.

120. Du Bois, "The Giant Stirs," 265–67; Von Eschen, *Race against Empire*, 145–46. Von Eschen notes that Du Bois makes similar comments in an article from 1954, "Africa and the American Negro Intelligentsia." A similar piece is "Africa and Afro-America," originally from *Spotlight on Africa: Newsletter*, a late publication of the CAA. This was the text of a keynote address to the "Working Conference in Support of African Liberation," which was held at Friendship Baptist

Church, New York, April 24, 1954. Reprinted in Aptheker, *Writings in Periodicals*, vol. 4, 215–20.

121. Von Eschen, *Race against Empire*, 125, 143–44, 158; Plummer, *Rising Wind*, 226–37. Plummer notes that these new directions in African studies were products of a segregated university system. Phelps-Stokes and SSRC conferences on Africa were generally not designed to include African American input, and there was very little exchange of resources between black and white universities in this period. Although some funding for African Americans was available through the Phelps-Stokes fund, it was the exception.

122. Von Eschen, *Race against Empire*, 150–63.

123. Ibid., 145–46; Plummer, *Rising Wind*, 239–40; Gaines, *American Africans in Ghana*, 11.

124. Du Bois, "The Future of Africa," in Du Bois, *The World and Africa*, 305–10.

125. Lewis, *W. E. B. Du Bois: The Fight for Equality*, 566–69; Gaines, *American Africans in Ghana*, 14–16, 140–142.

126. Du Bois to Gus Hall, October 1, 1961, in Aptheker, *The Correspondence of W. E. B. Du Bois*, vol. 3, 439–40.

127. Du Bois, "American Negroes and Africa's Rise to Freedom, *National Guardian* (February 13, 1961), in Du Bois, *The World and Africa*, 334–38.

128. See Horne, *Race Woman*, chapter 8; Gaines, *American Africans in Ghana*, 143.

129. Ferguson, *Global Shadows*, 49.

130. Mbembe, *On the Postcolony*, 197; emphasis in the original.

131. Goldberg, *The Racial State*, 43, 210.

132. Ferguson, *Global Shadows*, 189–90; emphasis in the original.

133. Wynter, "Is 'Development' a Purely Empirical Concept or also Teleological?," 300; emphasis in the original.

134. Ferguson, *Global Shadows*, 33.

135. Mbembe, *On the Postcolony*, 14; emphasis in the original.

136. Ibid., 12–13; emphasis in the original.

137. Ibid., 199.

138. Du Bois, "The Realities in Africa: European Profit or Negro Development?," *Foreign Affairs* 21 (July 1943), in Aptheker, *Writings in Periodicals*, vol. 3, 174.

139. Stecopoulos, "Putting Old Africa on the Map," 221–24.

140. Ibid., 243.

141. Wynter, "Is 'Development' a Purely Empirical Concept or also Teleological?," 312; emphasis in the original.

142. Von Eschen suggests that history proved Du Bois's warnings about the persistence of the colonial past correct: "As the inequitable social relations of empire came back home, these processes eventually eroded the industrial and public sectors where African American workers had made significant gains." See *Race against Empire*, 187.

143. Hardt and Negri, *Multitude*, 167; Gilroy, *Postcolonial Melancholia*, 45. Quoted material from Hardt and Negri; emphasis in the original.

144. Mbembe, *On the Postcolony*, 2.

145. Ferguson, *Global Shadows*, 69–88.

NOTES TO CHAPTER 4

1. Du Bois, "20th Century: The Century of the Color Line," in Aptheker, *Pamphlets and Leaflets*, 280. This piece was originally published in the January 14, 1950, issue of the newspaper.

2. Ibid., 283, 285.

3. Ibid., 286.

4. Ibid., 286.

5. Malveaux and Green, *The Paradox of Loyalty*, xix. The authors adopt their title from Mary Frances Berry, who uses the phrase in her co-written volume, with John Blassingame, *Long Memory: The Black Experience in America*.

6. Alexander, *Pedagogies of Crossing*, 235.

7. Carbado, "Racial Naturalization," 639. Although Carbado emphasizes the ways "blackness has often been included in the juridical order solely in the form of its exclusion (that is, its capacity to be subordinated)," his framework also acknowledges the ways "this inclusive exclusion historically has positioned black people both inside and outside America's national imagination — as a matter of law, politics, and social life."

8. Shirley Graham joined the group in early 1948 as well. She later took the lead role in passing a pro-Du Bois resolution after he had been dismissed by the NAACP. Horne, *Black and Red*, 107; Horne, *Race Woman*, 113.

9. Call characterized and quoted in Charles C. Price, "Cultural and Scientific Conference for World Peace," *Science*, March 18, 1949, 290.

10. Also on the panel were the journalists Richard Boyer and Ira Wolfert, the writer and editor Charles Madison, and the poet and session chair Louis Untermeyer, For accounts of panelists' and audience members' comments, see Gillmore, *Speaking of Peace*, and "Panel Discussions of the Cultural Conference Delegates Cover a Wide Range of Subjects," *New York Times*, March 27, 1949, 44–45.

11. Wittner, *One World or None*, 55–79.

12. Ibid., 171–90; Holloway, *Stalin and the Bomb*, 264–67, 287–92. The WPC admitted in 1989 that most of its funding in its early years had come from the Soviet Union. See *Peace Courier*, 1989, no. 4.

13. Wittner, *One World or None*, 203–9, 271–72; Gillmore, *Speaking of Peace*, 1–4; Marable, *W. E. B. Du Bois*, 176; Horne, *Black and Red*, 120–21; Horne, *Race Woman*, 119; Lewis, *W. E. B. Du Bois: The Fight for Equality*, 542–43; Du Bois, *His Day Is Marching On*, 103–9; Du Bois, *In Battle for Peace*, 26–27. Du Bois in his memoir references Singer, "An Analysis of the New York Press

Treatment of the Peace Conference at the Waldorf Astoria," as a source for the press coverage.

14. Wittner, *One World or None*, 205–6; Saunders, *The Cultural Cold War*, 45–56; Lewis, *W. E. B. Du Bois: The Fight for Equality*, 542–43; Gillmore, *Speaking of Peace*, 85–87; Norman Cousins, "A Dissenting Opinion," in Gillmore, *Speaking of Peace*, 15–17.

15. Du Bois, "The Nature of Intellectual Freedom," in Gillmore, *Speaking of Peace*, 77–78. Also reproduced in Aptheker, *Writings in Nonperiodical Literature*, 267–68.

16. Du Bois, "The Fight for World Peace," *The Papers of W. E. B. Du Bois*, reel 80, frames 1208–10. Portions of the speech with slightly different language are quoted in Du Bois, *His Day Is Marching On*, 109–10.

17. Plummer, *Rising Wind*, 4, 199. Nikhil Singh similarly notes that advocates of socialism and Soviet affinity threatened the putative political "consensus" in the United States that was achieved by mobilizing "anticommunism" to "articulate a structure of common differences that could sustain a more or less permanent wartime footing." Singh, *Black Is a Country*, 163.

18. Cain, "From Liberalism to Communism," 459.

19. Horne, *Black and Red*, 8–10, 289–311.

20. Baldwin, *Beyond the Color Line and the Iron Curtain*, 153. She continues: "The affective sweep and inspirational power of the explanatory framework offered him by Marxism and the Soviet model needs to be appreciated as one that appealed to both the unquestionable depth of his intellectual prowess and correlated to his unflagging commitment to global liberation, decolonization, and peace movements, as well as to his opposition to militarism, corporate tyranny, social inequality, and racial segregation."

21. Du Bois, "Social Medicine," in Aptheker, *Against Racism*, 275. This was an address delivered at College of Medicine, University of Illinois, Chicago, during Negro History week, February 8, 1950.

22. Cain, "From Liberalism to Communism," especially 456–57, 469–71.

23. For a series of interesting takes on this conundrum, see Nussbaum et al., *For Love of Country*.

24. Lewis, *W. E. B. Du Bois: The Fight for Equality*, 544–45; Horne, *Black and Red*, 122; Marable, *W. E. B. Du Bois*, 176–77; Du Bois, *In Battle for Peace*, 28.

25. Quoted in Singh, *Black Is a Country*, 163. Du Bois had been publicly critical of Byrnes before. See, for example, the discussion of Byrnes in his pamphlet "Behold the Land," based on a speech delivered on October 20, 1946, to the Southern Negro Youth Congress, in Aptheker, *Pamphlets and Leaflets*, 275–79; 276; the reference to Byrnes in *The World and Africa*, 254–55.

26. See Du Bois, *In Battle for Peace*, 182–86, for the text of his speech.

27. Ibid., 43–44.
28. Du Bois, "I Speak for Peace," in Aptheker, *Pamphlets and Leaflets*, 287–91; 291.
29. Carbado, "Racial Naturalization," 643–44. Carbado focuses more specifically on the Dred Scott decision, arguing that the decision is problematic not just because it excludes blacks from citizenship but because it includes them as property. But a similar point can be made about the 1850 law. Although it did not as explicitly deny black citizenship as Dred Scott, it limited the scope of African Americans' rights as citizens by denying their right to a jury trial or to testify on their own behalf.
30. Du Bois, "I Speak for Peace," in Aptheker, *Pamphlets and Leaflets*, 291.
31. Du Bois, "The Social Significance of These Three Cases (11 January 1951)," in Aptheker, *Against Racism*, 279, 281. These cases were *Sweatt v. Painter*, *McLaunin v. Oklahoma State Regents*, and *Henderson v. Insterstate Commerce Commission and Southern Railway*. See Aptheker's editor's note in *Against Racism*, 276.
32. Du Bois, *In Battle for Peace*, 34–35.
33. Ibid., 36–42; Horne, *Black and Red*, 125–31; Lewis, *W. E. B. Du Bois: The Fight for Equality*, 546–47; Wittner, *One World or None*, 182–90, 202–3. Wittner argues that the estimate of the total number of signatories across the globe was calculated, in part, by counting the entire adult population of the USSR.
34. Walter H. Waggoner, "Acheson Derides Soviet Peace Bids," *New York Times*, July 13, 1950, 1, 7. Portions of Acheson's statement are also quoted in Du Bois, *In Battle for Peace*, 37.
35. Horne, *Black and Red*, 132–33.
36. Lewis, *W. E. B. Du Bois: The Fight for Equality*, 547; press release reproduced in Du Bois, *In Battle for Peace*, 38–40. The press release was quoted in " 'Peace' Proponent Asks Atom Pledge," *New York Times*, July 17, 1950, 5. Although the teaser of the *Times* article stated that "Dr. Du Bois calls on Acheson to Promise U.S. Will 'Never Be First to Use Bomb,' " his press release did not say this outright, at least not the version in *In Battle for Peace*. Rather, the *Times* journalist seems to infer this from the fact that Du Bois so vigorously challenged Acheson's critique of the appeal.
37. Justice Department letter quoted in Du Bois, *In Battle for Peace*, 51. See also "Peace Group Told to File with U.S.," *New York Times*, August 25, 1950, 4; Horne, *Black and Red*, 132; Lewis, *W. E. B. Du Bois: The Fight for Equality*, 546.
38. "Peace Group Told to File with U.S.," *New York Times*, August 25, 1950, 4.
39. Du Bois, *In Battle for Peace*, 51–56, 63–71; Lewis, *W. E. B. Du Bois: The Fight for Equality*, 547–48. The discrepancy in the name of the organization likely stems from different translations from the French. The organization changed its name to the World Peace Council around the time of a November 1950 peace conference in Warsaw. On the name change see Wittner, *One World or None*, 184–85.

40. See Du Bois, *In Battle for Peace*, 57–63, for both W. E. B. and Shirley Graham Du Bois's accounts of the wedding; see also Horne, *Race Woman*, 134–35.

41. Lewis, *W. E. B. Du Bois: The Fight for Equality*, 549–51; Du Bois, *In Battle for Peace*, 62–65.

42. Du Bois, *In Battle for Peace*, 119–59; Lewis, *W. E. B. Du Bois: The Fight for Equality*, 551–53; Horne, *Black and Red*, 176–78.

43. Lewis, *W. E. B. Du Bois: The Fight for Equality*, 551–53.

44. Much of the account of the indictment and trial therein was reproduced almost verbatim in Du Bois's posthumous autobiography. See *Autobiography*, 343–95.

45. *In Battle for Peace*, 26–34, 117–18. Du Bois concludes his discussion of Rogge by refering to him as "Rogge the Rat."

46. Byerman, *Seizing the Word*, 207.

47. Du Bois, *In Battle for Peace*, 163–64.

48. Ibid., 152–55.

49. Ibid., 179–80.

50. Baldwin, *Beyond the Color Line and the Iron Curtain*, 157–59, 178, 183.

51. As Gerald Horne notes, NAACP activities in the late 1940s were often seen as disloyal. In one case, Frank Barnes, president of the Santa Monica branch, was suspended from his job at the post office for organizing a picket line at a Sears Roebuck store. The suspension was justified by Truman's Executive Order 9835, signed in 1947, which established processes for loyalty screenings for federal employees and applicants. See Horne, *Black and Red*, 59–61.

52. Muñoz, *Disidentifications*, 11. Building from Louis Althusser's notion of interpellation and Michel Pêcheux's work that builds from it, Muñoz defines disidentification as a third way, as distinct from identification or counteridentification, of negotiating dominant ideologies: "one that neither opts to assimilate within such a structure nor strictly opposes it; rather, disidentification is a strategy that works on and against dominant ideology."

53. Du Bois, *In Battle for Peace*, 71.

54. Ibid., 76, 152–53.

55. Ibid., 78–79.

56. Ibid., 164.

57. Ibid., 88–89.

58. Alexander, *Pedagogies of Crossing*, 181–83. Alexander subsequently writes: "Within the United States, the retrenchments in welfare not only bolster market principles that require a nuclear accumulating household, they also help to demystify other important public formations such as those of militarization. The military has been positioned as the new citizenship school for women and men removed from public assistance, thereby making the downsizing of the social wage the corollary to the increases in the military budget whose expenditures finance both the war abroad and strategies against 'domestic terrorism' at home.

This budget also finances the new kind of 'order maintenance' policing that is authorized in central cities, which utilizes 'warrior cops' trained in the military curriculum to police working-class communities that include immigrants. In addition, the police presence at toll booths, train stations, airports, bridges, and tunnels; the detention of large numbers of immigrants; the surveillance of foreign students; the wide diffusion of war propaganda on the Internet, on telephone, gas, and electricity bills, and public transportation media — all emendations of the private and the public — speak both to an escalation in the militarization of daily life, which the state positions as a necessary arm of the public war against domestic terrorism, and the safeguarding of the quasi-private/public space of the homeland as the basis of security. This public war is financed by the private tax-paying consumer, citizen and non-citizen alike, while private corporations intimately linked to public state managers, indeed state power, derive disproportionate profit." See page 233. See also Piven, *The War at Home*, 65–88.

59. Alexander, *Pedagogies of Crossing*, 234–35.

60. Ibid., 235–44. Alexander's analysis of the ways the construction of the enemy terrorist relies on sexual perversity draws from Puar and Rai, "Monster, Terrorist, Fag."

61. Alexander, *Pedagogies of Crossing*, 243, 249.

62. See *In Battle for Peace*, 14. She describes him inspiring her first poem, "Black Man's Music." Kate Baldwin calls attention to the irony of Graham's and Du Bois's "shared space" in the text ultimately reproducing a gendered hierarchy. Graham's "presence is always beside him as a loving support, confidant, and nurturing supplicant"; she comments "repeatedly . . . on the masterful clarity of Du Bois's intellect." Baldwin, *Beyond the Color Line*, 190.

63. Baldwin, *Beyond the Color Line*, 194.

64. Du Bois, *In Battle for Peace*, 179.

65. McAlister, *Epic Encounters*, 47. She argues that the doctrine of benevolent supremacy is expressed most notably by National Security Council document 68.

66. Ibid., 250, 259.

67. Ibid., 302.

68. Ibid., 255–57.

69. Volpp, "The Citizen and the Terrorist," 147.

70. See the USA Patriot Act, Title I, Section 102. Available at http://thomas.loc.gov.

71. Volpp, "The Citizen and the Terrorist," 151.

72. Alsultany, "The Primetime Plight of the Arab Muslim American After 9/11," 207–8.

73. Puar and Rai, "Monster, Terrorist, Fag," 138.

74. Two pieces that address this in the African American community are Karin L. Stanford, "The War Within: African American Public Opinion on the War

Against Terrorism," 95–116; and Laura Murphy, "White Man's Pass: The Heightened Danger of Racial Profiling in the Post 9/11 World," 175–84, in Malveaux and Green, *The Paradox of Loyalty*.

75. Volpp, "The Citizen and the Terrorist," 154; Puar and Rai, "Monster, Terrorist, Fag," 140. On the reproduction of normative genders and sexualities, see Faludi, *The Terror Dream*.

76. Holt, *The Problem of Race in the Twenty-First Century*, 102.

77. Gordon, *Her Majesty's Other Children*, 4–5.

78. Carbado, "Racial Naturalization," 652–53. Rereading Toni Morrison's critique of Elia Kazan's *America, America*, Carbado argues that the antiblack racism of the character Stavros is not merely the path toward his own Americanization—in terms of identity as citizen rather than formal citizenship status—but rather part of the process by which the object of his wrath is Americanized as well. "Stavros's attainment of white American identity depends upon an exclusion of the black shoe shiner . . . and that exclusion is precisely what renders the shoe shiner intelligible as an American. Indeed it is through Stavros's exclusion that the shoe shiner reexperiences his American belonging."

79. Wideman, "Whose War: The Color of Terror," in Malveaux and Green, *The Paradox of Loyalty*, 122.

80. See Kelley, *Freedom Dreams*.

81. Mosley, *What Next*, 26–27.

82. Ibid., 37. Or, in his words: "How can we, Black people of America, who have suffered so much under the iron heel of progress, stand back and allow people to starve and die as silently and unheralded as our own ancestors did on those slave ships so many years ago? How can we, the great defenders of liberty, allow our sweat and blood, taxes and minds to be bent toward the subjugation of the rest of the world? Not only do we stand silently by while Kurds, Mayans, Sudanese, and South Africans die from warfare, slavery, disease, and neglect, but we also sit almost passively—knowing full well that hundreds of thousands of young Black men and women are imprisoned and institutionalized by a police state organized around the principal [*sic*] of protecting the property of the rich."

83. Ibid., 7.

84. Mosley's intervention is framed very much along masculine lines, crafted as it is as a revision of lessons imparted by his father, who "told me what it meant to be a man and to be a Black man." Ibid., 10.

85. Roy, *An Ordinary Person's Guide to Empire*, 37–38, 67.

86. Sexton and Lee, "Figuring the Prison," 1012, 1016.

87. For a brief treatment of Durban, see Naomi Klein, "Obama's Big Silence: The Race Question," *The Guardian* (September 12, 2009).

88. Achcar, *The Clash of Barbarisms*, 114–15.

Achcar, Gilbert. *The Clash of Barbarisms: The Making of the New World Disorder*. Updated and expanded ed. Translated by Peter Drucker. Boulder, Colo.: Paradigm Publishers, 2006.

Adi, Hakim. "Pan-Africanism in Britain: Background to the 1945 Manchester Congress." In *The 1945 Manchester Pan-African Congress Revisited*, edited by Hakim Adi and Marika Sherwood, 9–32. London: New Beacon Books, 1995.

Agamben, Giorgio. *Homo Sacer: Sovereign Power and Bare Life*. Translated by Daniel Heller-Roazen. Stanford, Calif.: Stanford University Press, 1998.

Ahmed, Sara. "'Liberal Multiculturalism Is the Hegemony — It's an Empirical Fact' — A Response to Slavoj Žižek." *Dark Matter*, comment posted February 19, 2008. http://www.darkmatter101.org/site/2008/02/19/'liberal-multiculturalism-is-the-hegemony-its-an-empirical-fact'-a-response-to-slavoj-zizek/.

Alexander, M. Jacqui. *Pedagogies of Crossing: Meditations on Feminism, Sexual Politics, Memory, and the Sacred*. Durham, N.C.: Duke University Press, 2005.

Alsultany, Evelyn. "The Primetime Plight of the Arab Muslim American After 9/11." In *Race and Arab Americans Before and After 9/11: From Invisible Citizens to Visible Subjects*, edited by Amaney Jamal and Nadine Naber, 204–28. Syracuse, New York: Syracuse University Press, 2008.

Anderson, Carol. *Eyes off the Prize: The United Nations and the African American Struggle for Human Rights, 1944–1955*. New York: Cambridge University Press, 2003.

———. "From Hope to Disillusion: African Americans, the United Nations, and the Struggle for Human Rights, 1944–1947." *Diplomatic History* 20, no. 4 (Fall 1996): 531–63.

Anthony, David Henry III. *Max Yergan: Race Man, Internationalist, Cold Warrior*. New York: New York University Press, 2006.

Appiah, K. Anthony. "The Uncompleted Argument: Du Bois and the Illusion of Race." *Critical Inquiry* 12, no. 1 (Autumn 1985): 21–37.

Appiah, K. Anthony, and Amy Gutmann. *Color Conscious: The Political Morality of Race*. Princeton, N.J.: Princeton University Press, 1996.

Aptheker, Bettina. *Woman's Legacy: Essays on Race, Sex, and Class in American History*. Amherst: University of Massachusetts Press, 1982.

Aptheker, Herbert, ed. *Against Racism: Unpublished Essays, Papers, Addresses, 1887–1961, by W. E. B. Du Bois*. Amherst: University of Massachusetts Press, 1985.

——, ed. *The Correspondence of W. E. B. Du Bois*. Vol. 2, *Selections, 1934–1944*. Amherst: University of Massachusetts Press, 1976.

——, ed. *The Correspondence of W. E. B. Du Bois*. Vol. 3, *Selections, 1944–1963*. Amherst: University of Massachusetts Press, 1976.

——, ed. *A Documentary History of the Negro People in the United States, 1933–1945*. New York: Citadel Press, 1974.

——, ed. *Newspaper Columns by W. E. B. Du Bois*. Vol. 1, *1883–1944*. White Plains, N.Y.: Kraus-Thomson, 1986.

——, ed. *Newspaper Columns by W. E. B. Du Bois*. Vol. 2, *1945–1961*. White Plains, N.Y.: Kraus-Thomson, 1986.

——, ed. *Pamphlets and Leaflets by W. E. B. Du Bois*. White Plains, N.Y.: Kraus-Thomson, 1986.

——, ed. *Writings in Periodicals Edited by W. E. B. Du Bois: Selections from Phylon*. Millwood, N.Y.: Kraus-Thomson, 1980.

——, ed. *Writings by W. E. B. Du Bois in Non-Periodical Literature Edited by Others*. Millwood, N.Y.: Kraus-Thomson, 1982.

——, ed. *Writings by W. E. B. Du Bois in Periodicals Edited by Others*. Vol. 2, *1910–1934*. Millwood, N.Y.: Kraus-Thomson, 1982.

——, ed. *Writings by W. E. B. Du Bois in Periodicals Edited by Others*. Vol. 3, *1935–1944*. Millwood, N.Y.: Kraus-Thomson, 1982.

——, ed. *Writings by W. E. B. Du Bois in Periodicals Edited by Others*. Vol. 4, *1945–1961*. Millwood, N.Y.: Kraus-Thomson, 1982.

Armattoe, Raphael E. G. *The Golden Age of West African Civilization*. Londonderry: Lomeshie Research Centre, 1946.

Baker, Lee D. *From Savage to Negro: Anthropology and the Construction of Race, 1896–1954*. Berkeley: University of California Press, 1998.

Baldwin, Kate A. *Beyond the Color Line and the Iron Curtain: Reading Encounters between Black and Red, 1922–1963*. Durham, N.C.: Duke University Press, 2002.

Balfour, Lawrie. "Unreconstructed Democracy: W. E. B. Du Bois and the Case for Reparations." *Political Science Review* 97, no. 1 (February 2003): 33–44.

Balibar, Etienne, and Immanuel Wallerstein. *Race, Nation, Class: Ambiguous Identities*. London: Verso, 1991.

Barkan, Elazar. *The Retreat of Scientific Racism: Changing Concepts of Race in Britain and the United States Between the World Wars*. Cambridge: Cambridge University Press, 1992.

Bell, Bernard W., Emily Grosholz, and James B. Stewart, eds. *W. E. B. Du Bois on Race and Culture: Philosophy, Politics, and Poetics*. New York: Routledge, 1996.

Borgwardt, Elizabeth. *A New Deal for the World: America's Vision for Human Rights*. Cambridge: Harvard University Press, 2005.

Borstelmann, Thomas. *The Cold War and the Color Line: American Race Relations in the Global Arena*. Cambridge, Mass.: Harvard University Press, 2001.

Broderick, Francis. *W. E. B. Du Bois: Negro Leader in a Time of Crisis*. Stanford, Calif.: Stanford University Press, 1959.

Brown, Michael K., Martin Carnoy, Elliott Currie, Troy Duster, David B. Oppenheimer, Marjorie M. Shultz, and David Wellman. *Whitewashing Race: The Myth of a Color-Blind Society*. Berkeley: University of California Press, 2003.

Bunche, Ralph. *A World View of Race*. Port Washington, N.Y.: Kennikat Press, 1968.

Byerman, Keith E. *Seizing the Word: History, Art, and Self in the Work of W. E. B. Du Bois*. Athens: University of Georgia Press, 1994.

Cain, William. "From Liberalism to Communism: The Political Thought of W. E. B. Du Bois." In *Cultures of United States Imperialism*, edited by Amy Kaplan and Donald E. Pease, 456–73. Durham, N.C.: Duke University Press, 1993.

Carbado, Devon W. "Racial Naturalization." *American Quarterly* 57, no. 3 (September 2005): 639–53.

Carby, Hazel. *Race Men*. Cambridge, Mass.: Harvard University Press, 1998.

Committee on Africa, the War, and Peace Aims. *The Atlantic Charter and Africa from an American Standpoint*. New York, 1942.

Cruse, Harold. *The Crisis of the Negro Intellectual*. New York: William Morrow, 1967.

Davis, Angela Y. *Women, Race & Class*. New York: Random House, 1981.

Degler, Carl. *In Search of Human Nature: The Decline and Revival of Darwinism in American Social Thought*. New York: Oxford University Press, 1991.

Du Bois, Shirley Graham. *His Day Is Marching On: A Memoir of W. E. B. Du Bois*. New York: J. B. Lippincott Company, 1971.

Du Bois, W. E. B. *Africa, Its Geography, People and Products*. Vol. 5 of *The Oxford W. E. B. Du Bois*, edited by Henry Louis Gates Jr. New York: Oxford University Press, 2007.

——. *An Appeal to the World: A Statement on the Denial of Human Rights to Minorities in the Case of Citizens of Negro Descent in the United States of America and an Appeal to the United Nations for Redress*. New York: 1947.

——. *The Autobiography of W. E. B. Du Bois*. New York: International Publishers, 1968.

——. *Black Folk Then and Now*. Vol. 7 of *The Oxford W. E. B. Du Bois*, edited by Henry Louis Gates Jr. New York: Oxford University Press, 2007.

——. *Black Reconstruction in America, 1860 to 1880*. New York: Free Press, 1998.

——. *Color and Democracy: Colonies and Peace*. Reprint, with a new introduction by Herbert Aptheker. Millwood, N.Y.: Kraus-Thomson, 1975.

———. "The Conservation of Races." Reprinted in *Du Bois, Writings*, 815–26. New York: Library of America College Editions, 1996.

———. *Darkwater: Voices from within the Veil*. New York: Dover, 1999.

———. *Dusk of Dawn: An Essay toward an Autobiography of a Race Concept*. Reprinted in *Du Bois, Writings*, 549–802. New York: Library of America College Editions, 1996.

———. *In Battle for Peace: The Story of My 83rd Birthday*, with comment by Shirley Graham. New York: Masses and Mainstream, 1952.

———. *John Brown*. Millwood, N.Y.: Kraus-Thomson, 1973.

———. "My Evolving Program for Negro Freedom." In *What the Negro Wants*, edited by Rayford Logan, 31–70. Chapel Hill: University of North Carolina Press, 1944.

———. "Neuropa: Hitler's World Order." *Journal of Negro Education* 10, no. 3 (July 1941): 380–86.

———. *The Papers of W. E. B. Du Bois*. Microform. Sanford, N.C.: Microfilming Corp. of America.

———. *The Philadelphia Negro*. With a new introduction by Herbert Aptheker. Millwood, N.Y.: Kraus-Thomson, 1973.

———. *The Souls of Black Folk*. New York: Dover, 1994.

———. *The World and Africa: An Inquiry into the Part Which Africa Has Played in World History*. New York: International Publishers, 1965.

Dudziak, Mary L. *Cold War Civil Rights: Race and the Image of American Democracy*. Princeton, N.J.: Princeton University Press, 2000.

Edwards, Barrington. "W. E. B. Du Bois between Worlds: Berlin, Empirical Social Research, and the Race Question." *Du Bois Review* 3, no. 2 (September 2006): 395–424.

Eze, Emmanuel Chukwudi. *Achieving Our Humanity: The Idea of a Postracial Future*. New York: Routledge, 2001.

Ferguson, James. *Global Shadows: Africa in the Neoliberal World Order*. Durham, N.C.: Duke University Press, 2006.

Ferguson, Roderick. "W. E. B. Du Bois: Biography of a Discourse." In *Next to the Color Line: Gender, Sexuality, and W. E. B. Du Bois*, edited by Susan Gillman and Alys Eve Weinbaum, 269–88. Minneapolis: University of Minnesota Press, 2007.

Foucault, Michel. *Society Must Be Defended: Lectures at the College de France, 1975–1976*. Edited by Mauro Bertani and Alessandro Fontana; translated by David Macey. New York: Picador, 1997.

Gaines, Kevin K. *American Africans in Ghana: Black Expatriates and the Civil Rights Era*. Chapel Hill: The University of North Carolina Press, 2006.

Gates, Henry Louis Jr. "The Black Letters on the Sign: W. E. B. Du Bois and the Canon." In *The Oxford W. E. B. Du Bois*, edited by Henry Louis Gates Jr., New York: Oxford University Press, 2007.

Giddings, Paula. *When and Where I Enter: The Impact of Black Women on Race and Sex in America*. New York: William Morrow, 1984.

Gillman, Susan. *Blood Talk: American Race Melodrama and the Culture of the Occult*. Chicago: University of Chicago Press, 2003.

Gillman, Susan, and Alys Eve Weinbaum, eds. *Next to the Color Line: Gender, Sexuality, and W. E. B. Du Bois*. Minneapolis: University of Minnesota Press, 2007.

Gillmore, Daniel S., ed. *Speaking of Peace: An Edited Report of the Cultural and Scientific Conference for World Peace, New York, March 25, 26 and 27 1949 under the Auspices of the National Council of the Arts, Sciences and Professions*. New York: National Council of the Arts, Sciences and Professions, 1949.

Gilroy, Paul. *Against Race: Imagining Political Culture Beyond the Color Line*. Cambridge, Mass.: Harvard University Press, 2000.

———. *The Black Atlantic: Modernity and Double Consciousness*. Cambridge, Mass.: Harvard University Press, 1993.

———. *Postcolonial Melancholia*. New York: Columbia University Press, 2006.

Goldberg, David Theo. "Deva-Stating Disasters: Race in the Shadow(s) of New Orleans." *Du Bois Review* 3, no. 1 (March 2006): 83–95.

———. "The End(s) of Race." *Postcolonial Studies* 7, no. 2 (2004): 211–30.

———. *The Racial State*. Malden, Mass.: Blackwell, 2002.

———. *Racist Culture: Philosophy and the Politics of Meaning*. Malden, Mass.: Blackwell, 1993.

Gooding-Williams, Robert. *In the Shadow of Du Bois: Afro-Modern Political Thought in America*. Cambridge: Harvard University Press, 2009.

———. "Outlaw, Appiah, and Du Bois's 'The Conservation of Races.'" In *W. E. B. Du Bois on Race and Culture: Philosophy, Politics, and Poetics*, edited by Bernard W. Bell, Emily Grosholz, and James B. Stewart, 39–56. New York: Routledge, 1996.

Gordon, Lewis. *Her Majesty's Other Children: Sketches of Racism from a Neocolonial Age*. Lanham, Md.: Rowman and Littlefield, 1997.

Green, Dan S., and Edwin D. Driver, eds. *W. E. B. Du Bois on Sociology and the Black Community*. Chicago: University of Chicago Press, 1978.

Gregory, Derek. *The Colonial Present: Afghanistan, Palestine, Iraq*. Malden, Mass.: Blackwell, 2004.

Guterl, Matthew Pratt. *The Color of Race in America, 1900–1940*. Cambridge, Mass.: Harvard University Press, 2001.

Hall, Stuart. "Gramsci's Relevance for the Study of Race and Ethnicity." In *Stuart Hall: Critical Dialogues in Cultural Studies*, edited by David Morley and Kuan-Hsing Chen, 411–40. London: Routledge, 1996.

Hancock, Ange-Marie. "W. E. B. Du Bois: Intellectual Forefather of Intersectionality." *Souls* 7, no. 3–4 (2005): 74–84.

Harding, Vincent. "W. E. B. Du Bois and the Black Messianic Vision." *Freedomways* 9 (First quarter, 1969): 44–58.

Hardt, Michael, and Antonio Negri. *Multitude: War and Democracy in the Age of Empire*. New York: Penguin, 2004.

Harris, Cheryl I. "Whiteness as Property." In *Critical Race Theory: The Key Writings that Formed the Movement*, edited by Kimberlé Crenshaw, Neil Gotanda, Gary Pellar, and Kendall Thomas, 276–91. New York: New Press, 1995.

Harvey, David. *A Brief History of Neoliberalism*. New York: Oxford University Press, 2005.

Hollinger, David. *Postethnic America: Beyond Multiculturalism*. New York: Basic Books, 1995.

Holloway, David. *Stalin and the Bomb: The Soviet Union and Atomic Energy, 1939–56*. New Haven, Conn.: Yale University Press, 1994.

Holloway, Jonathan Scott. *Confronting the Veil: Abram Harris, Jr., E. Franklin Frazier, and Ralph Bunche, 1919–1941*. Chapel Hill: University of North Carolina Press, 2002.

Holt, Thomas C. "The Political Uses of Alienation: W. E. B. Du Bois on Politics, Race, and Culture, 1903–1940." *American Quarterly* 42, no. 2 (June 1990): 301–23.

———. *The Problem of Race in the Twenty-First Century*. Cambridge, Mass.: Harvard University Press, 2000.

Horne, Gerald. *Black and Red: W. E. B. Du Bois and the Afro-American Response to the Cold War, 1944–1963*. Albany, N.Y.: State University of New York Press, 1986.

———. *Race Woman: The Lives of Shirley Graham Du Bois*. New York: New York University Press, 2000.

Ignatiev, Noel, and John Garvey, eds. *Race Traitor*. New York: Routledge, 1996.

Isaacs, Harold. *The New World of Negro Americans*. New York: John Day, 1963.

James, Joy. *Transcending the Talented Tenth: Black Leaders and American Intellectuals*. New York: Routledge, 1997.

Janken, Kenneth R. "From Colonial Liberation to Cold War Liberalism: Walter White, the NAACP, and Foreign Affairs, 1941–1955." *Ethnic and Racial Studies* 21, no. 6 (November 1998): 1074–95.

Judy, Ronald A. T. "Introduction: On W. E. B. Du Bois and Hyperbolic Thinking." *boundary 2* 27, no. 3 (Fall 2000): 1–35.

Kaplan, Amy. *The Anarchy of Empire in the Making of U.S. Culture*. Cambridge, Mass.: Harvard University Press, 2002.

Katz, Maude White. "Learning from History—The Ingram Case of the 1940s." *Freedomways* 19, no. 2 (Second quarter 1979): 82–86.

Katz, Michael B., and Thomas J. Sugrue, eds. *W. E. B. Du Bois, Race, and the City: The Philadelphia Negro and Its Legacy*. Philadelphia: University of Pennsylvania Press, 1998.

Kelley, Robin D. G. *Freedom Dreams: The Black Radical Imagination*. Boston: Beacon Press, 2002.

King, Richard H. *Race, Culture, and the Intellectuals, 1940–1970*. Washington, D.C.: Woodrow Wilson Center Press; Baltimore: Johns Hopkins University Press, 2004.

Lenin, V. I. *Imperialism: The Highest Stage of Capitalism: A Popular Outline*. New York: International Publishers, 1988.

Lewis, David Levering. *W. E. B. Du Bois: Biography of a Race, 1868–1919*. New York: Henry Holt, 1993.

——. *W. E. B. Du Bois: The Fight for Equality and the American Century, 1919–1963*. New York: Henry Holt, 2000.

——. *W. E. B. Du Bois: A Reader*. New York: Henry Holt, 1995.

Lipsitz, George. *American Studies in a Moment of Danger*. Minneapolis: University of Minnesota Press, 2001.

Locke, Alain, ed. *The New Negro*. New York: Atheneum, 1977.

Logan, Rayford, ed. *W. E. B. Du Bois: A Profile*. New York: Hill and Wang, 1971.

Lott, Tommy L. *The Invention of Race: Black Culture and the Politics of Representation*. Malden, Mass.: Blackwell, 1999.

Malveaux, Julianne, and Regina A. Green, eds. *The Paradox of Loyalty: An African American Response to the War on Terrorism*. 2nd ed. Chicago: Third World Press, 2004.

Mamdani, Mahmood. Introduction to *The World and Africa*. Vol. 14 of *The Oxford W. E. B. Du Bois*, edited by Henry Louis Gates Jr., xxv–xxx. New York: Oxford University Press, 2007.

Marable, Manning. "The Pan-Africanism of W. E. B. Du Bois." In *W. E. B. Du Bois on Race and Culture: Philosophy, Politics, and Poetics*, edited by Bernard W. Bell, Emily Grosholz, and James B. Stewart, 193–218. New York: Routledge, 1996.

——. "Reconstructing the Radical Du Bois." *Souls* 7, no. 3–4 (2005): 1–25.

——. *W. E. B. Du Bois: Black Radical Democrat*. Boston: Twayne, 1986.

Martin, Charles. "Race, Gender, and Southern Justice: The Rosa Lee Ingram Case." *American Journal of Legal History* 29, no. 3 (July 1985): 251–68.

Mbembe, Achille. "Necropolitics." Translated by Libby Meintjes. *Public Culture* 15, no. 1 (2003): 11–40.

——. *On the Postcolony*. Berkeley: University of California Press, 2001.

McAlister, Melani. *Epic Encounters: Culture, Media, and U.S. Interests in the Middle East since 1945*. Updated ed., with a post-9/11 chapter. Berkeley: University of California Press, 2005.

McWilliams, Carey. *Brothers under the Skin*. Rev. ed. Boston: Little, Brown and Company, 1951.

Monteiro, Anthony. "Being an African in the World: The Du Boisian Epistemology." *Annals of the American Academy of Political and Social Science* 568, no. 1 (March 2000): 220–34.

Moon, Henry Lee, ed. *The Emerging Thought of W. E. B. Du Bois: Essays and Editorials from the Crisis*. New York: Simon and Schuster, 1972.

Moses, Wilson J. "Culture, Civilization, and the Decline of the West." In *W. E. B. Du Bois on Race and Culture: Philosophy, Politics, and Poetics*, edited by Bernard W. Bell, Emily Grosholz, and James B. Stewart, 243–60. New York: Routledge, 1996.

Mosley, Walter. *What Next: A Memoir toward World Peace*. Baltimore: Black Classic Press, 2003.

Mostern, Kenneth. *Autobiography and Black Identity Politics: Racialization in Twentieth-Century America*. Cambridge, Mass.: Harvard University Press, 1999.

Mudimbe, V. Y. *The Invention of Africa: Gnosis, Philosophy, and the Order of Knowledge*. Bloomington: Indiana University Press, 1988.

Mullen, Bill V. *Afro-Orientalism*. Minneapolis: University of Minnesota Press, 2004.

Muñoz, Jose. *Disidentifications: Queers of Color and the Performance of Politics*. Minneapolis: University of Minnesota Press, 1999.

Mustapha, Abdul-Karim. "Constituting Negative Geopolitics: Memorality and Event in *The World and Africa*." *boundary 2* 27, no. 3 (Fall 2000): 171–97.

Myrdal, Gunnar. *An American Dilemma: The Negro Problem and Modern Democracy*. New York: Harper and Brothers, 1944.

Nordstrom, Carolyn. *Shadows of War: Violence, Power, and International Profiteering in the Twenty-First Century*. Berkeley: University of California Press, 2004.

Nussbaum, Martha, and Respondents. *For Love of Country: Debating the Limits of Patriotism*. Edited by Joshua Cohen. Boston: Beacon Press, 1996.

Olson, Joel. *The Abolition of White Democracy*. Minneapolis: University of Minnesota Press, 2004.

———. "W. E. B. Du Bois and the Race Concept." *Souls* 7, no. 3–4 (2005): 118–28.

Omi, Michael, and Howard Winant. *Racial Formation in the United States: From the 1960s to the 1990s*. 2nd ed. New York: Routledge, 1994.

Outlaw, Lucius. "'Conserve' Races? In Defense of W. E. B. Du Bois." In *W. E. B. Du Bois on Race and Culture: Philosophy, Politics, and Poetics*, edited by Bernard W. Bell, Emily Grosholz, and James B. Stewart, 16–37. New York: Routledge, 1996.

Padmore, George. *Africa and World Peace:* London: Frank Cass and Company, 1937.

———, ed. *Colonial and Coloured Unity: A Programme of Action: History of the Pan-African Congress*. Manchester: Pan-African Service, 1946.

———. *Pan-Africanism or Communism*. Garden City, N.Y.: Doubleday, 1971.

Piven, Frances Fox. *The War at Home: The Domestic Costs of Bush's Militarism*. New York: New Press, 2004.

Plummer, Brenda Gayle. *Rising Wind: Black Americans and U.S. Foreign Affairs, 1935–1960*. Chapel Hill: University of North Carolina Press, 1996.

Prashad, Vijay. *Everybody Was Kung Fu Fighting: Afro-Asian Connections and the Myth of Cultural Purity*. Boston: Beacon Press, 2001.

Puar, Jasbir K., and Amit S. Rai. "Monster, Terrorist, Fag: The War on Terrorism and the Production of Docile Patriots." *Social Text* 20, no. 3 (Fall 2002): 117–48.

Rabaka, Reiland. *W. E. B. Du Bois and the Problems of the Twenty-First Century: An Essay on Africana Critical Theory*. Lanham, Md.: Rowman and Littlefield, 2007.

———. *Du Bois's Dialectics: Black Radical Politics and the Reconstruction of Critical Social Theory*. Lanham, MD: Lexington Books, 2008.

Rampersad, Arnold. *The Art and Imagination of W. E. B. Du Bois*. Cambridge, Mass.: Harvard University Press, 1976.

Reed, Aldolph L. Jr. *W. E. B. Du Bois and American Political Thought: Fabianism and the Color Line*: New York: Oxford University Press, 1997.

Robinson, Cedric J. *Black Marxism: The Making of the Black Radical Tradition*. London: Zed Books, 1983.

———. "W. E. B. Du Bois and Black Sovereignty." In *Imagining Home: Class, Culture and Nationalism in the African Diaspora*, edited by Sidney Lemelle and Robin D. G. Kelley, 145–57. London: Verso, 1994.

Roediger, David R. *Colored White: Transcending the Racial Past*. Berkeley: University of California Press, 2002.

———. *The Wages of Whiteness: Race and the Making of the American Working Class*. New York: Verso, 1999.

Roy, Arundhati. *An Ordinary Person's Guide to Empire*. Boston: South End Press, 2004.

Rudwick, Elliot. *W. E. B. Du Bois: A Study in Minority Group Leadership*. Philadelphia: University of Pennsylvania Press, 1960.

Saunders, Frances Stonor. *The Cultural Cold War: The CIA and the World of Arts and Letters*. New York: New Press, 1999.

Scott, David. *Conscripts of Modernity: The Tragedy of Colonial Enlightenment*. Durham, N.C.: Duke University Press, 2004.

Sexton, Jared, and Elizabeth Lee. "Figuring the Prison: Prerequisites of Torture at Abu Ghraib." *Antipode* (2006): 1005–22.

Shuford, John. "Four Du Boisian Contributions to Critical Race Theory." *Transactions of the Charles S. Peirce Society* 37, no. 3 (Summer 2001): 301–37.

Singer, Henry A. "An Analysis of the New York Press Treatment of the Peace Conference at the Waldorf Astoria." *Journal of Educational Sociology* 23 (January 1950): 258–70.

Singh, Nikhil Pal. *Black Is a Country: Race and the Unfinished Struggle for Democracy*. Cambridge, Mass.: Harvard University Press, 2004.

———. "Culture/Wars: Recoding Empire in an Age of Democracy." *American Quarterly* 50, no. 3 (September 1998): 471–522.

Stecopoulos, Harilaos. "Putting Old Africa on the Map: British Imperial Legacies and Contemporary U.S. Culture." In *Exceptional State: Contemporary U.S. Culture and the New Imperialism*, edited by Ashley Dawson and Malini Johar, 221–24. Durham, N.C.: Duke University Press, 2007.

Stephens, Michelle. *Black Empire: The Masculine Global Imaginary of Caribbean Intellectuals in the United States, 1914–1962.* Durham, N.C.: Duke University Press, 2005.

Sundquist, Eric. *To Wake the Nations: Race in the Making of American Literature.* Cambridge, Mass.: Harvard University Press, 1993.

Taylor, Ula Yvette. *The Veiled Garvey: The Life and Times of Amy Jacques Garvey.* Chapel Hill: University of North Carolina Press, 2002.

Torgovnick, Marianna. *The War Complex: World War II in Our Time.* Chicago: University of Chicago Press, 2005.

Tucker, William H. *The Science and Politics of Racial Research.* Champaign: University of Illinois Press, 1994.

UNESCO. *Race and Science.* New York: Columbia University Press, 1961.

Volpp, Leti. "The Citizen and the Terrorist." In *September 11 in History : A Watershed Moment?,* edited by Mary L. Dudziak, 147–62. Durham, N.C.: Duke University Press, 2003.

Von Eschen, Penny. *Race against Empire: Black Americans and Anticolonialism, 1937–1957.* Ithaca, N.Y.: Cornell University Press, 1997.

Wald, Priscilla. *Constituting Americans: Cultural Anxiety and Narrative Form.* Durham, N.C.: Duke University Press, 1995.

Wallerstein, Immanuel. *The Decline of American Power.* New York: New Press, 2003.

Washington, Mary Helen. "Introductory Essay." Anna Julia Cooper, *A Voice from the South.* New York: Oxford University Press, 1998.

Weinbaum, Alys. "Reproducing Racial Globality: W. E. B. Du Bois and the Sexual Politics of Black Internationalism." *Social Text* 19, no. 2 (Summer 2001): 15–41.

Williams, Robert W. "The Early Social Science of W. E. B. Du Bois." *Du Bois Review* 3, no. 2 (September 2006): 365–94.

Winant, Howard. *The World Is a Ghetto: Race and Democracy since World War II.* New York: Basic Books, 2001.

Wittner, Lawrence S. *One World or None: A History of the World Nuclear Disarmament Movement through 1953.* Stanford, Calif.: Stanford University Press, 1993.

Wolters, Raymond. *Du Bois and His Rivals.* Columbia: University of Missouri Press, 2002.

Wynter, Sylvia. "Is 'Development' a Purely Empirical Concept or also Teleological? A Perspective from 'We the Underdeveloped.'" In *Prospects for Recovery and Sustainable Development in Africa,* edited by Aguibou Y. Yansané, 299–316. Westport, Conn.: Greenwood Press, 1996.

Zamir, Shamoon. *Dark Voices: W. E. B. Du Bois and American Thought, 1888–1903.* Chicago: University of Chicago Press, 1995.

Zuberi, Tufuku, ed. "The Study of African American Problems: W. E. B. Du Bois's Agenda, Then and Now." *Annals of the American Academy of Political and Social Science* 568, no. 1 (March 2000).

Carnegie Corporation, 38, 106
Casely-Hayford, Joseph Ephriam, 104
China, 2, 16, 68–72, 83, 130, 137, 142, 178
"Chronicle of Race Relations, A" (Du Bois), 22, 49–52. See also *Phylon*
Churchill, Winston, 74–77, 94, 124
citizenship, 117, 129; black and African American claims of, 57, 67; changing nature of, 3; colonialism and, 138; exclusionary nature of, 12, 157, 170; loyalty and, 147–48, 162–67, 171, 173, 176; rights and responsibilities of, 57, 147–48, 176; suspect citizens, 148, 153, 158–60, 164, 166–67, 172
civilization discourse, 123, 129, 152, 178
civil rights movement (U.S.), 42, 157–58, 164–73; Du Bois impact on, 25, 33, 38, 145; internationalism and, 118–20, 136, 152–53; leaders of, 14, 22, 115; links with organizations of, 54–55, 73, 75, 81, 90–96, 105–7, 113; relationship with human rights of, 12, 16–18, 54, 106
Civil Rights Congress, 92
Cold War, 96–101, 138, 145, 168; Africa and, 130–37; hysteria of, 2; judicial legacies of, 18; liberalism and, 94; loyalty and, 149–55, 173–74; as a racial project, 158, 164–66; relationship to social movements of, 12, 120–21; U.S. in, 95. See also war
colonialism: Africa and, 104–12, 133; African Americans and, 90; anticolonialism and, 11, 15, 94, 104–5, 140; citizenship and, 117; economic development and, 85; European, 7, 26, 52, 78, 114, 117; history of, 138; neocolonialism and, 16, 97–98, 139–

41; postcolonial, 104, 138–39; present and, 106; racist legacies of, 3, 18, 107, 124–26, 140, 156; violence and, 67; war and, 46, 78, 82–90, 106; white supremacy and, 51
colonial subjects, 67, 73–75, 80, 89–90, 114
Color and Democracy: Colonies and Peace (Du Bois), 64, 82, 84–89, 100, 122, 153
colorblind/colorblindness, 17, 22, 58–60, 174; academics as, 59, 180 n. 16; work against, 23
"color line, the." *See* race
Committee on Africa, the War, and Peace Aims, 76, 108, 112, 118
communism, 45, 136–38, 146, 152–54, 163
Communist International, 26–27
Communist Party of the United States (CPUSA), 27–28, 116, 149–51, 162; Du Bois's joining of, 2, 5, 137–38; NAACP and, 94, 120
Congress of Industrial Organizations (CIO), 115
"Conservation of Races, The" (Du Bois), 9, 36
Council of African Affairs (CAA), 1, 18, 94, 105, 115–17, 131–37, 146, 208 n. 107
Counts, George, 151
Cousins, Norman, 151–52
Crisis (magazine), 67, 76; Du Bois as editor of, 1, 25; Marxian analysis in, 27; Du Bois's resignation from, 29
critical race studies: masculinism of, 6
Cultural and Scientific Conference for World Peace, 149, 154–55

Darkwater (Du Bois), 8, 26, 67, 80, 112
Davis, Ben, 133

dom and, 152; liberalism and, 42, 155; Marxian critique of, 22, 26, 32, 50, 164; morality and, 53–54; peace and, 63–64; political economy of, 124, 164; "post-race" and, 174–75; racial feeling, 31; racial knowledge, 40; self-determination and, 114–17; science and, 22–26, 31, 40–41, 52–58, 72, 186 n. 43; as social and political category, 7, 143; as social construction, 21–22, 32, 44; war and, 63–64, 101, 114, 123, 133–34; World War II and, 89, 105–6

"race concept," 21, 32–46; changes to, in Du Bois's work, 16, 50, 57; critiques of, 13; in Du Bois's early work, 6–7; in Du Bois's later work, 10, 50, 57; as globally recognized, 84, 89

racial formation(s), 11, 13, 72, 170–71

Rai, Amit, 170

Rampersad, Arnold, 5–6, 24, 197 n. 8

rape metaphors, 123–24, 128, 168, 207 n. 95

Reconstruction, 29, 34, 80

Redfield, Robert, 51

Reed, Adolph, 9, 14, 181 n. 22, 202 n. 29

Robeson, Paul, 94–95, 105, 113, 132, 155–56, 161

Robinson, Cedric, 5, 111

Robinson, Jackie, 156

Rockefeller Foundation, 29, 38, 136

Rogge, John, 162, 168

Romulo, Carlos, 93

Roosevelt, Eleanor, 93–94, 131

Roosevelt, Franklin D., 32–33, 72–77, 83–84, 117

Roy, Arundhati, 174

Roy, M. N., 26

Russia, 16, 88, 146, 154, 168, 172, 178. *See also* Soviet Union

Rwanda, 99

Schlesinger, Arthur, Jr., 94–95, 120

Schomburg Library, 90, 115

science: antiracism and, 55; Du Bois's critique of, 6, 17, 22–26, 43–44; propaganda and, 30, 34–35, 38; race and 22–26, 31, 40–41, 52–58, 72, 186–87 n. 43, white supremacy and, 37, 39, 51–52

Scott, David, 15, 184 n. 43

self-determination: Africa and, 110–14; in Atlantic Charter, 75–76, 114; for blacks in U.S., 27, 37; colonialism and, 90, 104; Du Bois's commitment to, 116; governmental, 75

September 11, 2001, 100, 147–48, 169–73

Shapley, Harlow, 149, 152

Sierra Leone, 113

Singh, Nikhil Pal, 12, 32–34, 73, 212 n. 17

slavery: Africa and, 120; industry and, 42, 124; racist legacies of, 3, 14, 81, 107, 123–26, 140; slave trade and, 68, 74, 98, 109, 176

Smuts, Jan Christian, 79, 117

sociology, 25, 29, 35–36, 39

Souls of Black Folk, The (Du Bois): 6, 23, 25, 182 n.23,

South Africa, 50, 70, 117, 132–33, 170, 208 n. 107

Southern Negro Youth Congress, 95

Soviet Africa Institute, 137

Soviet Union (USSR): Africa and, 105, 130, 135, 137, 142; conflict with U.S., 93–95, 97, 146–48; Du Bois on, 10, 26, 71, 146–55, 162, 166; peace movements and, 98–101, 133, 146, 148–57, 159, 161–64; position globally, 83, 89, 178; nationalism and, 153. *See also* Russia; Stalin, Joseph

Spain, 121

Spencer, Herbert, 36,

Stalin, Joseph, 10, 71, 75, 149–51, 153–54, 175. *See also* Soviet Union

Stecopoulos, Harilaos, 141

Stephens, Michelle, 129–30

Stettinius, Edward, 83–84, 91, 117, 135

Stimson, Henry L., 71

Stockholm Appeal, 159

Stokes, Anson Phelps, 108, 201 nn. 18–19, 202 n. 26, 209 n. 121

Sudan, 121

Sumner, Charles, 42, 55

Sundquist, Eric, 30

Supreme Court (U.S.), 158

Theroux, Paul, 103

Torgovnick, Marianna, 63, 70, 100

Truman Doctrine: 94–96, 149

Truman, Harry S., 131, 156, 159, 161, 165

"20th Century: The Century of the Color Line" (Du Bois), 145

UNESCO (United Nations Educational, Scientific and Cultural Organization), 54, 191 n. 98

United Kingdom, 69, 74, 83, 94, 110, 112–14, 149

United Nations (UN), 131, 141, 151, 160; Africa and, 113–21; colonialism and, 89–91, 127–28; Du Bois on, 64, 73–81, 91–94, 105, 117; formation of, 74, 82–84; Pan-Africanism and, 133–34. *See also* human rights; Universal Declaration on Human Rights

United States (U.S.), 56–67, 122–23, 171; Africa and, 103–10, 127; African Americans' relationship to, 33, 55, 121, 157; anticolonialism and, 78, 144, 146, 169; civil society in, 174;

Cold War and, 97–101, 148–51; Du Bois's critique of, 1–17, 53–55, 82–89, 95–101, 106–8, 146–49, 156–58; future and, 145, 167–78; government censorship of Du Bois in, 4; hegemony of, 19, 53–55, 60, 96, 125, 146, 153, 165, 169; as imperial power, 3, 7, 12, 52–57, 73–76, 95, 137, 145–46, 177; Justice Department of, 160, 165–6; liberalism in, 75, 86–87; State Department of, 111, 130–31, 150; Supreme Court of, 158; World War II and, 83, 88–89

Universal Declaration of Human Rights, 93, 131. *See also* human rights; United Nations

Universal Negro Improvement Association (UNIA), 111. *See also* Garvey, Marcus

USSR. *See* Soviet Union

Van Dieman, Roger, 55–57

Vassar College, 106–8

Volpp, Leti, 169–70

Von Eschen, Penny, 12, 137, 196 n. 41, 208 n. 107

Wallace, Henry, 73, 95, 168

Wallace-Johnson, I. T. A., 113–14

Wallerstein, Immanuel, 96, 98

Walters, Alexander, 104–5

war: African Americans and, 69–70, 77, 155–56; colonialism and, 46, 78, 82–90, 106; democracy and, 73–74, 80, 84, 89, 161; imperialism and, 64–72, 85, 148, 154–55; nation and, 65; race and, 63–64, 89, 101, 105–6, 114, 123, 133–34; on terrorism, 147–48. *See also* Cold War; Gulf War

Warren, Earl, 54

Weinbaum, Alys, 8, 128

West African Student's Union (WASU), 113

White, Hayden, 15

whiteness, 7, 29, 104, 171

white supremacy, 22–23, 58, 69, 85, 118; challenges to, 11, 55–57, 145, 158, 165; scholarship on, 34, 104; science and, 37, 39, 51–52

White, Walter: 28, 82, 91, 93, 118, 120–21, 130–31

Wideman, John Edgar, 172

Wilkins, Roy, 28

Williams, Henry Sylvester, 104–5, 113, 115

Wilson, Woodrow, 111

Winant, Howard, 11, 13

women of color, 61, 129

World and Africa, The (Du Bois), 10, 18, 105, 122, 125–128

World Colonial Council, 117

World Conference Against Racism (2001), 175–7

World Peace Council. *See* Partisans of Peace

World Trade Union Conference, 113–14

World War I, 26, 67, 77, 117, 164; Allies during, 109

World War II, 77, 80, 96–101, 134, 164, 173; Allies during, 77–79, 81, 114; post-war peace, 63–64, 82–83; relationship to social movements of, 12; race and, 89, 105–6

Wynter, Sylvia, 139–42

Yale University, 106–8, 158

Yergan, Max, 105, 113, 132

Zimbabwe, 125

Zionism, 176

Žižek, Slavoj, 60

ERIC PORTER is professor of American studies at the
University of California, Santa Cruz. He is the author of
*What Is This Thing Called Jazz? African American Musicians
as Artists, Critics, and Activists* (2002).

Library of Congress Cataloging-in-Publication Data
Porter, Eric (Eric C.)
The problem of the future world : W. E. B. Du Bois and
the race concept at midcentury / Eric Porter.
p. cm.
Includes bibliographical references and index.
ISBN 978-0-8223-4812-2 (cloth : alk. paper)
ISBN 978-0-8223-4808-5 (pbk. : alk. paper)
1. Du Bois, W. E. B. (William Edward Burghardt),
1868–1963 — Criticism and interpretation. 2. Du Bois,
W. E. B. (William Edward Burghardt), 1868–1963 — Political
and social views. 3. American literature — African American
authors — History and criticism. 4. Politics and literature —
United States — History — 20th century. I. Title.
PS3507.U147Z755 2010
305.896′0730092 — dc22   2010022497